LETTERS OF
FYODOR MICHAILOVITCH
DOSTOEVSKY
to his Family and Friends

FYODOR MICHAILOVITCH DOSTOEVSKY, PETERSBURG, 1879.

LETTERS OF
FYODOR MICHAILOVITCH
DOSTOEVSKY
to his Family and Friends

translated by
ETHEL COLBURN MAYNE

with an introduction by
AVRAHM YARMOLINSKY

HORIZON PRESS  NEW YORK

DOSTOEVSKY'S SELF-PORTRAIT

"The truth is, I find it terribly difficult to write letters; I have no talent for it" (no. LXVI).* Thus as an elderly man Dostoevsky ended a long missive. Nevertheless, he penned—literally—a considerable number of letters. The four-volume Moscow edition of them, which was completed last year, contains over nine hundred items, and undoubtedly many have not been preserved, while some may not yet have come to light. His not infrequent absences from home—one of them, which was involuntary, lasting a decade—his activities as author and editor, his position as a public figure to whom strangers turned for counsel and spiritual comfort—all served to swell his correspondence.

Aside from the semi-fictional record of his life in prison, and some fragmentary reminiscences in *A Writer's Diary*, a monthly which he issued intermittently in his last years and to which he was the sole contributor, he published nothing in the nature of memoirs. The autobiographical impulse asserted itself in his stories and novels. In fashioning them he drew heavily on his intimate experiences and rare self-knowledge. He placed his characters in situations in which he had found himself, endowed them with his own traits, made them the mouthpieces of his convictions and obsessions. It is as though he were driven by an urge to reveal what he felt and thought, to confess. Naturally, his avowals are often oblique, ambiguous, disguised. The letters, on the other hand, are direct, outspoken, unequivocal, if occasionally less than candid, for example when he tries to get an advance from a tight-fisted publisher. He had great powers of observation and a unique insight into the workings of the mind, but he was also a visionary

* Numerals refer to letters in the present collection.

v

and a man given to exaggeration and distortion. The scholar will
examine critically and as far as possibly verify some of the statements of fact made in the letters. Indubitably, however, they are
the prime source for the reconstruction of Dostoevsky's private
life, with which his art is so intimately bound up.

Among the more engaging of the early letters are those in which
the moody, sensitive adolescent, who is miserable in the uncon-
genial atmosphere of the school of military engineering he attends,
pours out his troubled heart to his brother Michael. He is haunted
by black thoughts and is tempted by the idea of suicide. Apparently as an escape from his oppressive surroundings, he conceives
the idea of simulating insanity. His mind is in a turmoil with fuzzy
philosophizing about God, Nature, the Soul. What adds to his
wretchedness is the fact that remittances from home are few and
far between. He has his first taste of the "iron poverty," to use
a phrase in one of his stiff, respectful letters to his father, which
was to dog him for many years and impose its indelible mark on
his character. But the picture is not without bright spots: passionate friendships with one or two kindred souls, and *books*. He
is a prodigious reader with an eclectic taste. Both Victor Hugo
and Racine command his admiration, his enthusiasm for Schiller
is boundless. Already he has begun to scribble ambitiously, and he
speaks of himself as a student of the mystery that man is. With
the approach of graduation he is confirmed in his resolution to
devote his life not to designing fortifications but to literature, and
in spite of fits of despondency he has moments when his heart lifts
as he dreams of the future. Such is the portrait that the letters
delineate of the novelist as a raw youth.

The later communications, mostly to the same correspondent,
disclose the circumstances of the budding author: the sudden
fame, dizzying and short-lived, the beginning of the literary peon-
age, which was to last most of his life, attacks of hideous depression, hypochondria, vague "moral" and nervous ailments, perhaps
the first signs of epilepsy, the disease that was to sap his energies
practically to the end. Naturally there is no hint in the letters of
his meetings with a handful of young men who gathered on Friday
evenings to air radical ideas challenging the authority of Church
and State, and to read subversive books and manuscripts. As a

result of this association he found himself in prison, and on the morning of December 22, 1849, he stood on a scaffold awaiting execution. Only after he, together with the other condemned men, had gone through all the grim preparations for it was the commutation of his death sentence to four years of hard labor in Siberia announced. He described those shattering moments drily enough in the opening paragraph of a letter (xx) that he wrote to Michael the same day. A psychologically subtle evocation of the experience appears in *The Idiot*, published nearly twenty years later, in the shape of an episode related to Prince Myshkin by a stranger.

As a convict, Dostoevsky was isolated from the outside world. He had been sentenced to serve in the army for an indefinite period on completing his term of hard labor, and so in due time he exchanged the prisoner's garb for the uniform of a private in a battalion stationed in a wretched Siberian town. His new status enabled him to resume contact with home. Few letters are more absorbing than the mammoth one (xxi) in which he told Michael what he had endured in the course of his penal servitude and what an extraordinary effect those hardships had had on his body and mind. This account is also in the nature of a preliminary sketch for that humane and enduring work, *The House of the Dead*, published after a lapse of eight years. Equally important for the understanding of what hard labor had done to Dostoevsky is the letter (xxii) that he addressed about the same time to the devout lady who had befriended him and his fellow convicts on their way to prison. It has to do with a matter central to his thinking: religion. Eventually he will envision the Orthodox Church as the ideal society destined in the fullness of time to replace the secular State. The credo which, as he tells his correspondent, he had formulated for himself in prison is the expression of a personal commitment to Christ, without concern for the body of the faithful. Curiously enough, this cherished credo of his, repeated verbatim, figures in *The Possessed*, written some sixteen years later. It is attributed to the protagonist, Stavrogin, as one of the beliefs that he professes—perhaps insincerely—before he lapses into atheism.

Other Siberian letters make it clear that the former political offender and freethinker has become not only an ardent, though somewhat unorthodox, Christian, but also a loyal subject of the Czar, a patriot believing in Russia's exalted, if otherwise unspecified, mission in Europe. And so when at the end of a decade of exile he was back in the capital, he aligned himself with those who set their faces against the materialistic, irreverent, irreligious, potentially revolutionary trend, known under the misnomer of "Nihilism," which had developed among the young. He brought home with him a consumptive wife, a widow he had married on borrowed money, and a stepson. In the course of his stormy courtship—the details of it may be gleaned from his correspondence—he had played the part of the hero of *The Insulted and Injured* (his first post-Siberian novel) who goes out of his way to promote the happiness of the girl he loves with his rival. What the letters have to say about the marriage suggests that it was an unhappy, though by no means loveless union, exemplifying the emotional ambivalence that is prominent in Dostoevsky's conception of the psyche. After his wife's death, in 1864, he continued to make a home for her son.

From other communications we learn something about his first trip abroad, in the summer of 1862, which intensified his hostility toward Western civilization, and of his second trip the following year. It was then that he visited Wiesbaden, where he contracted the gambling fever, which was to ravage him for years. Thence he traveled to Paris, where he joined by prearrangement Polina Suslova, an uninhibited and rather sadistic young woman, half his age. She had been his mistress for a short time, but now jilted him for another lover who proved faithless. She seems to have been the model for the heroine of *The Gamblers*, which is clearly based on the author's experiences at roulette. He could afford to do all this traveling because the magazine that Michael had launched as soon as his brother reappeared in the capital was doing rather well. The fat years came to an end with Michael's sudden death in the summer of 1864. Dostoevsky took over the monthly, which failed within a year, whereupon he assumed responsibility for the large debts that both Michael and he had incurred, and for the support of Michael's orphaned family. For the next dozen years or so money or, more truly, the lack of it, is a chief theme in his correspondence.

He secured a loan from the Fund for Needy Authors and an advance from a publisher on outrageous terms and, having paid off some urgent debts, with the remainder of the money again went abroad. He traveled to Wiesbaden, where he met Polina Suslova. The wicked girl, he wrote to her sister, continued to torment him, trading on the fact that he still loved her, though against his better judgment. He made no headway with the young woman, and a steady run of bad luck at roulette left him penniless. Polina having in the meantime departed, he wrote to her that for three days he had been living on tea, which was all the hotel keeper would allow him on credit, and that he was refused a candle at night, and he begged her to send him what she could. She was herself short of funds and did not reply. As he was later to write to his second wife, it was on one of those days that he conceived the idea of *Crime and Punishment*. The perennial borrower was able to return home by adding two old friends and the local Russian priest to the list of his creditors. Before leaving Wiesbaden, he offered the projected novel to a magazine in a letter of which only a rough draft is extant and which has since been much quoted. Therein he outlined the plot and indicated that the tale would show "Nihilism" as threatening to weaken the moral fibre of the nation. That morality cannot prevail without belief in God and personal immortality—in a later letter (LXX) he will say that the two "are one and the same"—was one of the cardinal dogmas of his faith. In this, as in later novels, his conscious purpose was to edify, without boring, an errant generation, to exorcise the demons that possessed it.

In 1867 he went abroad with his young bride, and stayed there over four years. He crossed the frontier ostensibly to consult foreign physicians about his epilepsy, but in fact mainly to keep out of debtors' prison. The letters dating from that period (many of them are included in the present collection) are the most poignant and dramatic portion of the epistolary material under consideration. In detailing the manifold miseries of what he called his "second exile," they cast a sharp light on his morbid temperament, on the torments and ecstasies that writing meant to him, on his sense of dedication to what he regarded as a high calling, a supreme duty. We learn something about what he sought to achieve in *The Idiot* and *The Possessed*, which he composed during those black years, and about the vicissitudes through which their plots passed. Like all his longer narratives, the two novels were serialized, and he complained bitterly that he was forced by penury to allow initial instalments to be printed before the rest was in shape, thus risking the ruin of his work. Some information is gained about one of his aborted literary projects: a sequence of novels under the general title, *The Life of a Great Sinner*.

Scattered through these communications are remarks that illuminate some facets of his thinking. The nations of the West are in a state of decadence, he asserts, for the reason that the Church of Rome has perverted the teachings of Christ. The Russian people alone have preserved the Christian religion in its purity. Hence his country's mission, and his own task as a writer, is to reveal the true Savior, the Christ of Russian Orthodoxy, to mankind. He also inveighs against socialism, seeing it as an attempt to set up a mechanical, irreligious, rationally planned collective, in which the individual will be degraded. These ideas, greatly elaborated, are woven into the texture of his novels and harped upon in his expository writings. Repeatedly he tried to body forth the Christian spirit of which, he believed, the Russian masses were the sole vessel. He was more successful in portraying a lost soul or an anguished sinner than a pious vagabond or a saintly Orthodox churchman.

The letters of Dostoevsky's last decade are of lesser import. They convey something of the tenor of less harried days. An author in vogue, a happily married man and a devoted paterfamilias, he is still racked by illness, but the wolf is no longer posted at the door. He appears at public meetings, is received in society and befriended by such pillars of the autocracy as Pobyedonostzev. The notes to his wife from Ems, where he goes nearly every year to take the waters, are marked by a uxorious eroticism which reminded one biographer of old Karamazov's sensuality. The letters to the same correspondent from Moscow—he is there to deliver a speech on the occasion of the unveiling of a statue of Pushkin—reveal his pretensions to being a leader of the conservative "party" that had a shadowy existence in the late eighteen-seventies. He receives a good deal of fan mail, including pleas for advice from perplexed souls. The few replies of his that are extant—all cordial, conscientious missives—add little regarding his views to what can be learned from the pages of *A Writer's Diary*. One of these communications (LXXIII) significantly amplifies his theory of emotional ambivalence, in the depiction of which he was a pioneer. Writing to a lady who complained that she was harassed by inward duality, he confesses that he is similarly afflicted, but that it is the source of "great delight" as well as "great torment," adding that only belief in Christ, or a strong desire to believe in Him, can alleviate the torment. Another remarkable letter interprets Christ's first temptation in the wilderness ("Command that these stones be made bread") as a prophecy of socialism. This bit of exegesis will figure in "The Grand Inquisitor," the pivotal chapter of *The Brothers Karamazov*. Dostoevsky's correspondence makes it possible to follow the stages of his work on that last and greatest novel of his, completed three months before his death. He takes pains to guard against factual errors in the narrative, but he is a realist only "in the higher sense," as he puts it. In commenting to his editor on what he calls a "climactic" instalment of the novel, he writes that his purpose is to refute socialism, a philosophy, he adds, that stems from the denial not of the existence of God, but of the meaning of the world that He created. The novelist goes on to say that the refutation will be effected by the section about Father Zossima, on which he is working "with fear, trepidation and awe," and that for the sake of those pages he is writing the entire book. He confides his anxiety in a letter to Pobyedonostzev: Has he succeeded in making his point? Will readers understand? It was apparently his belief that in *The Brothers Karamazov* he came closer than he had ever done to disburdening himself of the message with which he had been entrusted, and thus closer to writing his testament to Russia, to the world.

Dostoevsky does not rank with the great letter writers. The brief survey of the substance of his letters offered above should indicate, however, that those urgent, spontaneous pages are of no small interest and value. Without them, the chronicling of the works and days of one whose life moved from crisis to crisis and whose writings have so deeply impressed themselves on men's imagination, would be a hopeless task. They have much to tell about his

health, his material circumstances, his cast of mind. We learn a
great deal about his two marriages and something about an unhappy love affair that taught him much about what Henry James
called "the great constringent relation" between the sexes. Fur-
thermore, the letters bring into focus aspects of his thinking on
ethical and religious ultimates and on his country's mission—ideas
and ideals playing such an important part in his fictions. Above
all, they reveal the purposes he aimed at in his narratives and
clarify the conception and the long, difficult gestation of the
major novels on which his reputation rests. Not a few of the letters
are human documents, vibrant with pathos and drama. A selection
from the entire body of this epistolary material should reveal to
the general reader what amounts to a self-portrait of the novelist.

—AVRAHM YARMOLINSKY

TRANSLATOR'S PREFACE

In the German translator's[1] preface to this volume
it is pointed out that a complete collection of Dostoevsky's letters does not yet exist. "The first volume
of the first collected edition of Dostoevsky's works
(St. Petersburg, 1873) contains only a selection, which
is usually lacking in the later editions." Herr Eliasberg goes on to tell us that "a series of letters which
were to have been included in the present work was
at the last moment withdrawn by the novelist's
widow; the corrected proofs of these are to be preserved in a sealed portfolio at the Dostoevsky Museum
in Moscow."

The present volume derives chiefly from the book
by Tchechichin : "Dostoevsky in the Reminiscences
of his Contemporaries, and in his Letters and
Memoranda" (Moscow, 1912). The letters here
numbered XXXVIII., XLIV., L., LVI., and LVIII.
are lacking in Tchechichin's book, and were taken
from a Russian monthly journal, *Rousskaya Starina*.
Those numbered XXXIX., XLVI., XLVIII., and
LIX., which are incompletely given by Tchechichin,
are here given in full.

From Tchechichin's work were also taken a number

[1] Herr Alexander Eliasberg (R. Piper and Co., Munich).

xiii

of notes, as well as the reminiscences of Dostoevsky by his contemporaries, which here form an Appendix.

The present text, therefore, while it contains much that is relatively "inedited," yet cannot pretend to full completeness.   On comparing it with a French translation of some of the letters, issued by the Société du Mercure de France in 1908, it is seen to be a good deal the more judiciously edited of the two—the German translator has pared away many repetitions, much irrelevant and uninteresting matter, while he has used material of the highest biographical value which the French editor either unaccountably omitted, or, it may be, had not at disposal.   Of such are the letters enumerated above ; and, more than all, the peculiarly interesting passage in Letter XXXIV., which relates Dostoevsky's historic quarrel with Turgenev.

A word about the punctuation.   It has been, so far as was thought at all feasible, left as Dostoevsky offered it.   Like Byron, he "did not know a comma ; at least, where to put one"—or rather, in Dostoevsky's case, where *not* to put one, for his lavish use of the less important and lucid sign is very remarkable. Here and there, this predilection has been departed from by me, but only when it too deeply obscured the sense ; elsewhere, since even punctuation has its value for the student of character, Dostoevsky's " system " is retained in all its chaotic originality.

E. C. M.

CONTENTS

xvi CONTENTS

RECOLLECTIONS OF DOSTOEVSKY

CONTEMPORARY JUDGMENTS

ILLUSTRATIONS

*The illustrations are from photographs taken, by permission, from the
originals in the Moscow Museum.*

CHRONOLOGICAL TABLE OF DOSTOEVSKY'S LIFE

After V. TCHECHICHIN

1821. "In the parish of St. Peter and Paul at Moscow was born on October 30 of the year 1821, in the dwelling-house of the Workhouse Hospital, to Staff-Physician Michail Andreyevitch Dostoevsky, a male child, who was named Fyodor. Baptised on November 4."

1831. Dostoevsky's parents purchase a country-house in the Tula Government, where the family henceforth spends the summer.

1834. Dostoevsky enters the boys' school of L. J. Tchermak at Moscow.

1836. Great influence of the Literature-master upon the boys. Enthusiasm for Pushkin.

1837. On February 27, Maria Fyodorovna Dostoevsky, his mother, dies. Early in the year, Fyodor Dostoevsky goes with his elder brother Michael to Petersburg, and enters the Preparatory School of K. F. Kostomarov. In the autumn, he is admitted to the Principal College of Engineering.

1837-43. Study at the College of Engineering.

1838. Summer in camp. Enthusiasm for Balzac, Hugo, E. T. A. Hoffmann. In the autumn, failure in the examinations; is not promoted. In the winter, friendly relations with Schidlovsky and Berechetzky. Interest in Schiller.

1839. Death of his father, Michail Andreyevitch Dostoevsky.

1840. November 29: Promotion to non-commissioned officer's rank. December 27: To ensign's.

1841. Dramatic efforts, "Maria Stuart" and "Boris Godounov." (They have not come down to us.) August 5: Dostoevsky undergoes the examination for promotion to commissioned rank, and is promoted to be Field-Engineer's Ensign, on the recommendation of the College of Engineering.

1842. Promotion to Lieutenant's rank.

1843. August 12: Leaves the College. August 23: Obtains an appointment in the Department of Engineering.

1844. At the end of the preceding and in the beginning of this
year, Dostoevsky is occupied in translating Balzac's "Eugénie
Grandet." During the year he reads and translates works by
George Sand and Sue.
Works at " Poor Folk."
Project for a drama (Letter of September 30, 1844).
October 19 : Dostoevsky is by Royal permission discharged
with the rank of First-Lieutenant " on account of illness."
December 17 : He is struck off the lists of the Corps of
Military Engineers.

1845. In the beginning of May, the novel " Poor Folk " is finished.
Nekrassov and Grigorovitch pay the midnight visit after
reading " Poor Folk."
Intercourse with Bielinsky. In the summer he goes to his
brother Michael at Reval.
November 15 : Letter to his brother with news of his first
successes in literary circles.
At the end of the year, plans for the satirical journal,
Suboskal.
" Novel in Nine Letters."

1846. January 15 : Nekrassov's *Petersburg Almanac* appears, with
Dostoevsky's first book, " Poor Folk."
Bielinsky's article on " Poor Folk" in the *Otetschestvennia
Zapiski.*
February 1 : The story of "The Double " ("Goliadkin ")
appears in the *Otetschestvennia Zapiski.*
" The Whiskers that were Shaved Off" and the "Story of
the Abolished Public Offices." (Neither work has come down
to us.)
" Mr. Prochartschin" (*O.Z.*, No. 10).
In the summer, at Reval with his brother.
In the autumn, Dostoevsky thinks of issuing his collected
tales in volume form.
At the end of the year come misunderstandings, and a
breach with the editorial staff of the *Sovremennik.*

1847. The "Novel in Nine Letters" is published in the *Sovre-
mennik,* and " The Mistress of the Inn" in the *Otetschestvennia
Zapiski.*
" Poor Folk " appears in book form.

1848. The February Revolution in Paris.
Political groups, such as those around Petrachevsky, form in
Petersburg.
" The Stranger-Woman " (*O.Z.*, No. 1).
" A Weak Heart " (*O.Z.*, No. 2).
" Christmas and Wedding " (*O.Z.*, No. 10).
" Bright Nights " (*O.Z.*, No. 16).
" The Jealous Husband " (*O.Z.*, No. 12).

1849. " Netotchka Nesvanova" (*O.Z.*, Nos. 1-2, 5-6).

In March, Dostoevsky reads aloud [a revolutionary letter from Bielinsky to Gogol at Petrachevsky's rooms].[1]

On April 23, Dostoevsky, together with other members of the Petrachevsky circle, is arrested, and imprisoned in the Petropaulovsky Fortress. [He was accused of "having taken part in conversations about the severity of the Censorship; of having read, at a meeting in March, 1849, Bielinsky's revolutionary letter to Gogol; of having again read it at Dourov's rooms, and of having given it to Monbelli to copy; of having listened at Dourov's to the reading of various articles; of having knowledge of the plan to establish a clandestine printing-press," etc.][1]

December 19: Dostoevsky is condemned to degradation from military rank, and imprisonment.

December 22: Dostoevsky, and all the Petrachevsky group, hear read over them, first, the death-sentence, and then the commuted sentence of hard labour in the Siberian prisons.

December 24-25: On this night Dostoevsky is put in irons, and transported from Petersburg to Siberia.

1850. January 11: Arrival at Tobolsk. Meeting with the wives of the Decembrists.

January 17: Continues journey to Omsk.

1850-54. Serves his sentence in the prison at Omsk.

1854. February 15: Completion of sentence.

February 22: Letter to his brother with description of his life in the prison.

March 2: Dostoevsky is enrolled as private in the 7th Siberian Regiment of the Line.

In end of March, arrives at Semipalatinsk.

In May, writes his poem on the European incidents of 1854.

November 21: Baron Vrangel arrives at Semipalatinsk.

1855. February 19: The Tsar Alexander II. ascends the throne. Dostoevsky writes a poem on the death of Nicholas I. and the accession of Alexander II. (It has not come down to us.) He begins "The House of the Dead."

1856. January 15: Promotion to non-commissioned rank.

March 24: Letter to General Totleben, requesting his intercession with the Tsar.

October 1: By Imperial command, he is promoted to be Ensign in the same battalion.

1857. February 6: Dostoevsky's betrothal to the widowed Maria Dmitryevna Issayev takes place at Kusnezk.

---

[1] Translator's amplification.

April 18 : Imperial minute to the Commander of the Siberian Army Corps to the effect that Dostoevsky and his legal heirs regain the ancient title of nobility, though the confiscated property is not to be restored. Dostoevsky first hears of this in May.

At the end of the year, Dostoevsky sends in a petition, on discharge, begging to be allowed to live in Moscow.

" The Little Hero " (*O.Z.*, No. 8).

1859. March 18 : Discharged from military service with the rank of Lieutenant. Indication of the town of Tver as a suitable place of abode.

" Uncle's Dream " (*Roussky Viestnik*, No. 3).

July 2 : Departure from Semipalatinsk.

Autumn in Tver. Petition to the Tsar, that he may be allowed to live freely in all the towns of the Empire. Work at " The House of the Dead."

" Stepanchikovo Village " (*O.Z.*, Nos. 11-12).

At the end of November, permission to leave Tver. Leaves for Petersburg.

1860. Collected Edition of Works. Two volumes. Moscow : N. A. Osnovsky.

1861. Collaboration on the journal *Vremya*.

Publication of " Injury and Insult " in that journal and in book form.

1861-62. Publication of " The House of the Dead" (*Vremya*, 1861, Nos. 4, 9-11 ; and 1862, Nos. 1-3, 5, 12).

" A Silly Story " (*Vremya*, No. 11).

1862. Two editions in book form of " The House of the Dead."

June 7 : Departure for abroad.

Stays in Paris, London (meeting with Herzen), and Geneva.

1863. " Winter Notes on Summer Impressions " (*Vremya*, Nos. 2-3).

In May, suppression of the *Vremya*, in consequence of an article by Strachov on the Polish Question.

During the summer, travel in foreign lands. Stay in Rome. Plan for " The Gambler."

Wife's illness during the winter.

1864-65. Direction of *The Epoch*, which took the place of the *Vremya*.

1864. March 24 : Appears the first number of *The Epoch*. " From the Darkness of the Great City " (*Epoch*, Nos. 1-2 and 4).

April 16 : Death of his wife.

June 10 : Death of his brother Michael.

December 25 : Death of his friend and collaborator, Apollon Grigoryev.

1865. " An Unusual Occurrence " (*Epoch*, No. 2).
At the end of July, goes abroad. Begins the novel
" Rodion Raskolnikov " (" Crime and Punishment ").
Autumn in Wiesbaden.
October : Visit to Baron Vrangel at Copenhagen.
November : Return to Russia. Sale of his author's rights to
the publisher Stellovsky.

1865-66. First Collected Edition, in three volumes. Petersburg :
Stellovsky.
Publication of " Rodion Raskolnikov " (" Crime and Punish-
ment ") in the *Roussky Viestnik* (Nos. 1-2, 4, 6, 8, 11-12) and in
book form.
Summer at Lublin, near Moscow.
End of the year, at work on " The Gambler." Intercourse
with the stenographer Anna Grigorevna Snitkin.

1867. February 15 : Marriage to A. G. Snitkin.

1867-71. Life abroad.

1867. April 14 : Goes abroad. Two months in Dresden. Article
on Bielinsky (not preserved).
August 16 : Letter to Apollon Maikov on the quarrel with
Turgenev, and Dostoevsky's losses at roulette.
Plan for the " Diary of a Writer." (Letter to his niece of
September 29.)
At the end of the year, begins " The Idiot."
Third edition of " The House of the Dead "; second and
third editions of " Crime and Punishment."

1868. Publication of " The Idiot " in the *Roussky Viestnik* (Nos. 1,
2, 4-12) and in book form.
Summer in Switzerland and Italy.
Idea of a novel on Atheism (prototype of " The Brothers
Karamazov "). Letters about this to Maikov and his niece.

1869. Beginning of the year, in Florence. Connection with the
new journal *Sarya*, and lively interest in Danilevsky's essay on
" Russia and Europe."

1870. " The Permanent Husband " (*Sarya*, Nos. 1, 2). Beginning
of " The Possessed." Fourth edition of " Crime and Punishment."

1871-72. Publication of " The Possessed " (*Roussky Viestnik*, 1871,
Nos. 1-2, 4, 7, 9-12 ; and 1872, Nos. 11-12).

1871. July 8 : Return from abroad to Petersburg.

1872. Project of a trip to the East.
" The Permanent Husband " in book form.

1873. Joins editorial staff of *Grajdanin* (*The Citizen*), and publishes the " Diary of a Writer " (first sixteen chapters) and his " Survey of Foreign Occurrences."
   " The Possessed " in book form.

1874. At the end of March, arrest for infraction of the Censorship regulations.
   Autumn and winter, at Staraya-Roussa. Second edition of " The Idiot."
   Beginning of the novel, " The Hobbledehoy."

1875. " The Hobbledehoy " (*Otetschestvennia Zapiski*, Nos. 1, 2, 4, 5, 9, 11, 12), and in book form.
   Fourth edition of " The House of the Dead."
   Summer at Ems.

1876-77. " Diary of a Writer."

1876. Summer at Ems.
   Article (in the June number of the *Diary*) on the Balkan Question, and Dostoevsky's political creed.
   " The Hobbledehoy " in book form.

1877. " The Little Girl " (in the Supplement to *Grajdanin*).
   Summer in the Kursk Government.
   December 24 : " Memento for My Whole Life."

1878. In the summer, begins " The Brothers Karamazov."
   Fourth edition of " Crime and Punishment."

1879-80. Appearance of " The Brothers Karamazov " (*Roussky Viestnik*, 1879, Nos. 1, 2, 4-6, 8-11 ; 1880, Nos. 1, 4, 7-11), and in book form.

1879. Second edition of the " Diary of a Writer " from the year 1876.
   Fifth edition of " Injury and Insult."
   In June, goes with Vladimir Solovyov to the monastery at Optin.

1880. May 25 : Banquet of Moscow writers and journalists in Dostoevsky's honour.
   June 6 and 7 : Festivities at Moscow in connection with the unveiling of the Pushkin Memorial.
   June 8 : Dostoevsky's speech on Pushkin at the meeting of the Society of Lovers of Russian Literature. Takes part in the " Pushkin Evenings " got up by the Literary Fund.

1881. January 28 : At 8.38 o'clock p.m. Dostoevsky dies.
   January 31 : Public burial in the Cemetery of the Alexander Nevsky Monastery at Petersburg.

I

To his Father

MY DEAR GOOD FATHER,   *May* 10, 1838.

Can you really think that your son is asking too much when he applies to you for an allowance? God be my witness that not for self-interest, nor even in actual extremest need, could I ever wish to despoil you in any way. How bitter it is to have to ask my flesh and blood a favour which so heavily oppresses them! I have my own head, my own hands. Were I but free and independent, I should never have asked you for so much as a kopeck—I should have inured myself to the bitterest poverty. I should have been ashamed to write from my very death-bed, asking for support. As things are, I can only console you with promises for the future; however, that future is no longer a distant one, and time will convince you of its reality.

At present I beg you, dearest Papa, to reflect that in the literal sense of the word—I *serve*. I must, whether I wish it or not, conform to the obligations of my immediate environment. Why should I set up as an exception? Such exceptional attitudes, moreover, are often attended by the greatest un-

pleasantnesses. You will readily understand this,
dear Papa. You have mixed enough with men to do
that. And therefore consider, please, the following
points : Life in camp, for every student of the Military
Academy, demands at least forty roubles. (I write
this, because I am addressing my father.) In that
sum are not included such necessities as tea, sugar,
etc. Yet all those things I must have as well—
assuredly not only as comforts, but as sheer indis-
pensables. When one has to sleep in a canvas tent
during damp and rain, or when, in such weather, one
returns weary and chilled from practice, one may
easily fall ill for want of tea, as I have frequently
experienced in former years at these times. But I
want to consider your difficulties, and so I will give
up tea altogether, and ask you only for the barest
necessary of all—sixteen roubles for two pairs of
ordinary boots. Again : I *must* keep my things, such
as books, footgear, writing materials, paper, etc.,
somewhere or other. I need for that a trunk, for in
camp there is no kind of shelter but the tents. Our
beds are bundles of straw covered with sheets. Now
I ask you where, without a trunk, am I to keep my
things ? You must know that the Treasury does not
care in the least whether I have one or not. For the
exams will soon be over, and then I shall need no
books ; and as it is supposed to look after my uniform,
I ought not to require boots, etc. But how can I
pass the time without books ? and the boots with
which we are supplied are so bad that three pairs
scarcely see one through six months, even in the town.

[Here follows a further catalogue of necessary
purchases.]

From your last remittance I have laid by fifteen

roubles. So you see, dear Papa, that I need at least twenty-five more. We break up camp in the beginning of June. If you will stand by your son in his bitter need, send him this money by the first of June. I dare not insist upon my petition: I am not asking too much, but my gratitude will be boundless.

II

To his Brother Michael

PETERSBURG,
August 9, 1838.

[The letter begins with explanations of why Dostoevsky has not written to his brother for so long : he has not had a kopeck.]

It is true that I am idle—very idle. But what will become of me, if everlasting idleness is to be my only attitude towards life ? I don't know if my gloomy mood will ever leave me. And to think that such a state of mind is allotted to man alone—the atmosphere of his soul seems compounded of a mixture of the heavenly and the earthly. What an unnatural product, then, is he, since the law of spiritual nature is in him violated. . . . This earth seems to me a purgatory for divine spirits who have been assailed by sinful thoughts. I feel that our world has become one immense Negative, and that everything noble, beautiful, and divine, has turned itself into a satire. If in this picture there occurs an individual who neither in idea nor effect harmonizes with the whole— who is, in a word, an entirely unrelated figure—what must happen to the picture ? It is destroyed, and can no longer endure.

Yet how terrible it is to perceive only the coarse

veil under which the All doth languish! To know
that one single effort of the will would suffice to
demolish that veil and become one with eternity—to
know all this, and still live on like the last and least
of creatures. . . . How terrible! How petty is man!
Hamlet! Hamlet! When I think of his moving
wild speech, in which resounds the groaning of the
whole numbed universe, there breaks from *my* soul
not one reproach, not one sigh. . . . That soul is
then so utterly oppressed by woe that it fears to
grasp the woe entire, lest so it lacerate itself. Pascal
once said: He who protests against philosophy is
himself a philosopher. A poor sort of system!

But I have talked enough nonsense. Of your
letters I have had only two, besides the last of all.
Now, brother, you complain of your poverty. I am
not rich either. But you will hardly believe that
when we broke up camp I had not a kopeck. On
the way I caught cold (it rained the whole day and
we had no shelter), was sick with hunger as well, and
had no money to moisten my throat with so much as
a sip of tea. I got well in time, but I had suffered
the direst need in camp, till at last the money came
from Papa. I paid my debts, and spent the rest.

[Dostoevsky enlarges further on his brother's situation and his own financial difficulties.]

However, it is time to speak of other things. You
plume yourself on the number of books you have
read. . . . But don't please imagine that I envy you
that. At Peterhof I read at least as many as
you have. The whole of Hoffmann in Russian and
German (that is, "Kater Murr," which hasn't yet been
translated), and nearly all Balzac. (Balzac is great!

His characters are the creations of an all-embracing intelligence. Not the spirit of the age, but whole millenniums, with all their strivings, have worked towards such development and liberation in the soul of man.) Besides all these, I read Goethe's " Faust " and his shorter poems, Polevois' History, " Ugolino " and " Undine " (I'll write at length about " Ugolino " some other time), and, finally, Victor Hugo, except " Cromwell " and " Hernani." Farewell. Write to me, please, as often as you possibly can, for your letters are a joy and solace. Answer *this* at once. I shall expect your reply in twelve days at the very latest. Do write, that I may not utterly languish.

Thy brother,

F. DOSTOEVSKY.

I have a new plan : to go mad. That's the way : for people to lose their heads, and then be cured and brought back to reason ! If you've read all Hoffmann, you'll surely remember Alban. How do you like him ? It is terrible to watch a man who has the Incomprehensible within his grasp, does not know what to do with it, and sits playing with a toy called God !

III

To his Brother Michael

PETERSBURG,
October 31, 1838.

How long since I've written to you, dear brother ! That hateful examination—it prevented me from writing to you and Papa, and from looking up I. N. Schidlovsky.[1] And what came of it all ? I

---

[1] I. Nikolay Schidlovsky, a Treasury official, who wrote high-flown poems of abstract-ideal tendency. He later ruined himself by drink.

have not yet been promoted. O horror! to live another whole year in this misery! I should not have been so furious did I not know that I am the victim of the sheerest baseness. The failure would not have worried me so very much, if our poor father's tears had not burned into my soul. I had not hitherto known the sensation of wounded vanity. If such a feeling had got hold of me, I might well have blushed for myself. . . . But now you must know that I should like to crush the whole world at one blow. . . . I lost so much time before the examination, and was ill and miserable besides; but *underwent* it in the fullest and most literal sense of the word, and yet have failed. . . . It is the decree of the Professor of Algebra, to whom, in the course of the year, I had been somewhat cheeky, and who was base enough to remind me of it to-day, while ostensibly explaining to me the reason for my failure. Out of ten full marks I got an average of nine and a half, and yet I'm left. . . . But hang it all, if I must suffer, I will. . . . I'll waste no more paper on this topic, for I so seldom have an opportunity to talk with you.

My friend, you philosophize like a poet. And just because the soul cannot be for ever in a state of exaltation, your philosophy is not true and not just. To *know* more, one must *feel* less, and *vice versa*. Your judgment is feather-headed—it is a delirium of the heart. What do you mean precisely by the word *know?* Nature, the soul, love, and God, one recognizes through the heart, and not through the reason. Were we spirits, we could dwell in that region of ideas over which our souls hover, seeking the solution. But we are earth-born beings, and can

only guess at the Idea—not grasp it by all sides at
once.   The guide for our intelligences through the
temporary illusion into the innermost centre of the
soul is called *Reason*.   Now, Reason is a material
capacity, while the soul or spirit lives on the
thoughts which are whispered by the heart.
Thought is born in the soul.   Reason is a tool, a
machine, which is driven by the spiritual fire.   When
human reason (which would demand a chapter for
itself) penetrates into the domain of knowledge, it
works independently of the *feeling*, and consequently
of the *heart*.   But when our aim is the understanding
of love or of nature, we march towards the very
citadel of the heart.   I don't want to vex you, but I
do want to say that I don't share your views on
poetry or philosophy.   Philosophy cannot be regarded
as a mere equation where nature is the unknown
quantity !   Remark that the poet, in the moment of
inspiration, comprehends God, and consequently does
the philosopher's work.   Consequently poetic inspira-
is nothing less than philosophical inspiration.   Consequently philosophy is nothing but poetry, a higher
degree of poetry !   It is odd that you reason quite in
the sense of our contemporary philosophy.   What a
lot of crazy systems have been born of late in the
cleverest and most ardent brains !   To get a right
result from this motley troop one would have to
subject them all to a mathematical formula.   And
yet they are the " laws " of our contemporary philosophy !   I have jabbered enough.   And if I look
upon your flabby system as impossible, I think it
quite likely that my objections are no less flabby, so
I won't bother you with any more of them.

Brother, it is so sad to live without hope !   When

I look forward I shudder at the future. I move in a cold arctic atmosphere, wherein no sunlight ever pierces. For a long time I have not had a single outbreak of inspiration. . . . Hence I feel as the Prisoner of Chillon felt after his brother's death. The Paradise-bird of poetry will never, never visit me again—never again warm my frozen soul. You say that I am reserved ; but all my former dreams have long since forsaken me, and from those glorious arabesques that I once could fashion all the gilding has disappeared. The thoughts that used to kindle my soul and heart have lost their glow and ardency ; or else my heart is numbed, or else. . . . I am afraid to go on with that sentence. I won't admit that all the past was a dream, a bright golden dream.

Brother, I have read your poem. It urged some tears from my soul, and lulled it for a while by the spell of memories. You say that you have an idea for a drama. I am glad of that. Write your drama, then. If you had not these last crumbs from the Elysian feast, what would be left you in life ? I am so sorry that these last few weeks I have not been able to look up Ivan Nikolayevitch (Schidlovsky) ; I was ill. Now listen. I think that the poet's inspiration is increased by success. Byron was an egoist ; *his* longing for fame was petty. But the mere thought that through one's inspiration there will one day lift itself from the dust to heaven's heights some noble, beautiful human soul ; the thought that those lines over which one has wept are consecrated as by a heavenly rite through one's inspiration, and that over them the coming generations will weep in echo . . . that thought, I am convinced, has come to many a poet in the very

DOSTOEVSKY'S BIRTHPLACE.

(THE WORKHOUSE HOSPITAL AT MOSCOW.)

DOSTOEVSKY'S FATHER.

moment of his highest creative rapture.   But the
shouting of the mob is empty and vain.   There occur
to me those lines of Pushkin, where he describes the
mob and the poet :

"So let the foolish crowd, thy work despising, scream,
    And spit upon the shrine where burns thy fire supreme,
    Let them in childish arrogance thy tripod set a-tremble. . . ."

Wonderful, isn't it ?   Farewell.
                    Your friend and brother,
                        F. DOSTOEVSKY.

By the way, do tell me what is the leading idea
in Châteaubriand's work, " Génie du Christianisme."
I read lately in *Ssyn Otetschestva* an attack by
the critic Nisard on Victor Hugo.   How little the
French esteem him !   How low does Nisard rate
his dramas and romances !   They are unfair to him ;
and Nisard (though he is so intelligent) talks nonsense.   Tell me, too, the leading motive of your
drama ; I am sure it is fine.

I pity our poor father !   He has such a remarkable
character.   What trouble he has had.   It is so bitter
that I can do nothing to console him !   But, do you
know, Papa is wholly a stranger in the world.   He
has lived in it now for fifty years, and yet he has the
same opinions of mankind that he had thirty years
ago.   What sublime innocence !   Yet the world has
disappointed him, and I believe that that is the
destiny of us all.   Farewell.

IV

To his Brother Michael

PETERSBURG,
January 1, 1840.

I thank you from my heart, good brother, for your
dear letter.   I am certainly quite a different sort of
person from you ; you could never imagine how
delightfully my heart thrills when they bring me a
letter from you, and I have invented a new sort of
enjoyment : I put myself on the rack.   I take your
letter in my hand, turn it about for some minutes,
feel it to see whether it's long, and when I've satiated
myself with the sealed envelope, I put it in my
pocket.   You'd never guess what a pleasant state of
heart and soul I thus procure for myself.   I often
wait a quarter of an hour ; at last I fall greedily upon
the packet, unseal it, and devour your lines—your
dear lines !   Countless feelings awake in my heart
while I read your letter.   So many tender and painful, sweet and bitter, emotions crowd into my soul—
yes, dear brother, there are painful and bitter ones.
You cannot dream how bitter it is for me when
people don't understand me, when they mistake what
I say, and see it in the wrong light.   After I had
read your last letter, I was quite *enragé* because you
were not near me ; I saw the dearest dreams of my
heart, my most sacred principles, which I have won
by hard experience, wholly distorted, mutilated, de-
formed.   You said to me yourself : " Do write to me,
contradict me, dispute with me."   You anticipated
some profit therefrom.   Dear brother, it has not been
of the least use !   The only thing that you have got

from it is, that in your egoism (we are all egoists, for
that matter) you have formed just such an opinion
of me, my views, ideas, and peculiarities, as happens
to suit yourself.   And that is an extremely insulting
one!   No—polemics in intimate letters are a subtle
poison.   How will it be now, when we see one another again?   I believe that all this will be subject
for endless contention.   But enough of it.

Now for your verses—hear me yet again, dear
brother!   I believe that in human life are infinite
pain and infinite joy.   In the poet's life spring thorns
and roses.   The lyric is like the poet's shadow, always
with him, for he is an articulate creature.   Your lyric
poems are charming: "The Walk," "The Morning,"
"Visions of the Mother," "Roses," "The Horse of
Phœbus"—these and many others are lovely.   They
are all like a vital piece of news from you—and a
piece of news that moves me profoundly.   For in those
days I could understand you so well; and they are
months which have stamped themselves deeply in my
consciousness.   How many strange and wondrous
things had I just then lived through!   It is a long
story, and I shall never tell it to anyone.

When I last met Schidlovsky I took a walk with
him in Ekaterinhof.   What an amazing talk we had
that evening!   We were recalling the past winter,
when we talked much of Homer, Shakespeare,
Schiller, and Hoffmann — particularly Hoffmann.
We spoke of ourselves also, of the future, and of
you, my dear fellow.   But he has been away a long
time now, and I have no news of him.   Is he still
alive even?   For his health was very bad.   So do
write to him!

All through last winter I was in a strangely exalted

mood. Intercourse with Schidlovsky had procured
me many hours of fuller life, though that was not
the only reason for my inspired state. You were,
perhaps, hurt with me, and may even be so still,
because I did not write to you at that time. Stupid
service-matters were the hindrance. I must confess to you, my dear fellow, that though I have
always loved you, it was for your verses, for the
poetry of your life, for your sufferings . . . that was
all. It was neither brother-love nor comrade-love.
For I had with me at that time a friend, a man,
whom I *did* love so. You said once, brother, that I
had not read Schiller. You are mistaken. I have
him by heart, I have spoken his speech and dreamed
his dreams ; and I believe that it was a peculiarly
good stroke of luck that made me acquainted with
the great poet in that special period of my life. I
could never have learnt to know Schiller so well as
precisely in those days. When I read Schiller with
him, I saw *in him* the noble and fiery Don Carlos,
the Marquis Posa, and Mortimer. That friendship
was of great value to me, and has caused me great
pain. But I desire to keep silence about it for ever.
The name of Schiller is for me a beloved and intimate
password, which awakens countless memories and
dreams. Those memories are bitter, and that is why
I have always avoided talking with you about Schiller
and the impressions which I owe to him. Even to
hear his name sets my heart aching.

I meant to answer other of your reproaches, and
show you that you have misunderstood me. About
other things besides I wanted to speak ; but as I
write this letter, so many sweet remembrances and
dreams come over me that I can talk of nothing else.

Only one reproach will I refer to—namely, that those great poets whom, according to you, I do not know at all, I have nevertheless sought to compare closely with one another. I *never* drew such a parallel as one between Pushkin and Schiller. I can't imagine how you came to think so ; pray cite me the passage in my letter ; it is just possible that I may have happened to mention the names of Pushkin and Schiller in immediate juxtaposition, but I believe that you will find a comma between them. They have no smallest point of resemblance. Now between Pushkin and Byron one *might* speak of a likeness. But as to Homer and Victor Hugo, I positively believe that you have chosen to misunderstand me ! This is what I meant : Homer (a legendary figure, who was perhaps sent to us by God, as Christ was) can only be placed with Christ ; by no means with Victor Hugo. Do try, brother, to enter truly into the Iliad ; read it attentively (now confess that you never have read it). Homer, in the Iliad, gave to the ancient world the same organization in spiritual and earthly matters as the modern world owes to Christ. Do you understand me now ? Victor Hugo is a singer, clear as an angel, and his poetry is chaste and Christian through and through ; no one is like him in that respect—neither Schiller (if Schiller is a Christian poet at all), nor the lyric Shakespeare, nor Byron, nor Pushkin. I have read his Sonnets in French. Homer alone has the same unshakeable belief in his vocation for poetry and in the god of poetry whom he serves—in that sole respect his poetry is like Victor Hugo's, but *not* in the ideas with which Nature gifted him, and which he succeeded in expressing—I never meant the ideas at all, never. I even think that Dershavin stands higher as a lyricist than either of those two. Farewell, my dear fellow.

P.S.—I must give you one more scolding. When you talk about form in poetry, you seem to me quite crazy. I mean it seriously. I noticed a long time ago that in this respect you are not wholly normal. Lately you let fall a remark of the kind about Pushkin; I purposely did not take it up. Of your own forms I'll speak at length in my next letter ; now I have neither room nor time. But do tell me how, when you were talking about forms, you could advance the proposition that neither Racine nor Corneille could please us, because their forms were bad ? You miserable wretch ! And then you add with such effrontery : " Do you think, then, that they were both bad poets ?" Racine no poet—Racine the ardent, the passionate, the idealist Racine, no poet ! Do you dare to ask that ? Have you read his " Andromaque "—eh ? Have you read his " Iphigénie "? Will you by any chance maintain that it is not splendid ? And isn't Racine's Achilles of the same race as Homer's ? 1 grant you, Racine stole from Homer, but in what a fashion ! How marvellous are his women ! Do try to apprehend him. You say " Racine was no genius ; how could he possibly (?) produce a drama? He could only imitate Corneille." What about "Phèdre?" Brother, if you won't agree that " Phèdre " is the highest and purest poetry, I don't know what I shall think of you. Why, there's the force of a Shakespeare in it, if the medium *is* plaster of Paris instead of marble.

Now about Corneille. Listen again, brother ! 1

really don't know how to talk to you; perhaps, like
Ivan Nikiforovitch,[1] I ought to eat a substantial
portion of herbs first. I cannot believe that you've
read him at all; that's why you talk such nonsense.
Why, don't you know that Corneille, with his titanic
figures and his romantic spirit, nearly approaches
Shakespeare? You miserable wretch! Do you
happen to know that it was not until fifty years later
than the inept miserable Jodelle (author of that disgusting "Cléopâtre") and Ronsard, who was a fore-
warning of our own Trediakovsky, that Corneille
made his appearance, and that he was almost a contemporary of the insipid poetaster Malherbe? How
can you demand form from him? It was as much
as one could expect that he should borrow his form
from Seneca. Have you read his "Cinna"? What,
before the divine figure of Octavius, becomes of Karl
Moor, of Fiesco, of Tell, of Don Carlos? That
work would have done honour to Shakespeare. You
wretch! If you haven't read it yet, read now at
least the dialogue between Augustus and Cinna,
where he forgives him for his treachery. Good
Heavens! You will see that only offended seraphs
could so speak. Particularly the passage where
Augustus says: "*Soyons amis, Cinna.*" Have you
read his "Horace"? Decidedly only in Homer can
you find such figures. Old Horace is another
Diomedes; young Horace an Ajax, son of Telamon,
but with the spirit of an Achilles; Curias is Patrocles
and Achilles in one person; he is the very consum-
mation of conflicting love and duty. It's all so
lofty! Have you read "Le Cid"? Read it, unhappy
man, and fall in the dust before Corneille. You

---

[1] The hero of a novel by Gogol.

have blasphemed him. Anyhow, read him. What does the romantic stand for, if it doesn't reach its highest development in the " Cid "? How wonderful are the figures of Don Rodrigo, of his son, and of that son's beloved—and then, the end !

Please don't be offended with me for my insulting expressions ; don't bear me ill-will, as Ivan Ivanovitch Pererepenko did to Gogol.

V

To his Brother Michael

September 30, 1844.

[At first he speaks of the translation of Schiller, which the brothers wished to publish.]

Yes, brother, indeed I know that my position is desperate. I want to lay it before you now, just as it is. I am retiring because I can serve no longer. Life delights me not if I am to spend the best part of it in such a senseless manner. Moreover, I never did intend to remain long in the service—why should I waste my best years ? But the chief point is that they wanted to send me to the provinces. Now, tell me, pray, what should I be good for, out of Petersburg ? What could I do? You will assuredly understand me there.

As regards my future life, you really need not be anxious. I shall always find means to support myself. I mean to work tremendously hard. And I am *free* now. The only question is what I shall do just for the moment. Think of it, brother : I owe eight hundred roubles—five hundred and twenty-five for rent. (I have written home that I owe one thousand five hundred, for I know the gentry

there.[1]   They always send me a third of what I ask
for.)   Nobody knows yet that I am retiring.   Now,
what shall I do at first, when I am no longer in the
service?   I haven't even the money to buy civilian
clothes.   I retire on October 14.   If I don't receive
money from Moscow at once, I am lost.   Seriously,
they will put me in prison—this is certain.   It's a
quaint situation.

[There is further discussion of how he shall get
money from his relatives.]

You say that my salvation lies in my drama.   But
it will be a long time before it's played, and longer still
before I get any money for it.   Meanwhile, my retire-
ment stares me in the face.   (My dear fellow, if I had
not already sent in my papers, I should do so now ;
I in no wise regret that step.)   I have one hope more.
I am just finishing a novel,[2] about the length of
" Eugénie Grandet."   It is most original.   I am now
making the fair copy ; by the 14th I ought certainly
to have an answer from the editor.   I want to bring
it out in the *Otetchestvennia Zapiski*.[3]   (I am well
pleased with my work.)   I shall probably get four
hundred roubles for it—that is all I hope for.   I would
have liked to tell you more about the book, but I
haven't time.   (I shall certainly produce the play,
anyhow.   For that is the way I wish to make a
living.)

The Moscovians are incredibly stupid, conceited,
and priggish.   K.[4] in his last letter advises me, with
no apparent relevancy, not to let myself be so carried
away by Shakespeare.   He says that Shakespeare is

---

[1] His father was now dead, and an uncle-in-law acted as
Dostoevsky's guardian.   [2] His " Poor Folk."
[3] " Annals of the Fatherland."   [4] Dostoevsky's guardian.

only a soap-bubble. I wish you could explain to me
this ridiculous hostility against Shakespeare. Why
does he suddenly drag him in? You should have
seen the answer I sent him! It was a model in the
polemic style. I gave him a first-class snubbing.
My letters are masterpieces of the "literary art."

Brother, do, for God's sake, write home at once!
My situation is desperate. The 14th is the very
utmost limit of my time; I sent in my papers six
weeks ago. For Heaven's sake write to them, and
tell them to send me the money without delay! It is
urgent, for otherwise I shall have no clothes. Chles-
takov (in Gogol's "Revisor") was ready to go to
prison, but only "with all dignity." Now, how can
I, barefoot, go to prison "with all dignity"? . . .

My address : By the Vladimirkirche, care of Pryan-
ischnikof, Grafengasse.

I am extraordinarily pleased with my novel—beside
myself with joy. For *it* I shall certainly get money ;
but as for anything else. . . . Forgive this incoherent
letter.

VI

To his Brother Michael

March 24, 1845.

You must have been burning with impatience for
ever so long, dearest brother. The uncertainty of
my situation prevented me from writing. I can give
myself up to no employment, when only uncertainty
stares me in the face. Not that I have yet succeeded
in regulating my affairs in any way ; but despite this
unsettled state of things, I will write to you, for it is
so long since I have sent you a word.

I got five hundred roubles from the Moscow folk.
But I had so many old and new debts that the money
did not suffice for the printing. Still, it was not so
bad. I could either go on credit for the printing, or
else pay only half the household debts ; but the novel
was not ready. I *had* finished it in November, but
in December I decided to alter it radically. I did so,
and wrote it out fair again ; then in February I began
once more to fiddle at it, polishing, cutting, adding.
Towards the middle of March I was ready, and
satisfied with my work. But there arose a fresh
obstacle : the Censor wanted a whole month for the
reading. It couldn't be done quicker. The officials
at the Censorship are said to be loaded down with
work. I didn't know what to do, and asked for the
manuscript back. For besides the four weeks for the
Censor, I had to reckon on three more for the printing. So at earliest the book would appear in May.
That would have been too late ! Then people began
to urge me from all sides to send the novel to the
Otetchestvennia Zapiski. It would have been madness ; I should certainly have rued it. In the first
place, they wouldn't have read the manuscript at all,
or, if they *had*, not for at least six months. They
have enough manuscripts lying about without getting
mine. And if they did print, I shouldn't get a penny
for it ; for that paper is a pure oligarchy. What do
I want with fame, when I'm writing for daily bread ?
I took a desperate resolve—to wait a while longer,
and in the meantime incur fresh debts. Towards the
beginning of September, when everyone will be in
Petersburg, sniffing about like bloodhounds for something new, I'll try with my last kopecks (which
probably won't nearly suffice) to get the book printed.

If I published in a magazine, I should come under
the yoke of not only the head *maître d'hôtel*, but of
all the kitchen wenches and urchins who swarm
wherever culture is in the making. It's not a question of one dictator, but twenty. While if I print
the novel at my own expense, I may make my way
by my own ability ; and if the book is good, it won't
be overlooked—it may even get me out of debt, and
rescue me from anxiety about the means of subsistence.

And now to those means of subsistence ! You
know well, dear brother, that I have been thrown on
my own resources in that respect. But I have vowed
to myself that, however hard it may go with me, I'll
pull myself together, and in no circumstances will I
work to order. Work done to order would oppress
and blight me. I want each of my efforts to be
incontrovertibly good. Just look at Pushkin and
Gogol. Both wrote very little, yet both have de-
served national memorials. Gogol now gets a thousand
roubles a printed page, while Pushkin had, as you
know well, as much as a ducat a line of verse. Both
—but particularly Gogol—bought their fame at the
price of years of dire poverty. The old school is
going to pieces ; and the new school doesn't write—it
scribbles. Talent is universally squandered in striv-
ing after a " broad conception," wherein all one can
discover is a monstrous inchoate idea and colossal
muscular effort. There is hardly any real serious *work*
in the business. Béranger said of the modern French
feuilletonists that their work was like a bottle of
Chambertin in a bucket of water. And our people
are the same. Raphael worked for many years at
each picture, and lingered long over every detail,

therefore he created masterpieces. Gods grew under his brush! And to-day Vernet gets a picture ready in a month, and each needs a huge room, built expressly. The perspective is grandiose, the conception colossal—but there's not a ha'porth of serious work in the thing. They are all no better than house-painters.

I am really pleased with my novel. It is a serious and well-constructed work. But it has terrible shortcomings, too. Seeing it in print will make up to me for everything else. *Now*, while I have as yet no new ideas, I should rather like to write something that would introduce me to the public, or even for the mere money's sake ; not that I should at all wish to write rubbish, but for anything really serious I need a lot of time.

It is getting near the time, my dears, that I had hoped to spend with you all. But I shall not have the means, that is the money, for it. I have decided to stay on in my old abode. For here I have, at any rate, a contract with the landlord, and need not worry myself about anything for six months. It's simply a case of my novel covering *all!* If I fail in this, I'll hang myself.

I should like to have saved at least three hundred roubles by August. I can have the book printed for that. But the roubles run about like crabs in every direction. I had about four hundred worth of debts (including the new expenses and clothes) ; now I'm decently dressed for at least two years. But I really will come to you, anyhow. Write as soon as possible and say what you think about my staying on here. It is a crucial question. But what else can I do?

You write that you are terrified of the resourceless

future.   But Schiller will set right all that, and,
besides, my novel may bring in something.   Write
soon.   By the next post I'll tell you all my decisions.

*   *   *

Kiss the children from me, and greet Emilie
Fyodorovna.[1]   I often think of you all.   Perhaps it
will interest you to know what I do when I'm not
writing—well, I read.   I read a great deal, and it
has a curious effect on me.   When I re-read anything
that I knew years ago, I feel fresh powers in myself.
I can pierce to the heart of the book, grasp it entire,
and from it draw new confidence in myself.   Of
the writing of plays I don't want to know anything.
To do one I should need years of repose and hard
study.   It is easy enough, indeed, to write plays to-
day ; the drama is more like melodrama.   Shakespeare
disappears in the fog, he looks, amid the fumes of
our wretched modern drama, like a god, or a spectre
of the Brocken.   In the summer I shall, nevertheless,
perhaps try again to write one.   Just let us wait two
or even three years !   Brother, in literary matters
I am not the same person that I was a couple of
years ago.   Then it was all childishness and folly.
These two years of hard study have taken much from
me, and brought much to me.

In the *Invalide* lately I read in the feuilleton about
the German writers who died of hunger, cold, or in
a mad-house.   They were twenty in all—and what
names !   Even still it gives me the creeps.   It's
better to be a charlatan, really. . . .

[1] Michael Dostoevsky's wife.

VII

To his Brother Michael

DEAREST BROTHER,　　　　　　　　*May 4, 1845.*

Forgive my not having written for so long.
I have, as usual, had such a confounded lot to do.
My novel, which I simply can't break loose from,
keeps me endlessly at work.　If I had known beforehand how it would be, I should never have begun it
at all.　I decided to do it all over again, and, by
God! that has improved it a lot.　Now I'm ready with
it once more, and this revision is really the last.　I
have given myself my word not to touch it again.
After all, it's the fate of all first books to be altered
over and over again.　I don't know whether Châteaubriand's "Atala" was his first book, but I do know
that he re-wrote it seventeen times.　Pushkin did
just the same with quite short poems.　Gogol used
to polish away at his wonderful works for two years
at a time, and if you have read the "Sentimental
Journey," that witty book by Sterne, you'll very
likely remember what Walter Scott, in his article on
Sterne, says with reference to Sterne's servant, La
Fleur.　La Fleur declared that his master had filled
about two hundred quires of paper with the description of his journey through France.　Now, the question is, What became of all that paper?　The result
was a little book, for writing which a parsimonious
person (such as, for example, Plyushkin[1]) would have
used half a quire.　I can't understand at all how that
same Walter Scott could turn out such finished

[1] A character in Gogol's "Dead Souls"—the incarnation of
avarice.

works as "Mannering" in a few weeks. Perhaps only because at that time he was forty years old.

I don't in the least know, brother, what will become of me! You judge me falsely when you maintain that my situation doesn't trouble me a bit. It worries me frightfully, and I often cannot sleep for nights and nights because of my tormenting thoughts. Wise folk tell me that I shall come to the ground if I publish the novel as a book. They admit that the book will be a very good one, but say that I am no business man . . . and that the booksellers are usurers; that they will rob me as a matter of course, and I, as sure as death, shall let them.

For these reasons I have resolved to bring out the novel in a journal—for example, the *Otetchestvennia Zapiski*. That has an edition of 2,500 copies, consequently it is read by at least 100,000 people. If I let the novel appear in this journal, my literary career and my whole future life are assured. I might easily make my fortune by it. And thus I shall gain a firm footing in the paper, and shall always have money; and if my novel appears in the August or September number, I can bring it out as a book on my own account in October, and that with the certain prospect that everyone who buys novels at all will get it. Moreover, the advertisement will cost me nothing. Well, so things stand!

Until I have arranged for the novel, I cannot come to Reval; I don't want to waste any of my time. I must not flinch at any amount of hard work. I have, besides, a lot of new ideas, which will make a name for me in literature as soon as my first book has forged a path for me. These are, in short, my only views for the future.

But as to money, I have none, alas! The devil knows where it's gone to. But, at all events, I have few debts. . . .

When once I have produced the novel, I shall easily be able to arrange for your Schiller translation also, as true as I live! The "Juif Errant" isn't bad. But Sue strikes me as very limited in range.

I don't like to speak of it, dear brother, but your situation and the fate of your Schiller worry me so much that I often forget my own anxieties. And I really have not an easy time of it.

If I can't publish the novel, I shall probably go into the Neva. What else *should* I do? I have thought of every single thing. I could not survive the death of my fixed idea.

Write to me soon, for I am sick of myself.

VIII

To his Brother Michael

DEAREST BROTHER,　　　*October* 8, 1845.

Until now I have had neither time nor spirits to write you anything about my own affairs. Everything was disgusting and hateful, and the whole world seemed a desert. In the first place, I had no money all the time, and was living on credit, which is most unpleasant, my dear and only friend. In the second, I was in that wretched mood wherein one loses all courage, yet does not fall into dull indifference—rather, which is much worse, thinks a great deal too much about one's-self, and rages uncontrollably.

At the beginning of this month Nekrassov[1] came to me and paid me back part of his debt ; the rest I am to have in a few days. I must tell you that Bielinsky[2] gave me, a fortnight ago, a comprehensive lesson on how to live in the literary world. As a conclusion he told me that, for my soul's sake, I must not ask less than two hundred roubles a printed sheet. In that case my " Goliadkin "[3] would bring me in at least fifteen hundred roubles. Nekrassov, who was evidently conscience-stricken, anticipated him, and promised me on January 15 a hundred roubles more for my " Poor Folk," which he has acquired from me. He felt obliged to confess to me himself that a fee of a hundred and fifty roubles was absolutely un-Christian, so he has raised it by a hundred.

This is all very nice indeed. But it is most unpleasant to have still no word from the Censor about " Poor Folk." They have kidnapped that guileless novel, and I don't know what will be the end thereof. And suppose they forbid it to appear ? Or strike out every word of it ? It is a real calamity ! Nekrassov tells me, too, that his Almanac won't be able to appear at the right time, and that that undertaking has already cost him four thousand roubles.

Jakov Petrovitch Goliadkin is a bad hat ! He is utterly base, and I positively can't manage him. He won't move a step, for he always maintains that he isn't ready ; that he's mere nothingness as yet, but

[1] Nicolay Alexeyevitch Nekrassov (1821-77), a noted writer of Liberal tendencies ; he edited from 1846 to 1866 the monthly magazine established by Pushkin, *Sovremennik* (= *The Contemporary*).

[2] Vissarion Grigoryevitch Bielinsky, a most distinguished Russian critic, of extreme Liberal tendency.

[3] " The Double."

could, if it were necessary, show his true character;
then why won't he? And after all, he says, he's no
worse than the rest. What does *he* care about my
toil? Oh, a terribly base fellow! In no case can he
bring his career to a finish before the middle of
November. He has already had an interview with
His Excellency, and is not disinclined to take his
leave—as, indeed, he well may. Me, his poor author,
he is putting in a hole.

I often go to Bielinsky's. He's inordinately affectionate, seeing in me a vindication of his views to the
public. I have lately made the acquaintance of
Kroneberg, the translator of Shakespeare (he's a son
of the old Professor from Charkov). My future—and
certainly the immediate future—may shape itself, on
the whole, most favourably, but may also turn out
very badly indeed. Bielinsky urges me to finish my
"Goliadkin." He has already spread the fame of that
novel through the entire literary world, and almost
sold it to Krayevsky.[1] Half Petersburg is talking of
"Poor Folk." A good word from Grigorovitch[2] carries
weight, and he said to me myself the other day: "Je
suis votre claqueur-chauffeur."

Nekrassov is always full of wild schemes. It is a
condition of his being—he was born like that. Directly
he arrived here, he came to me one evening and unfolded a plan for a little "flying" Almanac into which
the whole literary community should put their backs;
but at the head of the editorial staff are to be myself,
Grigorovitch, and Nekrassov. The last will take the

[1] Editor of the *Otetchestvennia Zapiski*.
[2] Dmitri Vassilivitch Grigorovitch (1822-99), a popular writer;
author of numerous romances and novels. A colleague of Dostoevsky in the College of Engineering.

financial risk. The Almanac is to consist of two
sheets, and to appear fortnightly—on the 7th and 21st
of the month. It is to be called *Suboskal* (*The
Scoffer*). We mean to ridicule and jeer at everything
without mercy—the theatres, newspapers, society,
literature, daily happenings, exhibitions, advertise-
ments, foreign news—in short, everything; the whole
is to be done with *one* tendency and in *one* spirit.
The first number is to appear on November 7. It is
wonderfully compounded. In the first place, there are to
be illustrations as well. As motto we take the famous
words of Bulgarin* in his feuilleton in the *Sévernaïa
Ptchéla* (*Northern Bee*): "We are ready to die for
the truth, for we cannot live without truth," etc.
Underneath we shall put Faddey Bulgarin's signature.
The prospectus, which will appear on November 1,
will have the same motto. The first number will
contain the following contributions: A sort of
"send-off," by Nekrassov, "On Certain Petersburg
Basenesses" (those, of course, which have just then
been perpetrated); an "anticipated" novel by Eugène
Sue, "The Seven Deadly Sins" (the whole thing will
be in three pages); a review of all the journals; a
lecture "after" Schevirov, on Pushkin's verses:
they are so harmonious, that when Schevirov once at
the Coliseum in Rome, in company with some ladies,
recited a few strophes, all the frogs and lizards that
house there came creeping out to hear the wondrous
stanzas (Schevirov gave just such a discourse in the
Moscow University). Then comes a report of the
last sitting of the Society of Slavophils, whereat it
was solemnly maintained that Adam was a Slav and

---

[1] Faddey Bulgarin (1789-1859), a journalist in the pay of the
police; hated and feared as a denouncer and secret agent.

lived in Russia; it will be pointed out how important and useful is the settling of this question for the well-being of the whole Russian nation. In the art section, our *Suboskal* will declare itself at one with Kukolnik's *Illustration*, and call particular attention to the following passage in that journal [one where the letters and words were printed upside down and in the wrong order], for it is well known that the *Illustration* is so badly edited and proof-read that topsy-turvy letters and words running into one another are quite normal occurrences. Grigorovitch will write a " Chronicle of the Week," and take a rise out of people with his " things seen." I am to write " Observations of a Valet on his Master." The paper will, as you see, be highly diverting—something in the style of the *Guèpes* of Alphonse Karr. The notion is dazzling, for to me alone will come, at the very lowest estimate, from a hundred to a hundred and fifty roubles a month. The sheet will succeed. Nekrassov will do some verse, too.

. . . On no account miss reading " Teverino " (by George Sand, in the *Otetchestvennia Zapiski* for October). There has been nothing like it in our century. It gives us absolute archetypes of human character. . . .

IX

To his Brother Michael

November 16, 1845.

DEAREST BROTHER,

I write in great haste, for my time is very short. "Goliadkin" is still not ready, but I absolutely *must* have him finished by the 25th. You haven't written to me for so long that I have been worried about you. Do write oftener; what you say about lack of time is nonsense. Does one really need much time to write a letter? Provincial life, with its eternal do-nothingness, is simply ruining you, my dear fellow—that's all.

Well, brother, I believe that my fame is just now in its fullest flower. Everywhere I meet with the most amazing consideration and enormous interest. I have made the acquaintance of a lot of very important people. Prince Odoyevsky begs me for the honour of a visit, and Count Sollogub is tearing his hair in desperation. Panayev told him that a new genius had arisen who would sweep all the rest away. S. tore round, called on Krayevsky among others, and asked him quite bluntly: " Who is Dostoevsky? Where can I get hold of Dostoevsky?" Krayevsky, who is without respect of persons and snubs everybody, gave him for answer: " Dostoevsky won't be at all inclined to give you the honour and pleasure of his acquaintance." It was just the right word, for the youngster is now on his high horse, and hopes to crush me to the earth with his gracious condescension. Everybody looks upon me as a wonder of the world. If I but open my mouth, the air resounds with what Dostoevsky said, what Dostoevsky means to do. Bielinsky loves me unboundedly. The writer Turgenev, who has just returned from Paris, has from the first been more than friendly; and Bielinsky declares that Turgenev has quite lost his heart to me. T. is a really splendid person! I've almost lost my own heart to *him*. A highly gifted writer, an aristocrat, handsome, rich, intelligent, cultured, and only twenty-five—I really don't know what more he could ask from fate. Besides all that, he has an unusually upright, fine, well-disciplined nature. Do read his story, " Andrey Kolossov," in the *Otetchestvennia Zapiski*. The hero is himself, though he did not intend to depict his own character.

I am not rich yet, though I can't complain of poverty. Lately I was quite penniless for the moment ; Nekrassov has since then taken up the idea of publishing a most attractive sort of humorous Almanac, to be called *Suboskal*, and I have written the prospectus. It made a great sensation, for it is the first attempt there has been to write such productions in a light and humorous manner. It reminded me of the first feuilleton of Lucien de Rubempré.[1] It has already appeared in the *O. Z.*, and in another paper. I got twenty roubles for the job. When I found myself without a penny in my pocket, I went to call on Nekrassov. While I was sitting with him, I had a sudden idea of writing a novel in nine letters. As soon as I got home, I wrote it in one night ; it takes about half a sheet. In the morning I took the manuscript to Nekrassov, and got 125 roubles for it, so the *Suboskal* pays me at the rate of 250 roubles a sheet. In the evening my novel was read aloud in our circle—that is, before an audience of twenty, and had a colossal success. It will appear in the first number of the *Suboskal*. I'll send you the number for December 1. Bielinsky says he is quite sure of me now, for I have the faculty of grasping the most diverse subjects. When Krayevsky heard lately that I had no money, he begged me quite humbly to accept a loan of 500 roubles. I think that I shall get 200 roubles a sheet from him.

[1] In Balzac's " Illusions perdues."

I have a lot of new ideas—and if I confide any of
them to anybody, for instance Turgenev, by next
morning it will be rumoured in every corner of
Petersburg that Dostoevsky is writing this or that.
Indeed, brother, if I were to recount to you all my
triumphs, this paper would by no means suffice.   I
think that I shall soon have plenty of money.
" Goliadkin " thrives mightily ; it will be my masterpiece.   Yesterday I was at P.'s house for the first
time, and I have a sort of idea that I have fallen in
love with his wife.   She is wise and beautiful,
amiable, too, and unusually direct.   I am having a
good time.   Our circle is very extensive.   But I'm
writing about nothing but myself—forgive me, dear
fellow ; I will frankly confess to you that I *am* quite
intoxicated by my fame.   With my next letter I'll
send you the *Suboskal.*   Bielinsky says that I pro-
faned myself by collaborating in it.

Farewell, my friend.   I wish you luck, and congratulate you on your promotion.   I kiss the hands
of your Emilie Fyodorovna, and hug the children.
How are they all ?

P.S.—Bielinsky is keeping the publishers from
tearing me to pieces.   I've read this letter over, and
come to two conclusions—that I write atrociously,
and that I'm a boaster.

Farewell, and for God's sake write.   Our Schiller
will certainly come off.   Bielinsky praises the idea of
publishing the collected works.   I believe that in
time I shall be able to make good terms for the
work—perhaps with Nekrassov.   Farewell.

All the Minnas, Claras, Mariannas, etc., have got
amazingly pretty, but cost a lot of money.   Turgenev
and Bielinsky lately gave me a talking-to about my

disorderly way of life. Those fellows really don't know how they can best prove their affection—they are all in love with me.

X

To his Brother Michael

DEAREST BROTHER,   *February 1, 1846.*

   To begin with, don't be angry because I haven't written for so long. I swear to God that I've had no time, as I shall now show you. I was prevented chiefly by that rascal "Goliadkin," with whom I never finished till the 28th. It's frightful! And it's always the same whenever one promises one's-self anything. I meant to get done with him in August, but had to put off till February. Now I am sending you the Almanac. "Poor Folk" appeared on the 15th. If you only knew, brother, how bitterly the book has been abused! The criticism in the *Illustration* was one unbroken tirade. And that in the *Sévernaïa Ptchéla* (*Northern Bee*) is incredible, too; but at all events, I can remind myself how Gogol was received by the critics, and we both know the things that were written about Pushkin. Even the public is quite furious: three-fourths of my readers abuse, and a quarter (or even less) praise the book beyond measure. It is the subject of endless discussion. They scold, scold, scold, yet they read it. (The Almanac has gone off amazingly well. The whole edition is certain to be sold out in a fortnight.) And it was the same with Gogol. They abused, abused, but read him. Now they've made up *that* quarrel, and praise him. I've thrown a hard bone to the dogs, but let them worry

at it—fools! they but add to my fame.   The notice
in the *Northern Bee* is a disgrace to their critic.   It's
stupid beyond belief.   But then, the praise I get,
too!   Only think, all our lot, and even Bielinsky,
consider that I have far surpassed Gogol.   In the
Book-lovers' Library, where the critiques are written
by Nikitenko, there is soon to be a very long and
favourable notice of " Poor Folk."   Bielinsky will
ring a full peal in March.   Odoevsky is devoting
his whole article to " Poor Folk " alone; my friend
Sollogub likewise.   So I'm in the empyrean, brother,
and three months hence I'll tell you in person of all
my experiences.

Our public, like the crowd everywhere, has good
instincts, but no taste.   They cannot understand how
anyone can write in such a style.   They are accustomed to be treated, in every work, to the author's
own fads and fancies.   Now I have chosen not to
show mine.   They *will* not perceive that this or
that view is expressed by Dyevuschkin, not by me,
and that *he* could not speak otherwise.   They find
the book too drawn-out, and yet there is not a single
superfluous word in it.   Many, like Bielinsky, think
very original my manner of proceeding by analysis
rather than by synthesis—that is, I pierce to the
depths, trace out the atoms, and from them construct
the whole.   Gogol always works on the broad lines,
and so he never goes as deep as I do.   When you
read my book, you'll see this for yourself.   I have a
brilliant future before me!   To-day my " Goliadkin " appears.   Four days ago I was still working at
him.   He will fill eleven sheets of the *Otetschestvennia Zapiski*.   " Goliadkin " is ten times better than
" Poor Folk."   Our lot say that there has been

nothing like it in Russia since " Dead Souls," and
that it is a truly brilliant achievement; they even
say more.   What don't they look for from me!
" Goliadkin " really has come off well.   You will be
sure to like him enormously.   Do they take the *O. Z.*
in your part of the world ?   I don't know if Krayevsky
will give me a free copy.

I haven't written to you for so long, dear brother,
that I really don't know what I told you last.   So
much has been happening!   We shall soon see one
another again.   In the summer I shall positively
come to you, my friends, and shall write tremendously
the whole time.   I have ideas; and I'm writing now,
too.

For "Goliadkin" I got exactly 600 roubles.   And
I've earned a lot of money besides, so that since
our last meeting I've run through more than
3,000 roubles.   I do live in a very disorderly way,
and that's the truth! . . .   My health is utterly
shattered.   I am neurotic, and dread low fever.   I am
so dissolute that I simply can't live decently any
more. . . .

XI

To his Brother Michael

April 1, 1846.

You do reproach me, don't you, because I have not
written for so long ?   But I take my stand upon
Poprischtschin's[1] saying: " Letters are rubbish; only
apothecaries write letters."   What could I have said
to you ?   If I had told all I had to tell, it would have
taken volumes.   Every day brings me so much that

[1] Hero of Gogol's " Memoirs of a Madman."

is new, so many changes and impressions, agreeable and disagreeable, lucky and unlucky, matters, that I have no time to reflect upon them. In the first place, I'm always busy. I have heaps of ideas, and write incessantly. But don't imagine that mine is a bed of roses. Far from it. To begin with, I've spent a very great deal of money—that is to say, exactly 4,500 roubles—since our last meeting, and got about a thousand for my wares. Thus, with that economy of mine which you know so well, I have positively robbed myself, and so it often happens that I am quite penniless. . . .

But that doesn't signify. My fame has reached its highest point. In the course of two months I have, by my own reckoning, been mentioned five-and-thirty times in different papers. In certain articles I've been praised beyond measure, in others with more reserve, and in others, again, frightfully abused. What could I ask for more? But it does pain and trouble me that my own friends, Bielinsky and the others, are dissatisfied with my " Goliadkin." The first impression was blind enthusiasm, great sensation, and endless argument. The second was the really critical one. They all—that is, my friends and the whole public— declare with one voice that my " Goliadkin " is tedious and thin, and so drawn-out as to be almost unreadable. One of our lot is now going in for the perusal of one chapter a day, so that he may not tire himself, and in this way he smacks his lips with joy over it. Some of the public say emphatically that the book is quite impossible, that no one could really read it, that it's madness to write and print such stuff; others, again, declare that everything is from the life, and that they recognize themselves in the book; now

and again, it is true, I hear such hymns of praise that
I should be ashamed to repeat them.   As to myself,
I was for some time utterly discouraged.   I have
one terrible vice : I am unpardonably ambitious and
egotistic.   The thought that I had disappointed all
the hopes set on me, and spoilt what might have
been a really significant piece of work, depressed me
very heavily.   The thought of " Goliadkin " made me
sick.   I wrote a lot of it too quickly, and in moments
of fatigue.   The first half is better than the second.
Alongside many brilliant passages are others so dis-
gustingly bad that I can't read them myself.   All
this put me in a kind of hell for a time ; I was actually
ill with vexation.   Dear brother, I'll send you the
book in a fortnight.   Read it, and give me your honest
opinion.

I'll go over my life and work of late and tell you
some bits of news :

1st. A big bit : Bielinsky is giving up the editor-
ship of the *O. Z.*   His health is sadly shattered, and
he is going to a spa, perhaps in foreign parts.   For a
couple of years or so he will write no criticism at all.
To bolster up his finances, he is publishing an Almanac
of fabulous size—sixty sheets.   I am writing two tales
for him : " The Whiskers that were Shaved Off," and
" The Story of the Abolished Public Offices."   Both
are overwhelmingly tragic, and extraordinarily interesting—told most curtly.   The public awaits them
eagerly.   Both are short tales. . . .   Besides these, I
am to do something for Krayevsky, and write a novel
for Nekrassov.   The whole lot will take about a year.
The " Whiskers " are ready now.

2nd bit of news : A whole crowd of new writers
have popped up.   In some I divine rivals.   Particu-

larly interesting are Herzen (Iskander) and Gontscharov.   Herzen   has   published   some   things.
Gontscharov is only beginning, and has not yet been
printed.   Both   are   immensely   praised.   But at
present I have the top place, and hope to keep it for
ever.   In literary life there was never such activity as
now.   It is a good sign.

[Here follow some unimportant details of Dostoevsky's life.   He gives his brother, among other
things, the advice to translate Goethe's " Reineke
Fuchs."]

XII

To his Brother Michael

September 17, 1846.

I have already told you that I've rented a house.
I'm not in distress, but I have no outlook for the
future.   Krayevsky has given me fifty roubles, but I
could read in his face that he'll give me no more, so I
shall have a pretty stiff time.

In a certain quarter (the Censorship) they have
mutilated my "Prochartschin" frightfully.   The gentlemen have even—God knows why—struck out the word
" official."   The whole thing was, for that matter, entirely without offence, yet they've cut it to pieces.
They've simply killed the book dead.   There is only
a skeleton left of what I read to you.   Henceforth I
renounce that work of mine. . . .   I am still writing
at the " Whiskers."   The work goes very slowly.   I
fear it won't be ready in time.   I heard from two
men, namely Grigorovitch and a certain Beketov II.,
that the *Petersburg Almanac*[1] is known in the

[1] *Peterbourgsky Shornik.*

provinces only by the name of " Poor Folk." The
rest of the contents don't interest people in the least ;
and the sale in the provinces is colossal, they often
pay double prices. At the booksellers' in Pensa and
Kiev, for instance, the Almanac is officially priced at
from 25 to 30 roubles. It is really remarkable ; here
the book fell flat, and *there* they scramble for it.

Grigorovitch has written a truly wonderful story.
Myself and Maikov (who, by-the-bye, wants to write
a long article on me) have arranged for it to appear
in the *O. Z.* That journal is, by the way, in very low
water ; they haven't a single story in reserve.

Here we are frightfully dull. And so work goes
badly. I lived in a sort of paradise with you ; when
things do go well with me, I ruin everything by my
damnable character. . . .

XIII

To his Brother Michael

DEAREST BROTHER,   [*Undated*] 1846.

I mean to write to you only a few lines, for I
have a terrible crop of worries, and my situation is
desperate. The truth is that all my plans have come
to naught. The volume of stories is done for, because not a single one of the tales I told you about
lately has come off. Even the "Whiskers" I have
abandoned. I've abandoned the whole lot, for they
are nothing but a repetition of old stuff, long since
given forth by me. I have heaps of original, vital,
and lucid thoughts that all yearn to come to the
birth. When I had written the conclusion of the
" Whiskers " I saw this all by myself. In my position, any monotony is fatal.

I am writing a new story, and the work, as with " Poor Folk," goes easily and lightly. I had intended this tale for Krayevsky. The gentlemen on the *Sovremennik* may resent this ; it will affect me but little. If I have this story ready in January, I shall print nothing till the following year ; I want to write a novel, and shan't rest till I do.

But that I may live in the meantime, I intend to bring out " Poor Folk " and the over-written "Goliadkin" in book-form. . . .

XIV

To his Brother Michael

November 26, 1846.

All my plans about publishing have fallen through. The whole idea, however, was doubtfully profitable, needed much time, and was possibly premature. The public might have held off. I mean to postpone all that till next autumn. I shall by then be better known, and my position will be more defined. Besides, I have some money coming in. "Goliadkin" is now being illustrated by an artist in Moscow, and two artists here are doing pictures for " Poor Folk." Whichever does them best, gets the commission. Bernardsky[1] tells me that in February he wants to do business with me, and will pay me a certain sum for the right to publish my works with his illustrations. Till now he has been occupied with the illustrations to " Dead Souls." In a word, the publishing plans no longer interest me. Moreover,

---

[1] At that time a popular engraver and book-illustrator.

I have no time. I have a lot of work and commissions. I must tell you that I have broken off all relations with the *Sovremennik* as far as Nekrassov represents it. He was vexed because I wrote also for Krayevsky (as I *had* to do, so as to work off his advances of money to me), and because I would not make the public declaration which he desired, saying that I no longer was on the editorial staff of the *O. Z.* When he saw that he could get no new work from me in the immediate future, he flung various rudenesses at my head, and was foolish enough to demand money from me. I took him at his word, and drew up a promissory note which covered the whole amount, payable on December 15. I mean to see them coming to me hat in hand. As soon as I roundly abused Nekrassov, he curtsied and whimpered like a Jew that's been robbed. In short, it's a shabby story. Now they are spreading it about that I'm off my head with conceit, and have sold myself to Krayevsky, because Maikov praises me in his paper. Nekrassov henceforth means to drag me down. But as to Bielinsky, he is so pliable that even about literary matters he changes his views five times a week. With him alone have I kept up my former happy relations. He's a thoroughly good fellow. Krayevsky was so delighted by this whole affair that he gave me money, and promised besides to pay all my debts up to December 15. Therefore I must work for him until the early New Year.

Now look, brother—from the whole business I have deduced a sage rule. First, the budding author of talent injures himself by having friendly relations with the publishers and proprietors of journals, the consequence of which is that those gentry take

liberties and behave shabbily. Moreover, the artist
must be independent ; and finally, he must conse-
crate all his toil to the holy spirit of art—such toil
is holy, chaste, and demands single-heartedness ; my
own heart thrills now as never before with all the
new imaginings that come to life in my soul.
Brother, I am undergoing not only a moral, but a
physical, metamorphosis. Never before was there in
me such lucidity, such inward wealth ; never before
was my nature so tranquil, nor my health so satisfactory, as now. I owe this in great measure to my
good friends : Beketov, Saliubezky, and the others
with whom I live. They are honest, sensible fellows,
with fine instincts and affections, and noble, steadfast
characters. Intercourse with them has healed me.
Finally, I suggested that we should live together.
We took a big house all to ourselves, and go share
and share alike in all the housekeeping expenses,
which come, at the most, to 1,200 roubles a head
annually. So great are the blessings of the com-
munal system ! I have a room to myself, and work
all day long.

XV

To his Brother Michael

1847.

DEAR BROTHER,

I must once more beg you to forgive me for
not having kept my word, and written by the next
post. But through all the meantime I have been so
depressed in spirit that I simply *could not* write. I
have thought of you with so much pain—your fate
is truly grievous, dear brother ! With your feeble

MICHAEL DOSTOEVSKY.

DOSTOEVSKY'S MOTHER.

health, your turn of mind, your total lack of companionship, living in one perpetual tedium unvaried by any little festive occasions, and then the constant care about your family—care which is sweet to you, yet nevertheless weighs you down like a heavy yoke —why, your life is unbearable. But don't lose courage, brother. Better days will come. And know this, the richer we are in mind and spirit, the fairer will our life appear. It is indeed true that the dissonance and lack of equilibrium between ourselves and society is a terrible thing. External and internal things should be in equilibrium. For, lacking external experiences, those of the inward life will gain the upper hand, and that is most dangerous. The nerves and the fancy then take up too much room, as it were, in our consciousness. Every external happening seems colossal, and frightens us. We begin to fear life. It is at any rate a blessing that Nature has gifted you with powers of affection and strength of character. You have, besides, a vigorous, healthy mind, sparkles of diamond-like wit, and a happy nature. This is your salvation. I always think of you a great deal. My God, there are so many sour-faced, small-souled, narrow-minded, hoary-headed philosophers, professors of the art of existence, Pharisees, who pride themselves on their " experience of life "—that is to say, their lack of individuality (for they are all cut on the same pattern) ; and who are good for nothing at all, with their everlasting preachments about contentment with one's destiny, faith in something or other, modest demands from life, acceptance of the station one finds one's-self in, and so on—never once thinking about the sense of any of those words ; for *their* con-

tentment is that of cloistered self-castration; they
judge with unspeakably paltry animosity the vehe-
ment, ardent nature of him who refuses to accept
their insipid " daily-task " calendar of existence.   Oh,
how vulgar are all these preachers of the falseness of
earthly joys—how vulgar, every one !   Whenever I
fall into their hands, I suffer the torments of hell. . . .

[Here follows the description of a visitor who had
enraged Dostoevsky with his " vulgarities."]

I wish so much to see you again.   Sometimes a
nameless grief possesses me.   I can't help thinking
perpetually how moody and "edgey" I was when
with you at Reval.   I was ill then.   I remember still
how you once said to me that my behaviour towards
you excluded all sense of equality between us.   My
dear brother, that was unjust.   I have indeed, it is
true, an evil, repellent character.   But I have always
ranked you above myself.   I could give my life for you
and yours; but even when my heart is warm with
love, people often can't get so much as one friendly
word out of me.   At such times I have lost control of
my nerves.   I appear ludicrous, repellent, and have to
suffer inexpressibly from the misunderstanding of my
fellow-creatures.   People call me arid and heartless.
How often have I been rude to Emilie Fyodorovna,
your wife, who is a thousand times my superior.   I
remember, too, that frequently I was cross with your
son Fedya for no reason at all, though at the very time
I loved him perhaps even more than I love you.   I
can show myself to be a man of feeling and humour
only when external circumstances lift me high above
the external daily round.   When that is not my
state, I am always repellent.   I account for these

disparities by my malady. Have you read " Lucretia
Floriani"? Take a look at the "King" too. But soon
you'll be able to read my " Netotschka Nesvanova."
That story, like " Goliadkin," will be a self-confes-
sion, though different in tone. About " Goliadkin "
I often happen to hear such expressions of opinion
that I get quite frightened. Many say that it is a
veritable, as yet uncomprehended, marvel, that it will
have enormous significance in the future, and that by
itself alone it is enough to make me famous ; some
think it more exciting than Dumas. Now I'm
beginning again to praise myself. But it is so delightful, brother, to be rightly understood ! For what,
actually, do *you* love me so much ? I'll see to it that
somehow we meet again very soon. Won't we love
one another, that's all ! Wish me success. I am now
working at " The Mistress of the Inn." It is getting
on more easily than "Poor Folk" did. The story is in
the same manner. A flow of inspiration, which comes
from my inmost soul, is guiding my pen. It is quite
different from what it was with " Prochartschin,"
from which I suffered the whole summer through.
How I wish I could *soon* help you, brother. Depend,
as on a rock, on the money that I promised you. Kiss
all your dear ones for me. In the meantime I am

THY DOSTOEVSKY.

XVI

To his Brother Michael

[Postscript to a longer business letter, early in the
year 1847.]

You will scarcely believe it. Here is the third year
of my literary activity, and I am as if in a dream. I

don't see the life about me at all, I have no time to become conscious of it; no time, either, to learn anything. I want to attain to something steadfast. People have created a dubious fame for me, and I know not how long this hell of poverty and constant hurried work will last. Oh, if I could but once have rest!

XVII

To his Brother Michael

[FROM THE FORTRESS],
July 18, 1849.

DEAR BROTHER,

I was inexpressibly glad of your letter, which I got on July 11. At last you are free, and I can vividly imagine how happy you were when you saw your family again. How impatiently they must have awaited you! I seem to see that your life is beginning to shape itself differently. With what are you now occupied, and, above all, what are your means of support? Have you work, and of what sort? Summer is indeed a burden in the town. You tell me only that you have taken a new house; and probably it is much smaller. It is a pity you couldn't spend the whole summer in the country. I thank you for the things you sent; they have relieved and diverted me. You write, my dear fellow, that I must not lose heart. Indeed, I am not losing heart at all; to be sure, life here is very monotonous and dreary, but what else could it be? And after all it isn't invariably so tedious. The time goes by most irregularly, so to speak—now too quickly, now too slowly. Sometimes I have the feeling that I've grown accustomed to this sort of life, and that nothing matters very much. Of course, I try to keep all alluring thoughts out of my head, but can't always succeed; my early days, with their fresh impressions, storm in on my soul, and I live all the past over again. That is in the natural order of things. The days are now for the most part bright, and I am somewhat more cheerful. The rainy days, though, are unbearable, and on them the casemate looks terribly grim. I have occupation, however. I do not let the time go by for naught; I have made out the plots of three tales and two novels; and am writing a novel now, but avoid over-working. Such labour, when I do it with great enjoyment (I have never worked so much *con amore* as now), has always agitated me and affected my nerves. While I was working in freedom I was always obliged to diversify my labours with amusements; but here the excitement consequent on work has to evaporate unaided. My health is good, except for the hæmorrhoids, and the shattered state of my nerves, which keeps up a constant *crescendo*. Now and then I get attacks of breathlessness, my appetite is as unsatisfactory as ever, I sleep badly, and have morbid dreams. I sleep about five hours in the daytime, and wake four times at least every night. This is the only thing that really bothers me. The worst of all are the twilight hours. By nine o'clock it is quite dark here. I often cannot get to sleep until about one or two in the morning, and the five hours during which I have to lie in darkness are hard to bear. They are injuring my health more than anything else. When our case will be finished I can't say at all, for I have lost all sense of time, and merely use a calendar upon which I stroke out, quite passively,

each day as it passes: "That's over!" I haven't read
much since I've been here: two descriptions of travel
in the Holy Land, and the works of Demetrius von
Rostov. The latter interested me very much; but that
kind of reading is only a drop in the ocean; any other
sorts of books would, I imagine, quite extraordinarily
delight me, and they might be very useful, for thus I
could diversify my own thoughts with those of others,
or at all events capture a different mood.

There you have all the details of my present existence—I have nothing else to tell you. I am glad
that you found your family in the best of health.
Have you yet written of your liberation to Moscow?
It is a pity that nothing is done there. How I should
like to spend at least one day with you! It is now
three months since we came to this fortress: what
may not still be in store for us! Possibly I shall not,
the whole summer through, see so much as one green
leaf. Do you remember how in May they would
take us to walk in the little garden? The green was
just beginning then, and I couldn't help thinking of
Reval, where I was with you at about that season, and
of the garden belonging to the Engineering College.
I imagined that you *must* be making the same comparison, so sad was I. And I should like to see a lot
of other people besides. Whom do you see most of
now? I suppose everybody's in the country. But
our brother Andrey must surely be in town? Have
you seen Nikolya? Greet them all from me. Kiss
all your children for me. Greet your wife, and tell
her that I am greatly touched by her thinking of me.
Don't be too anxious on my account. I have but one
wish—to be in good health; the tedium is a passing
matter, and cheerfulness depends in the last resort

upon myself. Human beings have an incredible amount of endurance and will to live ; I should never have expected to find so much in myself; now I know it from experience. Farewell ! I hope that these few lines will give you much pleasure. Greet every one you see whom I have known—forget no one. I have not forgotten anybody. What can the children be thinking of me, and how do they explain to themselves my disappearance ! Farewell. If you can at all manage it, send me the *O. Z.* Then I should at any rate have something to read. Write me a few lines—it would extraordinarily cheer me.

Till next time !

XVIII

To his Brother Michael

[From the Fortress],
August 27, 1849.

I rejoice that I may answer **you, dear** brother, and thank you for sending the books. I rejoice also that you are well, and that the imprisonment had no evil effects upon your constitution. I am most particularly grateful to you for the *O. Z.* But you write far too little, and my letters are much more comprehensive than yours. This only by the way—you'll do better next time.

I have nothing definite to tell you about myself. As yet I know nothing whatever about our case. My *personal* life is as monotonous as ever ; but they have given me permission to walk in the garden, where there are almost seventeen trees ! This is a great happiness for me. Moreover, I am given a candle in the evenings—that's my second piece of luck. The third will be mine if you answer as soon as possible, and send me the next number of the *O. Z.* I am in the same position as a country subscriber, and await each number as a great event, like some landed proprietor dying of boredom in the provinces. Will you send me some historical works ? That would be splendid. But best of all would be the Bible (both Testaments). I need one. Should it prove possible, send it in a French translation. But if you could add as well a Slav edition, it would be the height of bliss.

Of my health I can tell you nothing good. For a month I have been living almost exclusively on castor oil. My hæmorrhoids have been unusually tormenting; moreover I detect a pain in the breast that I have never had before. My nervous irritability has notably increased, especially in the evening hours; at night I have long, hideous dreams, and latterly I have often felt as if the ground were rocking under me, so that my room seems like the cabin of a steamer. From all this I conclude that my nerves are increasingly shattered. Whenever formerly I had such nervous disturbances, I made use of them for writing; in such a state I could write much more and much better than usual; but now I refrain from work that I may not utterly destroy myself. I took a rest of three weeks, during which time I wrote not at all; now I have begun again. But anyhow, all this is nothing: I can stick it out to the end. Perhaps I shall get quite right again.

You most tremendously astonish me when you write that you believe they know nothing of our adventure in Moscow. I have thought it over, and come to the conclusion that that's quite impossible.

They simply *must* know, and I attribute their silence to another reason. And that was, after all, to be expected. Oh, it's quite clear. . . .

[The letter goes on to speak of his brother's family. Dostoevsky also makes some unimportant remarks on the articles in the *O. Z.*]

XIX

To his Brother Michael

[FROM THE FORTRESS],
September 14, 1849.

I have received, dear brother, your letter, the books (Shakespeare, the Bible, and the *O. Z.*) and the money (ten roubles): thank you for all. I am glad that you are well. I go on as before. Always the same digestive troubles and the hæmorrhoids. I don't know if all this will ever leave me. The autumn months, which I find so trying, are drawing near, and with them returns my hypochondria. The sky is already grey ; my health and good heart are dependent on those little tatters of blue that I can see from my casemate. But at any rate I'm alive, and comparatively well. This fact I maintain : therefore I beg you not to think of my state as wholly grievous. My health *is* at present good. I had expected worse, and now I see that I have so much vitality in me that it simply won't allow itself to be exhausted.

Thank you again for the books. They divert me at all events. For almost five months I have been living exclusively on my own provisions—that is to say, on my own head alone and solely. That machine is still in working order. But it is unspeakably hard to think *only*, everlastingly to think, without any of

those external impressions which renew and nourish
the soul.   I live as though under the bell of an air-
pump, from which the air is being drawn.   My whole
existence has concentrated itself in my head, and
from my head has drifted into my thoughts, and
the labour of those thoughts grows more arduous
every day.   Books are certainly a mere drop in the
ocean, still they do always help me ; while my own
work, I think, consumes my remains of strength.
Nevertheless it gives me much happiness.

I have read the books you sent.   I am particularly
thankful for the Shakespeare.   That was a good idea
of yours.   The English novel in the *O. Z.* is very
good.   On the other hand, Turgenev's comedy is unpardonably bad.   Why has he always such ill-luck ?
Is he fated to ruin every work of his which runs to
more than one printed sheet ?   I simply could not
recognize him in this comedy.   Not a trace of
originality ; everything in the old, worn-out groove.
He has said it all before, and much better.   The last
scene is puerile in its feebleness.   Here and there
one thinks to see signs of talent, but only for want
of something better.   How splendid is the article on
the Banks—and how universally true !   I thank all
who remember me ; greet your Emilie Fyodorovna
from me, our brother Andrey too, and kiss the children, who, I greatly hope, are better.   Truly I don't
know, brother, when and how we shall meet again !
Farewell, and please don't forget me.   Write to me,
even if it can't be for a fortnight.   Till next time !

Thy
F. DOSTOEVSKY.

Pray do not be anxious about me.   If you can get
hold of any books, send them.

XX

To his Brother Michael

[FROM THE FORTRESS],
December 22, 1849.

To-day, the 22nd of December, we were all taken
to Semjonovsky Square. There the death-sentence
was read to us, we were given the Cross to kiss, the
dagger was broken over our heads, and our funeral
toilet (white shirts) was made. Then three of us
were put standing before the palisades for the execution of the death-sentence. I was sixth in the row;
we were called up by groups of three, and so I
was in the second group, and had not more than a
minute to live. I thought of you, my brother, and
of yours; in that last moment you alone were in my
mind; then first I learnt how very much I love
you, my beloved brother! I had time to embrace
Plestcheiev and Dourov, who stood near me, and
to take my leave of them. Finally, retreat was
sounded, those who were bound to the palisades
were brought back, and it was read to us that His
Imperial Majesty granted us our lives. Then the
final sentences were recited. Palm alone is fully
pardoned. He has been transferred to the line with
the same rank.

F. DOSTOEVSKY.

XXI

To his Brother Michael

[FROM OMSK],
February 22, 1854.

At last I can talk with you somewhat more ex-
plicitly, and, I believe, in a more reasonable manner.

But before I write another line I *must* ask you :
Tell me, for God's sake, why you have never written
me a single syllable till now ?   Could I have expected
this from you ?   Believe me, in my lonely and isolated
state, I sometimes fell into utter despair, for I
believed that you were no longer alive ; through
whole nights I would brood upon what was to become
of your children, and I cursed my fate because I
could not help them.   But whenever I heard for
certain that you were still alive, I would get furious
(this happened, however, only in times of illness,
from which I have suffered a very great deal), and
begin to reproach you bitterly.   Then those states of
mind would pass, and I would excuse you, I would
exert myself to find a justification for you, and grow
tranquil as soon as I discovered any—nor did I ever
for a moment utterly lose faith in you : I know that
you love me, and keep me in kindly remembrance.
I wrote you a letter through our official staff; you
simply must have got it ; I expected an answer from
you, and received none.   Were you then forbidden
to write to me ?   But I know that letters are allowed,
for every one of the political prisoners here gets
several in the year.   Even Dourov had some ; and we
often asked the officials how it stood about correspondence, and they declared that people had the
right to send us letters.   I think I have guessed the
real reason for your silence.   You were too lazy to
go to the police-office, or if you did go once, you
took the first " No " for an answer—given you, probably, by some functionary or other who knew nothing
rightly about the matter.   Well, you have caused
me a great deal of selfish anxiety, for I thought : If
he won't take any trouble about a letter, he certainly

won't either about more important things ! Write
and answer me as quickly as possible ; write, without
awaiting an opportunity, *officially*, and be as explicit
and detailed as you possibly can. I am like a slice
cut from a loaf nowadays ; I long to grow back again,
but can't. *Les absents ont toujours tort.* Is that saying to come true of us two ? But be easy in your
mind : I trust you.

It is a week now since I left the prison. I am
sending this letter in the strictest secrecy ; say not a
syllable about it to anyone. I shall send you an
official one too, through the staff of the Siberian
Army Corps. Answer the official one instantly, but
this—on the first suitable occasion. You must, though,
write very circumstantially in the official letter of
what you have been doing during these four years.
For my part I should like to be sending you volumes.
But as my time scarcely suffices for even this sheet,
I shall tell you only the most important thing.

What *is* the most important ? What was the most
important to me in the recent past ? When I reflect,
I see that even to tell that, this sheet is far too small.
How can I impart to you what is now in my mind—
the things I thought, the things I did, the convictions
I acquired, the conclusions I came to ? I cannot
even attempt the task. It is absolutely impracticable.
I don't like to leave a piece of work half done ; to say
only a part is to say nothing. At any rate, you now
have my detailed report in your hands : read it, and
get from it what you will. It is my duty to tell you
all, and so I will begin with my recollections. Do
you remember how we parted from one another, my
dear beloved fellow ? You had scarcely left me when
we three, Dourov, Yastrchembsky, and I, were led

out to have the irons put on.   Precisely at midnight
on that Christmas Eve (1849), did chains touch me
for the first time.   They weigh about ten pounds,
and make walking extraordinarily difficult.   Then
we were put into open sledges, each alone with a
gendarme, and so, in four sledges—the orderly opening the procession—we left Petersburg.   I was
heavy-hearted, and the many different impressions
filled me with confused and uncertain sensations.
My heart beat with a peculiar flutter, and that
numbed its pain.   Still, the fresh air was reviving
in its effect, and, since it is usual before all new
experiences to be aware of a curious vivacity and
eagerness, so *I* was at bottom quite tranquil.   I
looked attentively at all the festively-lit houses of
Petersburg, and said good-bye to each.   They drove
us past your abode, and at Krayevsky's the windows
were brilliantly lit.   You had told me that he was
giving a Christmas party and tree, and that your
children were going to it, with Emilie Fyodorovna ;
I did feel dreadfully sad as we passed that house.   I
took leave, as it were, of the little ones.   I felt so
lonely for them, and even years afterwards I often
thought of them with tears in my eyes.   We were
driven beyond Yaroslavl ; after three or four stations
we stopped, in the first grey of morning, at Schlüssel-
burg, and went into an inn.   There we drank tea
with as much avidity as if we had not touched anything for a week.   After the eight months' captivity,
sixty versts in a sledge gave us appetites of which,
even to-day, I think with pleasure.

   I was in a good temper, Dourov chattered incessantly, and Yastrchembsky expressed unwonted
apprehensions for the future.   We all laid ourselves

out to become better acquainted with our orderly.
He was a good old man, very friendly inclined
towards us; a man who has seen a lot of life; he
had travelled all over Europe with despatches. On
the way he showed us many kindnesses. His name
was Kusma Prokofyevitch Prokofyev. Among
other things he let us have a covered sledge, which
was very welcome, for the frost was fearful.

The second day was a holiday; the drivers, who
were changed at the various stations, wore cloaks
of grey German cloth with bright red belts; in the
village-streets there was not a soul to be seen. It
was a splendid winter-day. They drove us through
the remote parts of the Petersburg, Novgorod, and
Yaroslavl Governments. There were quite insignificant little towns, at great distances from one another.
But as we were passing through on a holiday, there
was always plenty to eat and drink. We drove—
drove terribly. We were warmly dressed, it is true,
but we had to sit for ten hours at a time in the
sledges, halting at only five or six stations: it was
almost unendurable. I froze to the marrow, and
could scarcely thaw myself in the warm rooms at the
stations. Strange to say, the journey completely
restored me to health. Near Perm, we had a frost
of forty degrees during some of the nights. I don't
recommend that to you. It was highly disagreeable.
Mournful was the moment when we crossed the
Ural. The horses and sledges sank deep in the
snow. A snow-storm was raging. We got out of
the sledges—it was night—and waited, standing, till
they were extricated. All about us whirled the
snow-storm. We were standing on the confines of
Europe and Asia; before us lay Siberia and the

mysterious future—behind us, our whole past; it was very melancholy. Tears came to my eyes. On the way, the peasants would stream out of all the villages to see us; and although we were fettered, prices were tripled to us at all the stations. Kusma Prokofyevitch took half our expenses on himself, though we tried hard to prevent him; in this way each of us, during the whole journey, spent only fifteen roubles.

On January 12 (1850) we came to Tobolsk. After we had been paraded before the authorities, and searched, in which proceeding all our money was taken from us, myself, Dourov, and Yastrchembsky were taken into one cell; the others, Spyechnyov, etc., who had arrived before us, were in another section, and during the whole time we hardly once saw each other. I should like to tell you more of our six days' stay in Tobolsk, and of the impressions it made upon me. But I haven't room here. I will only tell you that the great compassion and sympathy which were shown us there, made up to us, like a big piece of happiness, for all that had gone before. The prisoners of former days[1] (and still more their wives) cared for us as if they had been our kith and kin. Those noble souls, tested by five-and-twenty years of suffering and self-sacrifice! We saw them but seldom, for we were very strictly guarded; still, they sent us clothes and provisions, they comforted and encouraged us. I had brought far too few clothes, and had bitterly repented it, but *they* sent me clothes. Finally we left Tobolsk, and reached Omsk in three days.

[1] These were the participators in the *coup d'état* of December 14, 1825 ("Decembrists"), who had been banished to Siberia.

While I was in Tobolsk, I gathered information about my future superiors. They told me that the Commandant was a very decent fellow, but that the Major, Krivzov, was an uncommon brute, a petty tyrant, a drunkard, a trickster—in short, the greatest horror that can be imagined. From the very beginning, he called both Dourov and me blockheads, and vowed to chastise us bodily at the first transgression. He had already held his position for two years, and done the most hideous and unsanctioned things ; two years later, he was court-martialled for them. So God protected me from him. He used to come to us mad drunk (I never once saw him sober), and would seek out some inoffensive prisoner and flog him on the pretext that *he*—the prisoner—was drunk. Often he came at night and punished at random—say, because such and such an one was sleeping on his left side instead of his right, or because he talked or moaned in his sleep—in fact, anything that occurred to his drunken mind. I should have had to break out in the long run against such a man as that, and it was he who wrote the monthly reports of us to Petersburg.

I had made acquaintance with convicts in Tobolsk ; at Omsk I settled myself down to live four years in common with them. They are rough, angry, embittered men. Their hatred for the nobility is boundless ; they regard all of us who belong to it with hostility and enmity. They would have devoured us if they only could. Judge then for yourself in what danger we stood, having to cohabit with these people for some years, eat with them, sleep by them, and with no possibility of complaining of the affronts which were constantly put upon us.

" You nobles have iron beaks, you have torn us to pieces. When you were masters, you injured the people, and now, when it's evil days with you, you want to be our brothers."

This theme was developed during four years. A hundred and fifty foes never wearied of persecuting us—it was their joy, their diversion, their pastime; our sole shield was our indifference and our moral superiority, which they were forced to recognize and respect; they were also impressed by our never yielding to their will. They were for ever conscious that we stood above them. They had not the least idea of what our offence had been. We kept our own counsel about that, and so we could never come to understand one another; we had to let the whole of the vindictiveness, the whole of the hatred, that they cherish against the nobility, flow over us. We had a very bad time there. A military prison is much worse than the ordinary ones. I spent the whole four years behind dungeon walls, and only left the prison when I was taken on " hard labour." The labour was hard, though not always; sometimes in bad weather, in rain, or in winter during the unendurable frosts, my strength would forsake me. Once I had to spend four hours at a piece of extra work, and in such frost that the quicksilver froze; it was perhaps forty degrees below zero. One of my feet was frost-bitten. We all lived together in one barrack-room. Imagine an old, crazy wooden building, that should long ago have been broken up as useless. In the summer it is unbearably hot, in the winter unbearably cold. All the boards are rotten. On the ground filth lies an inch thick; every instant one is in danger of slipping and

coming down.   The small windows are so frozen
over that even by day one can hardly read.   The ice
on the panes is three inches thick.   The ceilings drip,
there are draughts everywhere.   We are packed like
herrings in a barrel.   The stove is heated with six
logs of wood, but the room is so cold that the ice
never once thaws ; the atmosphere is unbearable—
and so through all the winter long.   In the same
room, the prisoners wash their linen, and thus make
the place so wet that one scarcely dares to move.
From twilight till morning we are forbidden to leave
the barrack-room ; the doors are barricaded ; in the
ante-room a great wooden trough for the calls of
nature is placed ; this makes one almost unable to
breathe.   All the prisoners stink like pigs ; they say
that they can't help it, for they must live, and are
but men.   We slept upon bare boards ; each man was
allowed one pillow only.   We covered ourselves with
short sheepskins, and our feet were outside the covering all the time.   It was thus that we froze night
after night.   Fleas, lice, and other vermin by the
bushel.   In the winter we got thin sheepskins to wear,
which didn't keep us warm at all, and boots with
short legs ; thus equipped, we had to go out in the frost.

To eat we got bread and cabbage-soup ; the soup
should, by the regulations, have contained a quarter-
pound of meat per head ; but they put in sausage-
meat, and so I never came across a piece of genuine
flesh.   On feast-days we got porridge, but with
scarcely any butter.   On fast-days—cabbage and
nothing else.   My stomach went utterly to pieces,
and I suffered tortures from indigestion.

From all this you can see for yourself that one
couldn't live there at all without money ; if I had

had none, I should most assuredly have perished ; no one could endure such a life. But every convict does some sort of work and sells it, thus earning, every single one of them, a few pence. I often drank tea and bought myself a piece of meat ; it was my salvation. It was quite impossible to do without smoking, for otherwise the stench would have choked one. All these things were done behind the backs of the officials.

I was often in hospital. My nerves were so shattered that I had some epileptic fits—however, that was not very often. I have rheumatism in my legs now, too. But except for that, I feel right well. Add to all these discomforts, the fact that it was almost impossible to get one's-self a book, and that when I did get one, I had to read it on the sly ; that all around me was incessant malignity, turbulence, and quarrelling ; then perpetual espionage, and the impossibility of ever being alone for even an instant— and so without variation for four long years ; you'll believe me when I tell you that I was not happy. And imagine, in addition, the ever-present dread of drawing down some punishment on myself, the irons, and the utter oppression of spirits—and you have the picture of my life.

I won't even try to tell you what transformations were undergone by my soul, my faith, my mind, and my heart in those four years. It would be a long story. Still, the eternal concentration, the escape into myself from bitter reality, did bear its fruit. I now have many new needs and hopes of which I never thought in other days. But all this will be pure enigma for you, and so I'll pass to other things. I will say only one word : Do not forget me, and do help me.　I need books and money.　Send them me, for Christ's sake.

Omsk is a hateful hole.　There is hardly a tree here.　In summer—heat and winds that bring sand-storms; in winter—snow-storms.　I have scarcely seen anything of the country round.　The place is dirty, almost exclusively inhabited by military, and dissolute to the last degree.　I mean the common people.　If I hadn't discovered some human beings here, I should have gone utterly to the dogs.　Con-stantine Ivanovitch Ivanov is like a brother to me.　He has done everything that he in any way could for me.　I owe him money.　If he ever goes to Peters-burg, show him some recognition.　I owe him twenty-five roubles.　But how can I repay his kindness, his constant willingness to carry out all my requests, his attention and care for me, just like a brother's ?　And he is not the only one whom I have to thank in that way.　Brother, there are very many noble natures in the world.

I have already said that your silence often tortured me.　I thank you for the money you sent.　In your next letter (even if it's " official," for I don't know yet whether it is possible for me to correspond with you)—in your next, write as fully as you can of all your affairs, of Emilie Fyodorovna, the children, all relations and acquaintances ; also of those in Moscow —who is alive and who is dead ; and of your business : tell me with what capital you started it,[1] whether it is lucrative, whether you are in funds, and finally, whether you will help me financially, and how much you will send me a year.　But send no money with

[1] Michael Dostoevsky had at this time a tobacco and cigarette factory.

the official letter—particularly if I don't find a covering address. For the present, give Michael Petrovitch as the consignor of all packets (you understand, don't you ?). For the time I have some money, but I have no books. If you can, send me the magazines for this year, or at any rate the *O. Z.* But what I urgently need are the following : I need (very necessary) ancient historians (in French translations); modern historians : Guizot, Thierry, Thiers, Ranke, and so forth ; national studies, and the Fathers of the Church. Choose the cheapest and most compact editions. Send them by return. They have ordered me to Semipalatinsk, which lies on the edge of the Kirghiz steppes ; I'll let you have the address. Here is one for the present, anyhow : " Semipalatinsk, Siberian Regiment of the Line, Seventh Battalion, Private F. Dostoevsky." That's the official style. To this one send your letters. But I'll give you another for the books. For the present, write as Michael Petrovitch. Remember, above all things, I need a German dictionary.

I don't know what awaits me at Semipalatinsk. I don't mind the service much. But what I *do* care about is—exert yourself for me, spend yourself for me with somebody or other. Could they not transfer me in a year or two to the Caucasus ? Then I should at least be in European Russia ! This is my dearest desire, grant it me for Christ's sake ! Brother, do not forget me ! I write and scold you and dispose of your very property ! But my faith in you is not yet extinguished. You are my brother, and you used to love me. I need money. I must have something to live on, brother. These years shall not have been in vain. I want money and books. What you spend on me will not be lost. If you give me help, you won't be robbing your children. If I live, I'll repay you with interest—oh, a thousandfold. In six years, perhaps even sooner, I shall surely get permission to print my books. It may indeed be quite otherwise, but I don't write recklessly now. You shall hear of me again.

We shall see one another some day, brother. I believe in that as in the multiplication-table. To my soul, all is clear. I see my whole future, and all that I shall accomplish, plainly before me. I am content with my life. I fear only men and tyranny. How easily might I come across a superior officer who did not like me (there are such folk !), who would torment me incessantly and destroy me with the rigours of service—for I am very frail, and of course in no state to bear the full burden of a soldier's life. People try to console me : " They're quite simple sort of fellows there." But I dread simple men more than complex ones. For that matter, men everywhere are just— men. Even among the robber-murderers in the prison, I came to know some men in those four years. Believe me, there were among them deep, strong, and beautiful natures, and it often gave me great joy to find gold under a rough exterior. And not in a single case, or even two, but in several cases. Some inspired respect ; others were downright fine. I taught the Russian language and reading to a young Circassian—he had been transported to Siberia for robbery with murder. How grateful he was to me ! Another convict wept when I said good-bye to him. Certainly I had often given him money, but it was so little, and his gratitude so boundless. My character, though, was deteriorating ; in my relations with others I was ill-tempered and impatient. They accounted for it by my mental condition, and bore all without grumbling. Apropos : what a number of national types and characters I became familiar with in the prison ! I lived *into* their lives, and so I believe I know them really well. Many tramps' and thieves' careers were laid bare to me, and, above all, the whole wretched existence of the common people. Decidedly I have not spent my time there in vain. I have learnt to know the Russian people as only a few know them. I am a little vain of it. I hope that such vanity is pardonable.

Brother ! Be sure to tell me of all the most important events in your life. Send the official letter to Semipalatinsk, and the unofficial—whither you soon shall know. Tell me of all our acquaintances in Petersburg, of literature (as many details as possible), and finally of our folks in Moscow. How is our brother Kolya ? What (and this is much more important) is sister Sacha doing ? Is Uncle still alive ? What is brother Andrey about ? I am writing to our aunt through sister Vera. For God's sake, keep this letter a dead secret, and burn it ; it might compromise various people. Don't forget, dear friend, to send me books. Above all things histories and national studies, the *O. Z.*, the Fathers of the Church, and churchhistories. Don't send all the books at once, though as soon after one another as possible. I am dispensing your money for you as if it were my own ; but only because your present situation is unknown to me. Write fully about your affairs, so that I may have some idea of them. But mark this, brother : books are my life, my food, my future ! For God's sake, don't abandon me. I pray you ! Try to get permission to send me the books quite openly. But be

cautious. If it can be done openly, send them openly.
But if it can't, then send them through brother
Constantine Ivanovitch, to his address. I shall get
them. Constantine Ivanovitch, by-the-bye, is going
this very year to Petersburg; he'll tell you everything. What a family he has! And what a wife!
She is a young girl, the daughter of the Decembrist
Annenkov. Such a heart, such a disposition—and to
think of what they've all been through! I shall set
myself, when I go to Semipalatinsk in a week, to
find a new covering-address. I am not quite strong
yet, so must remain here a while. (Send me the
Koran, and Kant's " Critique of Pure Reason "), and
if you have the chance of sending anything *not*
officially, then be sure to send Hegel—but particularly
Hegel's "History of Philosophy." Upon that depends my whole future. For God's sake, exert yourself for me to get me transferred to the Caucasus;
try to find out from well-informed people whether I
shall be permitted to print my works, and in what
way I should seek this sanction. I intend to try for
permission in two or three years. I beg you to sus-
tain me so long. Without money I shall be destroyed
by military life. So please!

Perhaps in the beginning the other relatives would
support me too? In that case they could hand the
money to you, and you would send it to me. In my
letters to Aunt and to Vera, though, I never ask for
money. They can guess themselves that I want it,
if they think about me at all.

Filippov, before he left for Sebastopol, gave me
twenty-five roubles. He left them with the Commandant, Nabokov, and I knew nothing about it
beforehand. He thought that I should have no

money.   A kind soul!   All our lot are doing not so
badly in banishment.   Toll has done his time, and
now lives quite tranquilly in Tomsk.   Yastr-
chemsky is in Tara; his time is drawing to an end.
Spyechayov is in the Irkutsk Government; he has
won general liking and respect there.   That man's is a
curious destiny!   Wherever, and in whatever circumstances, he may appear, even the most inaccessible
people show him honour and respect.   Petrachevsky
is now as then not in his right mind; Monbelli and
Loov are well; poor Grigoryev has gone clean out of
his senses and is in hospital.   And how goes it with
you?   Do you still see a great deal of Mme.
Plestcheiev?   What is her son doing?   From
prisoners who passed through here, I heard that he is
alive and in the fortress at Orsk, and that Golovinsky
has long been in the Caucasus.   How goes your
literature, and your interest in literature?   Are you
writing anything?   What is Krayevsky about, and
what are your relations with him?   I don't care for
Ostrovsky; I have read nothing by Pissemsky;
Drushinin I loathe.   I was enchanted with Eugénie
Tur.   I like Krestovsky too.

I should like to have written much more; but so
much time has gone by that even this letter was
somewhat difficult to write.   But it really cannot be
that our relation is altered in any respect.   Kiss your
children.   Can they remember Uncle Fedya at all?
Greet all acquaintances—but keep this letter a dead
secret.   Farewell, farewell, dear fellow!   You shall
hear from me again, and perhaps even see me.   Yes—
we shall most certainly see one another again!   Farewell.   Read attentively all that I write to you.
Write to me as often as possible (even if officially).

I embrace you and all yours more times than I can
count.

Thy
DOSTOEVSKY.

P.S.   Have you received my children's story,[1] that
I wrote in the fortress ?   If it is in your hands, don't
do anything with it, and show it to no one.   Who is
Tschernov, that wrote a " Double " in 1850 ?

Till next time !

Thy
DOSTOEVSKY.

XXII

To Mme. N. D. Fonvisin[2]

OMSK,
Beginning of March, 1854.

At last I am writing to you, my kind N. D., after
leaving my former place of abode.   When I last
wrote, I was sick in body and soul.   I was consumed
with longings, and I daresay my letter was quite
senseless.   That long, colourless, physically and
morally difficult life had stifled me.   It is always
grievous to me to write letters at such times ; and I
regard it as cowardice to force one's sorrow on others,
even when they are very fond of one.   I send you
this letter indirectly, and I am glad to be able to
speak with you quite unconstrainedly at last; all
the more because I have been transferred to Semipalatinsk to the seventh battalion, and therefore

[1] He means " The Little Hero."   The story did not appear till
1857 (in the *O. Z.*, under the pseudonym " M—y.").

[2] Wife of the Decembrist M. A. Fonvisin.   Dostoevsky had met
her in Tobolsk in 1850.   During his captivity, when he himself
was not allowed to correspond with his brother, she was his only
medium of communication with the outside world.

don't at all know in what way I may be able to correspond with you in future.

[Dostoevsky further discusses the question of how
he may most safely correspond with his brother and
with Mme. Fonvisin.]

With what delight I read your letter, dearest
N. D. You write quite admirable letters, or, more
precisely, your letters flow easily and naturally from
your good kind heart. There are reserved and embittered natures, which only in very rare moments
are expansive. I know such people. They are not
necessarily bad people—quite the contrary, indeed.

I don't know why, but I guess from your letter that
you returned home in bad spirits. I understand it; I
have sometimes thought that if ever I return home, I
shall get more grief than joy from my impressions
there. I have not lived your life, and much in it is
unknown to me, and indeed, no one can really know
exactly his fellow-mortal's life; still, human feeling is
common to us all, and it seems to me that everyone
who has been banished must live all his past grief
over again in consciousness and memory, on his return
home. It is like a balance, by which one can test the
true gravity of what one has endured, gone through,
and lost. God grant you a long life! I have heard
from many people that you are very religious. But
not because you are religious, but because I myself
have learnt it and gone through it, I want to say to
you that in such moments, one does, "like dry grass,"
thirst after faith, and that one finds it in the end,
solely and simply because one sees the truth more
clearly when one is unhappy. I want to say to you,
about myself, that I am a child of this age, a child of

unfaith and scepticism, and probably (indeed I know
it) shall remain so to the end of my life.   How dreadfully has it tormented me (and torments me even
now)—this longing for faith, which is all the stronger
for the proofs I have against it.   And yet God gives
me sometimes moments of perfect peace ; in such
moments I love and believe that I am loved ; in such
moments I have formulated my creed, wherein all is
clear and holy to me.   This creed is extremely
simple ; here it is : I believe that there is nothing
lovelier, deeper, more sympathetic, more rational,
more manly, and more perfect than the Saviour ; I
say to myself with jealous love that not only is there
no one else like Him, but that there could be no one.
I would even say more : If anyone could prove to me
that Christ is outside the truth, and if the truth really
did exclude Christ, I should prefer to stay with Christ
and not with truth.

I would rather not say anything more about it.
And yet I don't know why certain topics may never
be touched on in society, and why, if anyone does
introduce them, it makes the others uncomfortable.
Still, enough of it.   I heard that you were desirous
of travelling somewhere in the South.   God grant
that you may succeed in obtaining permission to do
so.   But will you please tell me when we shall be
quite free, or at any rate as free as other people ?   Perhaps only when we no longer need freedom ?   For my
part, I want all or nothing.   In my soldier's uniform
I am the same prisoner as before.   I rejoice greatly
that I find there is patience in my soul for quite a
long time yet, that I desire no earthly possessions,
and need nothing but books, the possibility of writing,
and of being daily for a few hours alone.   The last

troubles me most. For almost five years I have been constantly under surveillance, or with several other people, and not one hour alone with myself. To be alone is a natural need, like eating and drinking ; for in that kind of concentrated communism one becomes a whole-hearted enemy of mankind. The constant companionship of others works like poison or plague ; and from that unendurable martyrdom I most suffered in the last four years. There were moments in which I hated every man, whether good or evil, and regarded him as a thief who, unpunished, was robbing me of life. The most unbearable part is when one grows unjust, malignant, and evil, is aware of it, even reproves one's-self, and yet has not the power to control one's-self. I have experienced that. I am convinced that God will keep you from it. I believe that you, as a woman, have more power to forgive and to endure.

Do write me a line, N. D. I am now going to a veritable desert, to Asia, and there, in Semipalatinsk, it seems to me that all my past, all memories and impressions, will leave me ; for the last human beings whom I still had to love, and who were like a shadow of my past, will now have to desert me. I get so dreadfully quickly used to people, and grow into my environment so tenaciously, that I never can tear myself away, when the time comes, without great pain. I wish for *you*, N. D., that you may live as happily and as long as possible ! If we ever meet again, we shall learn to know one another afresh, and each of us may perhaps still have many happy days. I live in constant expectancy ; I am always rather ill now, and I feel that soon, very soon, something decisive must happen, that I am nearing the crucial moment of my whole life, am ripe for anything that may come—and that perhaps something tranquil and bright, perhaps something menacing, but in any case something inevitable, closely impends.   Otherwise my whole life would be a failure.   Perhaps it has all been but a sick delirium !   Farewell, N. D., or rather au revoir ; we'll hope, won't we ? that we *shall* see one another again !

Your,

D.

P.S.   For goodness' sake forgive this untidy, greasy letter !   But on my sacred honour, I can't write without erasures.   Don't be cross with me.

XXIII

To Mme. Maria Dmitryevna Issayev[1]

FROM SEMIPALATINSK TO KUSNEZK
[IN THE TOMSK GOVERNMENT],
June 4, 1855.

A thousand thanks for your dear letter on the journey, my dear and unforgettable friend Maria Dmitryevna.   I hope that you and Alexander Ivanovitch[2] will allow me to call you both friends.   We certainly were friends here, and I trust we shall remain so.   Is mere separation to alter us ?   I believe not ; for the parting from you, my dear friends, lies so heavily upon me that by that alone I can judge how very much I cling to you.   Just imagine : this is the second letter I have written to you.   I had an answer to your dear cordial letter ready for the earlier post, dear Maria Dmitryevna, but I never sent it.   Alex-

---

[1] Dostoevsky's future wife.   Compare the reminiscences of Baron Vrangel, in the Appendix.

[2] The lady's husband.

ander Yegorovitch,[1] who was to have taken it to the
post, quite suddenly left for Smyev last Saturday,
and I never heard of his departure till Sunday.   His
servant simultaneously disappeared for two days, and
the letter remained in my pocket.   Hard luck!   I
am now writing to you again, but know not if this
letter will get off either.   Alexander Yegorovitch is
not back yet.   But they have sent a special messenger
after him.

Here we hourly expect the Governor-General ; he
may perhaps be already arrived.   It is said that he
will spend about five days here.   But enough of
that.   How did you arrive at Kusnezk?   I hope
and pray that nothing happened to you on the
way.   You write that you are depressed and even ill.
So I am most anxious about you.   The mere move
caused you such trouble and such unavoidable discomforts, and now there's this illness added!   How
are you to bear it all?   I can think of nothing but
you.   You know how apprehensive I am, so you can
picture my anxiety.   My God, how little you—*you*,
who might be an ornament to any society—deserve
this fate with all its petty cares and contrarieties!
Accursed destiny!   I await your letter with impatience.   If only it would come by this post!   I
went several times to find out if it had ; but Alexander Yegorovitch is not back yet.   You ask me how
I pass the time, and how I arrange my day without
you.   For a fortnight I have not known what to do
with myself, so sad am I.   If you only knew how
orphaned I now feel!   It is just like the time when
they arrested me in 1849, put me in prison, and tore
me from all that I loved and prized.   So very much

[1] Baron Vrangel.

had I grown to you. I never looked upon our intercourse as an ordinary acquaintanceship, and now, when
I no longer have you near me, I begin to understand
many things. I have lived for five years entirely
without human relations—quite alone, without a
creature to whom I could open my heart. But you
two treated me like a brother. I remember that
from the very first, I felt at home in your house.
Alexander Ivanovitch could not have been kinder to
his own brother than he was to me. With my unendurable character, I must have caused you much
vexation, and yet you both loved me. I recognize it
and feel it, for indeed I am not quite heartless. You
are a wonderful woman ; you have a heart of rare
child-like kindliness, and you were like a sister to me.
The mere fact that a woman should treat me in so
friendly a way was a great event in my life. For
even the best man is often, if I may say so, a block.
Woman's heart, woman's compassion, woman's sympathy, the endless kindness of which we have no
clear perception, and which, in our obtuseness, we
often do not even notice—these are irreplaceable.
All *that* I found in you ; even apart from my many
failings, a sister could not have been kinder and
more tactful to me than you were. If we did go
through some violent upheavals, it was always
because I was ungrateful, and you were ill, ex-
acerbated, and wounded ; you were wounded because the disgusting society-folk neither prized nor
understood you, and anyone with your energy *must*
revolt against all injustice, and that revolt is noble
and dignified. These are the essential features of
your character ; suffering and circumstances have
naturally distorted much in you—but, by God, with

what usurer's interest was any such failing always
redeemed !   And since I was not stupid all the time,
I saw and treasured it.   In one word, I *had* to love
your house as my very own home—I could not do
otherwise.   I shall never forget you both, and shall
be ever grateful to you.   For I am convinced that
neither of you has the least idea of all you did for
me, and how very necessary to me were just such
people as you.   If I had not had you, I should most
likely have turned into a block of wood; but now I
am a human being again.   But enough ; it is not to
be expressed, least of all in a letter.   I curse this
letter, because it reminds me of our parting ; everything reminds me of that.   In the twilight, in those
hours when I used to go to you, such grief over-
whelms me that I could weep if I were at all prone
to do so ; and I know you would not laugh at my
tears.   Once for all, my heart is so constituted that
everything it loves and treasures grows deeply rooted
in it, and when uptorn, causes wounds and suffering.
I live quite solitary here now, and have no idea what
to do with myself, everything is spoilt for me.   A
frightful blank !   I have only Alexander Yegorovitch
now ; but in his company I always feel sad, for always
I involuntarily compare myself with him, and you
can easily imagine what that results in.   In any case,
he's away just at present.   During his absence I have
been twice in the Kasakov Gardens, and I did feel so
sad !   When I think of last summer, when *you*, poor
dear, had only one wish, to get out into the country
so that you might have a breath of fresh air—great
grief comes over me, and I feel frightfully sorry for
you.   Do you remember how we—you, Alexander
Ivanovitch, I, and Elena—were once in the Kasakov

Gardens ? How vivid was the sense of it, when I went
there again ! In the Gardens nothing is changed, and
the seat on which we sat is still standing there. . . .
And I felt so sad. You write suggesting that I
should live with Vrangel ; but I don't want to do
that, for I have several weighty reasons against it.
First, the question of money. If I lived with him, I
should of course have to spend much more money
on rent, servants, and food, for I wouldn't live at his
expense. Second: my character. Third: his character.
Fourth : I have noticed that he is much visited by all
sorts of people. I don't mean to shut myself off from
society, but I can't stand strangers. Finally : I love
solitude, I am used to it, and use is second nature.
Enough. I have really told you nothing yet. After I
had accompanied you to the forest and taken leave of
you under a pine-tree (which I've marked), I returned
arm-in-arm with Vrangel (who was leading his horse
by the bridle) to the Pechechonov's hospitable abode.
It was there that I first realized my desolate state.
At first I could see your travelling-carriage in the
distance, then only hear it, and at last it was quite
gone. We got into the droschky, and sat talking of
you both and of how you would bear the journey ;
and it was then that Vrangel told me something that
greatly rejoiced me. On the day of your departure,
early in the morning, it appears that Pyotr Michailovitch suggested that they should spend the whole
evening together somewhere. Vrangel refused the
offer, and when Pyotr Michailovitch asked him why,
he answered : " Because I must see the Issayevs off."
There were some other people there. Pyotr Michailovitch asked at once : " Then you know that pair
very well ?" Vrangel answered somewhat stiffly

that he had only known you for a short time, but
thought your house one of the pleasantest possible,
and that its mistress—that is, you—was a woman such
as he had seen none to equal since he had been in
Petersburg, and probably never would see again ; a
woman " such as *you* have never seen at all," he added,
"and I consider her acquaintance the greatest honour."

This story of Vrangel's gave me extraordinary joy.
I think the opinion of a man like that, who knows
ladies in the best society (for in such society he was
born), is quite decisive.   Talking of similar subjects,
and continually abusing the Pechechonovs, we reached
the town about sunrise.   And the driver, to whom
we had given no orders, took us straight to my house.
In this way the proposed tea fell through, of which
I was very glad, for I was longing to be alone.   I
stayed at home a good while, walking up and down
in my room, looking at the sunrise, and going over
the whole past year, which had flown by so rapidly for
me ; all the memories came up, and I grew very sad,
thinking of my future.   From that day I wander
about aimlessly, like the Wandering Jew.   I go
scarcely anywhere.   Everything seems tiresome.
I've been once to Grischin's, who is going to Kopal,
and is now breaking up house (he s going to Vyerny
too) ; to Mader's, who says I've grown thin ; to
Schulitchka's (I took him my birthday greetings),
where I met the Pechechonovs and talked with them ;
I visit Byelichov now and then ; and finally, go to
camp for drill.   I am frequently ill.   How impatiently
I awaited the return of the Tartar guides !   Every
minute I was running to Ordynsky's to find out
something about it, and so was Silota.   I have also
been once to your house, brought away the ivy (it's

here now), and saw the orphaned Surka, who ran to
meet me, crazy with joy, but will not be induced to
leave the house. At last the guides came back.
Your letter, for which I thank you infinitely, was a
great joy to me. I asked the Tartars many a question. They told me a lot, and praised you above all
things (everyone praises you, Maria Dmitryevna!).
I gave them a little money. The next day I met
Koptyov at Vrangel's. He told me things too, but
I couldn't ask him about what interested me most of
all, namely, how your travelling-expenses had worked
out. The question was too "ticklish." To this
day I can't imagine how you ever got over the
journey! How dear your letter is, Maria Dmitryevna!
I expected just such an one. It is so full of detail;
write me letters like that always. I can see your
grandmother as if she were before my eyes. The
bad old woman! How she adds to your troubles
and embitters your life. May she stay with her lap-
dog to the end of her days! I hope that Alexander
Ivanovitch will squeeze that last will and testament
out of her, without ever letting her enter the house in
person. She must be made to see that it's the best
arrangement even for herself; otherwise, she must
undertake in writing to die within three months (and
for each month pay 1,000 roubles); on that condition
alone should you receive her. Shall you really, with
your feeble health, be obliged to attend to all the
lap-dogs? Such old women are truly unbearable!
I read your letter to Vrangel—only parts of it, of
course. I could not help going once to see Elena:
the poor thing is so lonely. I am so immensely sorry
that you were ill on the way! When *shall* I get a
letter from you? I am so anxious! How were you

on arrival? I shake Alexander Ivanovitch mightily
by the hand, and kiss him. I hope he'll soon write
to me. I embrace him warmly as friend and brother,
and wish him better health than he had here. And
does he mean to be as entirely indiscriminate about
people in Kusnezk as he was in Semipalatinsk? Are
all those fellows really worth associating with, eating
and drinking with, and, afterwards, taking all conceivable basenesses from? In that way one injures one's-
self with eyes wide open. What a loathsome lot
they are, and above all, what a dirty lot! When
one was in their company, one often felt one's soul to
be as soiled as if one were in a low dram-shop. I hope
Alexander Ivanovitch won't be angry with me for
my wishes and my advice. Farewell, unforgettable
Maria Dmitryevna—farewell! We *shall* meet again,
shan't we? Write to me very often and very much,
write to me about Kusnezk, about the new people you
know, and as much as possible about yourself. Kiss
Pasha from me. Farewell, farewell—oh, *when* shall
we see one another again?

FYODOR DOSTOEVSKY.

XXIV

To Mme. Praskovya Yegorovna Annenkov.[1]

SEMIPALATINSK,
October 18, 1855.

PRASKOVYA YEGOROVNA!

I wanted to write to you long ago, and have
waited so long for a suitable opportunity that I will
not delay now that one presents itself. The bearer
of this letter, Alexey Ivanovitch Bachirev, is a very
modest and very excellent young man, a simple and
honest soul. I have known him now for a year and

[1] Wife of the well-known Decembrist Annenkov.

a half, and am sure that I am not mistaken in his qualities.

I shall ever remember the full, cordial sympathy which you and your whole excellent family showed to me and my companions in misfortune on my arrival in Siberia. I think of that sympathy with a quite peculiar sense of solace, and shall never, I think, forget it. He who has learnt by his own experience what " hostile destiny " means, and in certain moments has savoured the full bitterness of such a lot, knows also how sweet it then is to meet, quite unexpectedly, with brotherly compassion.

It was thus that you showed yourselves to me, and I often recall my meeting with you, when you came to Omsk and I was still in the prison.

Since my arrival at Semipalatinsk, I have heard almost nothing of Constantine Ivanovitch, and the much-honoured Olga Ivanovna[1]; my intercourse with Olga Ivanovna will for ever be one of the pleasantest memories of my life. Eighteen months ago, when Dourov and I left the prison, we spent nearly a month in her house.

You can well imagine the effect that such intercourse must have had on a man who for four years, adapting myself, as I did, to my fellow-prisoners, had lived like a slice cut from a loaf, or a person buried underground. Olga Ivanovna held out her hand to me like a sister, and the memory of that beautiful, pure, proud, and noble nature will be clear and radiant all my life long. May God shower much happiness on her, happiness for herself and for those who are dear to her. I should like to hear something of her. I believe that such

[1] These were the son-in-law and the daughter of Mme. Annenkov, Constantine Ivanovitch Ivanov, and Olga Ivanovna.

beautiful natures as hers must always be happy ; only
the evil are unhappy. I believe that happiness lies in
a clear conception of life and in goodness of heart, not
in external circumstances. Is it not so ? I am sure
that you will understand me rightly, and that is why
I write thus to you.

My life goes by somehow or other ; but I may confide to you that I have great hopes. . . . My hopes
are based on certain facts ; various people are taking
the greatest trouble for me in Petersburg, and I shall
perhaps hear something in a few months. You will
probably have heard that Dourov has been released
from military service on account of his health, and
has now entered the Civil Service. He is in Omsk.
Perhaps you have news of him. We don't correspond,
though we keep one another in good remembrance.

Baron Vrangel, whom you know, sends you
greeting. I am friendly with him. His is a fine,
fresh nature ; God grant it may always so remain.

My profound, entire, and sincere respects to your
husband. I wish you perfect happiness. Do you
happen to have heard anything from a certain oracle,[1]
who was consulted during my stay at Omsk ? I
remember still what a deep impression it made upon
Olga Ivanovna.

Farewell, most honoured Praskovya Yegorovna.

I am sure that we shall meet again, and perhaps quite
soon. It is my sincere wish. I think with veneration
of you and all yours.

I remain, in deepest reverence,

F. DOSTOEVSKY.

[1] The allusion is to a spiritualistic séance, at which Mme. Ivanovna
heard an astonishing prophecy with regard to a question of in-
heritance.

I had a few lines from Constantine Ivanovitch this summer.

Though I much esteem the bearer of this letter, A. I. Bachirev, I don't confide all things to him.

XXV

To Apollon Nikolayevitch Maikov[1]

SEMIPALATINSK,
January 18, 1856.

I meant to answer your kind letter long ago, my dear Apollon Nikolayevitch. As I read it, there came to me a breath of the past. I thank you a thousand times for not having forgotten me. I don't know why, but I always had the feeling that you wouldn't forget me ; perhaps because I can't forget you. You write that much has altered in this interval, and that we've both been through many transformations. For myself I can answer. I could tell you many interesting things about myself. But please don't be angry with me for writing now in all haste, so that my letter must be broken, and even perhaps confused. I am feeling just what you felt, as you wrote—the impossibility of expressing one's-self fully after so many years, even though one should write fifty pages. One must have the word of mouth and the personal contact, so that one can read the countenance and hear the heart speak in the tone. One word, spoken frankly, two-by-two, face speaking to face, means more than dozens of sheets of writing. I thank you most particularly for all you told me about yourself.

[Here follow some remarks about people with whom Maikov was connected.]

[1] The well-known author (1821-97).

Perhaps you have heard something of me from my brother. In my hours of leisure I am putting down a good many notes of my prison-memories.[1] There are but few personal details in these sketches, though; when I've finished them, and if a really good opportunity offers, I'll send you a manuscript copy as a keepsake.

[Here follows a cordial recommendation of the bearer of this letter, Baron A. Vrangel.]

You write that you have thought of me warmly, and always asked yourself, " To what end, to what end ?" And I too have thought warmly of you, but your question " To what end ?" I shall answer not at all ; for whatever I might say must necessarily be waste of words. You write that you have done a great deal, thought a great deal, got a great deal that is new from life. It could not have been otherwise, and I'm sure that we should now agree in our views. For I too have thought a great deal and done a great deal ; such unusual circumstances and influences have combined in my experience that I have *had* to undergo, think, and weigh far too much, more than my strength was equal for. As you know me very well, you'll easily believe that in all things I was guided by those considerations which seemed to me to be just and upright, that I never played the hypocrite, and that when I took up any particular matter, I put my whole soul into it. Don't think, though, that I mean by these words to refer to the circumstances which have brought me here. I am speaking now of more recent experiences ; nor would it be relevant to allude to those gone-by occurrences—they were nothing but an

[1] " The House of the Dead," published 1861-62.

episode, after all. One's views alter; one's heart
remains the same. I have read your letter through,
but failed to understand the most essential part of it.
I mean about patriotism, the Russian Idea, the sense
of duty, national honour, and all those things of
which you speak with such enthusiasm. But, my
friend! were you ever any different? For *I* was
always inspired by those very emotions and convictions. Russia, Duty, Honour? Why, I always
was Russian through and through, and I say it most
decidedly. What then is "new" about the movement which is becoming perceptible around you, and
of which you write as of a novel tendency? I tell you
quite frankly that I don't understand you. I have
read your poem, and thought it exquisite; I wholly
share your patriotic emotion, your efforts towards the
moral emancipation of the Slavs. It is there that
Russia's mission lies—our noble, mighty Russia, our
holy mother. How beautiful are the concluding lines
of your "Council at Clermont"! Whence do you
draw the eloquence with which you have so magnifi-
cently expressed those powerful thoughts? Yes—
indeed I *do* share your idea that in Russia Europe
will find her final account; it is Russia's true mission.
That was always clear to me. You write that our
society "seems to be awakened from its apathy." Yet
you know that our society never does make manifestations; and who shall conclude therefrom that it is
nerveless? Once an idea is really made clearly manifest, and society called upon to examine it—society has
always grasped it at once. And so it is now : the Idea
has been grandly, most nationally and chivalrously
(one must declare *that*) made manifest—and behold,
that very political ideal which Peter the Great

fashioned for us has at once been universally accepted.
Perhaps you were and are offended by the fact that
in those strata of society where people consciously
think, feel, and investigate, French ideas are gaining
ground ? Undoubtedly there is a tinge of exclusiveness
in that ; still it is in the nature of all exclusiveness
instantly to produce its own antithesis. You will
admit yourself that all reasonable, thinking men—and
that means, those who set the tone in everything—have
ever regarded French ideas from a purely scientific
standpoint, and that even they who most leaned
towards exclusiveness, remained unchangingly Russian
throughout. What do you see new in that ? I
assure you that *I*, for example, feel so near to all
Russians that even the convicts never alarmed me ;
they were Russian, they were my brothers in misfortune ; and I often had the joy of discovering magna-
nimity in the soul of a robber and murderer ; but it
was only because I am Russian myself that I could
thus understand him. I have to thank my ill luck
for many practical experiences, which probably have
had a great influence upon me ; but I learnt at the
same time that in my very inmost being I always
have. been Russian. One may be mistaken in an
idea, but one can't mistake one's heart, and lose one's
conscience by reason of the mental error—by which I
mean, one can't act against one's convictions.

But why am I writing all this to you ? I know
well that these lines don't in the least express what I
mean ; then why do I go on writing ? I'll tell you,
instead, some things about myself. In prison I read
only very little, for I couldn't get any of the books I
wanted, though often books of a sort came into my
hands. Since I've been here in Semipalatinsk, I've

read rather more ; but still I have no books, not even
necessary ones, at hand, and time is going by. I
couldn't at all tell you how very much I suffered
from not being allowed to write in prison. My
mental labour comes only thus " to the boil." Some
things were all right ; I felt it. I planned out in that
way a great novel, which I consider will be my defini-
tive work. I was dreadfully afraid that the first
passion for my work would have gone cold when the
years had passed, and the hour of realization struck
at last—that passion without which one cannot write.
But I was mistaken: the figure which I had conceived,
and which is the basis of the whole book, needed some
years for its development, and I am convinced that I
should have ruined all if I had then, unready as I
was, begun the work in the first flush of zeal. But
even when I left the prison, I did not set to, though
all was quite ready in my mind. I simply could not
write. A circumstance, a contingency, which long
had delayed to enter my life and then at last did
invade it, wholly carried me away, intoxicated me.
I was happy, I could not work. Later I was to know
grief and sadness. I lost something which was my
all. Hundreds of versts now divide us.[1] I won't
speak more precisely, but will perhaps explain all at
some other time; now I cannot. . . . However, I have
not been wholly idle. I have done some work; but
the carrying-out of my *chef d'œuvre* I have postponed.
For that I need to be in a more tranquil mood. I
began for fun to write a comedy ; I invented so
many droll characters and episodes, and liked my hero
so much, that I abandoned the form of comedy
(although I quite enjoyed it) solely that I might

[1] The reference is to Mme. Issayev, later Dostoevsky's wife.

prolong as far as possible the pursuit of this new
hero's experiences, and my own laughter at him. He
is like myself in many respects. In a word, I am
writing a comic novel[1]; hitherto I have been describ-
ing only separate adventures, but now I've had
enough of that, and am unifying the whole.

There's my full report of work ; I can't help writing
it all to you ; when I talk *with you*, my unforgettable friend, I keep thinking of our past. Indeed, I
was so often happy in your company—how could I
forget you ? You write of literature—for a year I've
hardly read anything. I'll give you my impressions,
such as they are : Turgenev pleases me best ; it is
only a pity that he's so often unequal to his great
talent. L. T.[2] I like very well, but I have an idea
that he won't do much (perhaps I'm mistaken, however). Ostrovsky I don't know at all ; I've read
nothing of his, though I've seen many extracts from
his works in the articles about him. He may know
a certain section of Russian society very accurately,
but I don't believe he's an artist. Moreover he
seems to me *a writer utterly without ideals*. Please
try to persuade me to the contrary ; for goodness'
sake, send me those works of his which you consider
the best, that I may not be acquainted only with the
criticisms of him. Of Pissemsky I know only the
" Swaggerer " and the " Rich Suitor "—nothing else.
I like him very much. He is sane, good-humoured,
and even naive ; he can tell a story like a master.
One thing is a pity : he writes too fast. He writes
much too fast, and much too much. A man should
have more ambition, more respect for his talent and
his craft, and more love for art. When one's young,

[1] " Uncle's Dream."   [2] Leo Tolstoy.

ideas come crowding incredibly into one's head; but one should not capture each and all of them as it flies, and rush to give it forth. One should rather await the synthesis, and think more; wait till the many single details which make up an idea have gathered themselves into a nucleus, into a large, imposing picture; then, and not till then, should one write them down. The colossal figures, created by the colossal writers, have often grown out of long, stubborn labour. But the attempts and sketches that go to the picture should not be displayed at all. I don't know if you'll understand me! But, as far as Pissemsky goes, I think that he doesn't hold his pen sufficiently in check. Our literary ladies write like other literary ladies—that is, cleverly, neatly, and with much fluency of expression. Tell me, please, why a woman - writer is almost never a serious artist? Even the undoubtedly colossal artist, George Sand, often spoilt herself by her purely feminine traits. . . . *During the whole time there*, I came across many of your short poems in the newspapers. . . . I liked them greatly. Be strong and labour. I'll tell you in confidence, in strict confidence : Tyutchev[1] is very remarkable, but . . . etcetera. What Tyutchev is it, by-the-bye—is it *our* one ? Many of his poems are excellent.

Farewell, my dear friend. Excuse the incoherence of this letter. One never can say anything properly in a letter. On that account alone I can't bear Mme. de Sévigné. She wrote much too good letters. . . . Who knows ? Perhaps I shall some day clasp you in my arms again. May God so appoint it !

[1] Fyodor Tyutchev (1803-73), the most profound of Russian poet-philosophers.

For God's sake, show my letter to *nobody* (really nobody)! I embrace you.

XXVI

To General E. I. Totleben[1]

SEMIPALATINSK,
March 24, 1856.

Your Excellency Eduard Ivanovitch! Forgive me for daring to ask your attention to this letter. I fear that when you see the signature and my name, which you may indeed have forgotten—though many many years ago I had the honour of being known to you—you will be angry with me and toss the letter aside without reading it. I beg for your indulgence. You might well rebuke me if I failed to realize the quite unfathomable gulf between my position and yours. But I have gone through too many sorrowful experiences in my life to be capable of overlooking that gulf. I know very well indeed that I have no right whatever to remind you that you once knew me, and thus to make even the shadow of a claim on your attention. But I am so unhappy that, almost against my will, I must yield to the hope that you will not close your heart to an unfortunate exile, and will grant him a moment's attention.

I have requested Baron Alexander Vrangel to take you this letter. During his stay in Semipala-tinsk, he has done more for me than my own brother could have done. His friendship made me happy. He knows all my circumstances. I begged him to

---

[1] Eduard Totleben (1818-84), the distinguished soldier and engineer ; builder of the fortifications of Sebastopol, which resisted the united armies for twelve months.

take you this letter in person; he will do so, although
I could not tell him with any conviction that you
would receive the letter indulgently.　Such doubts
are easily comprehensible in the heart of a one-time
prisoner.　I have a great favour to ask of you, and
only a faint hope that you will hear me.

Perhaps you have heard something of my arrest,
my trial, and the supreme ratification of the sentence
which was given in the case concerning me in the
year 1849.　Perhaps you also bestowed some attention
on my fate.　I base that supposition on the fact that
I once was great friends with your brother Adolf
Ivanovitch — as a child, even, I loved him very
sincerely.　Although of late years I have not come
in contact with him, I am still sure that he pitied
me, and perhaps told you something of my sad story.
I dare not take up your time with an account of my
trial.　I was guilty, and am very conscious of it.　I
was convicted of the intention (but only the intention) of acting against the Government; I was law-
fully and quite justly condemned; the hard and
painful experiences of the ensuing years have sobered
me, and altered my views in many respects.　But
then, while I was still blind, I believed in all the
theories and Utopias.　When I went to Siberia, I
had at least the one comfort of having borne myself
honestly before the tribunal, of not having tried to
shift my guilt on others, and even of having sacrificed
my own interests, if thereby I thought I could save
those others.　But I was at that time still convinced
of the truth of my opinions; I would not confess all,
and so was the more sternly punished.　Previously
I had suffered for two years from a strange moral
disease: I had fallen into hypochondria.　There was

a time when I even lost my reason. I was exaggeratedly irritable, had a morbidly developed sensibility,
and the power of distorting the most ordinary events
into things immeasurable. But I felt that though
this disease had had a really evil influence upon my
destiny, it was nevertheless a poor and even a de-
grading excuse for me. And I was not so entirely
convinced, either, that it *had* had that influence.
Forgive these details. Be generous, and hear me
further.

I went to prison—four sad, terrible years. My
companions were criminals, men quite without human
emotions, and with perverted morals; for those four
years I beheld nothing uplifting—only the blackest
and ugliest "realities." I had not one single being
within reach with whom I could exchange a cordial
word; I endured hunger, cold, sicknesses; I suffered
from the hard labours and the hatred of my companions the criminals, who bore me a grudge for
being an officer and a well-born person. And yet
I swear to you that none of those torments was
greater than that which I felt when I realized my
errors, and saw that in banishment I was cut off from
my fellow-creatures and unable to serve them with
all my powers, desires, and capacities. I know that
I was punished for my ideas and theories. But ideas
and even convictions alter, nay, one's very self
alters; thus, it is very grievous for me to be now
expiating things that are no more, that have, indeed,
actually, in me, turned to their very contraries; to be
suffering for my former errors, which I now perceive
in all their folly—to feel that I have the power and
the talent to do something which would really atone
for the worthlessness of my earlier activities, and yet

to languish in impotence. I am now a soldier; I am
serving at Semipalatinsk, and this summer was promoted to the rank of non-commissioned officer. I
know that many people felt and feel genuine
sympathy for me; they have exerted themselves on
my behalf, have restored me to hope, and still do
much to solace me. The monarch is kind and com-
passionate. Lastly, I know that it goes very hard
with anyone who undertakes to prove that an unlucky
man is capable of doing something worth while, if
the proof should fail. But I *can* do something worth
while; I am not, indeed I am not, without talent,
feeling, and principle. I have a great favour to ask
of you, Eduard Ivanovitch. Only one thing troubles
me: I have not the least right to worry you about
my affairs. But you have a great noble heart. I
may say this frankly, for you have recently proved
it to all the world. Moreover *I* long since had the
happiness—longer since than others—of forming for
myself that opinion of you; I had long learnt to
esteem you. A word from you can now accomplish
much with our gracious monarch, who is grateful to
you, and loves you. Think of the poor exile, and
help him. I want to employ myself usefully. When
one has spiritual and mental powers which one cannot
turn to account, one suffers deeply from inactivity.
For the military career I am not fitted. I earnestly
desire, so far as in me lies, to do my utmost therein;
but I am sickly, and feel strongly desirous of another
sphere of action, more suited to my capabilities. My
dearest wish would be to be released from military
service and to enter the civil service somewhere in
European Russia, or even here; and also to have
some liberty of choice as to my place of abode. But

neither form of State service do I regard as the real
purpose of my life. Some years ago, the public gave
me a very hearty and encouraging welcome in the
literary sphere. I very much desire permission to
publish my works. And there are precedents for
this: many political offenders have been graciously
pardoned and given permission to write and print.
I have always considered the calling of an author to
be an honourable and useful one. I am certain that
in that sphere alone can I do valuable work; therein
I could attract attention, retrieve my good name, and
make my life to some extent easier, for I possess
nothing but this assured, though possibly quite
modest, literary talent. But I should like to say
quite frankly: besides the honest desire to change my
present lot for one that will better correspond with
my talents, another circumstance, upon which perhaps the happiness of my whole life depends[1] (it is
a wholly personal matter), has given me courage to
turn to you and recall myself to your mind. But
of course I am not asking for everything at once:
I am asking only for the possibility of giving up
the military, and entering the civil, service.

Read this my prayer, but do not call me poor-
spirited. I have suffered much, and by the very fact
that I have borne so many sorrows have proved my
patience and a certain degree of bravery. But now
I *have* lost courage—I realize that, myself. I used
always to think it cowardly to trouble anyone, who-
ever it might be, with my affairs. And now, I trouble
you! But I implore you to have mercy on me. Till
now I have borne my misfortune patiently. Now I
have broken down under the weight of circumstances

1 He hints here at his projected marriage.

and have resolved to make this attempt—it is nothing
but an attempt. I swear to you that the thought of
writing to you, and importuning you, never occurred
to me before. It would have been painful and
difficult to me to recall myself to you. In an
enthusiastic and wholly unself-seeking spirit, I have
lately followed your heroic career. If you knew with
what delight I spoke of you to others, you would
believe me. If you knew with what pride I declared
that I had the honour of knowing you personally!
When your glorious deeds were recounted here, I
was overwhelmed with questions about you, and it
was a joy to me that I was able to tell of you. I do
not fear to write this to you. Your deeds are so
great that even these words can hardly appear as
flattery. The bearer of this letter will be able to tell
you how sincere and unself-seeking are my feelings
towards you. The gratitude of a Russian towards
him who, at a time of national disaster, crowned the
terrible defence of Sebastopol with eternal, undying
glory, is comprehensible enough. I repeat that it
had not been my intention to trouble you in any
way. But now, when I have lost all courage, and
scarcely know to what side I shall turn, I have
reminded myself how kind, cordial, and natural you
always were with me. I thought of your ever gallant
and noble impulses, and began to hope. I asked
myself if you, who have now attained to so lofty and
glorious a position, would repulse me, who am fallen
so low? Forgive my boldness, forgive this long
(much too long, I realize) letter; and if you can do
anything for me, do it, I implore you. And I have
yet another great request; don't refuse it me. Recall
me, sometimes, to your brother Adolf Ivanovitch's

remembrance, and tell him that I still love him as
before, and often found him among my memories
during the four years in prison, when in spirit I
would live my whole past over again, day by day
and hour by hour. But he knows himself how dearly
I love him. I do happen to know that he has lately
been ill. Is he well again? Is he alive? Forgive
me this request also. But I know not through
whom I may attain my heart's desire, and so turn
to you. I am aware that this letter is a grave breach
of discipline. A common soldier writes to an
Adjutant-General! But you are generous-hearted,
and I confide in that.

With deepest respect and the sincere thanks of a
Russian,

I remain

Your Excellency's most devoted servant,

FYODOR DOSTOEVSKY.[1]

XXVII

To the Baron A. E. Vrangel

SEMIPALATINSK,
April 13, 1856.

[The letter begins with some not very interesting
details of Dostoevsky's material circumstances.]

You write that we political offenders may expect

---

[1] Totleben's minute ran: " His Majesty is pleased to order me
to suggest to the Minister of War that Fyodor Dostoevsky be promoted to the rank of ensign in a regiment of the Second Army
Corps. Should this not be possible, he is to be transferred to the
Civil Service with the rank of an official of the fourteenth class; in
both cases he is to be permitted to employ himself in literature,
and is to be given the right to print his works on condition of their
generally lawful tendency."

certain indulgences, which, however, are still kept a
secret.　Do me the kindness, dear friend, to try to
discover something concerning myself.　I *must* know
it.　If you learn anything, impart it to me without
delay.　About the transfer to the Caucasus I no
longer think—nor to the battalion at Barnaul.　All
that is unimportant to me now.

You write that everybody loves the new Tsar.
I myself idolize him.　I must confess that it is a
great object to me to be promoted ; but I may still
have to wait a long time for my promotion to commissioned rank ; and I should like to have something
now, at once, on the occasion of the Coronation
festivities.　The best and wisest would be of course
that I should ask for permission to publish.

I think of sending you very soon, privately, a poem
I have written about the Coronation.　I might even
send it "officially."　You will be sure to meet
Hasford.[1]　He soon starts, of course, for the Coronation.　Could you not persuade him to present my
poem to the Tsar ?　Would it not do ?　Tell me too
up to what time I am safe in writing to you, for if
you leave Petersburg, my letters might be lost, and
that would be tiresome.　I have already told you
about my article on Russia.　It has turned into a
regular political pamphlet.　Yet I should not like
to erase a single word of that article.　They will
scarcely allow me to begin my literary activity with
a pamphlet, however patriotic its contents may be.
But the article was good, and I was satisfied with it.
It interested me extraordinarily.　Still, I have abandoned the task.　For if I can't get permission to
publish it, why should I have all my trouble for

[1] Governor-General of Siberia.

nothing? Time is too precious now for me to
waste it in writing for mere amusement. Besides,
the political atmosphere has changed. And so, I
have begun a new article: " Letters on Art." The
Grand-Duchess Maria Nikolayevna is President of
the Academy of Arts. I intend to ask permission
to dedicate this piece to her, and let it then appear
anonymously. It is the fruit of ten years' delibera-
tion. I thought it out to the last detail as long ago
as Omsk. It will have many original and burning
passages, but I can't answer for the execution of the
whole. Probably many will disagree with me on
various points. But I believe in my ideas, and that
suffices me. I should like to ask Apollon Maikov to
read it beforehand. Certain chapters contain whole
pages from the pamphlet. It deals directly with the
place of Christianity in art. But where shall I bring
it out? If I let it appear as a separate publication,
at most a hundred people will read it, for it is no
novel, while in a journal I might get paid for it.
Now, the *Sovremennik* was always hostile to me, and
so was the *Moskvityanin*. In the *Roussky Viestnik*
there has appeared the prelude to an article by
Katkov on Pushkin, where the ideas expressed are in
disaccord with mine. So there remains only the
Otetschestvennia Zapiski. But I don't know how
matters stand with that journal. Would you therefore find out from Maikov and your brother
whether there is any chance of publishing and
being paid for the article, and tell me what they
say; just speak of it casually, as it were. The
principal thing is that the novel at which I'm now
working affords me great enjoyment. Only with
novels shall I ever make a name and attract public

attention.   All the same, it would be wiser to begin
with a serious article (upon art) and try for permission to publish such an one ; for nowadays people
regard a novel as an inferior sort of thing.   So I
believe, at any rate. . . .

[Dostoevsky reiterates his request that Vrangel
will exert himself on his behalf.]

XXVIII

To his Brother Michael

SEMIPALATINSK,
May 31, 1858.

You beg me, my friend, to send you everything
I write.   I can't remember (my memory is mostly
very bad now)—I can't remember whether I told you
that I had approached Katkov (*Roussky Viestnik*)
and offered him my co-operation on his paper ; I
promised that this very year I'd write a long tale for
him if he would at once send me 500 roubles.   Four
or five weeks ago I got those 500 roubles and a very
sensible and friendly letter from him.   He writes
that he is very glad of my co-operation, and at once
responds to my request (about the 500 roubles).   He
begs me not to hurry myself in any way, and to write
only at my leisure.   That's splendid.   So now I am
to write a long story for the *Roussky Viestnik ;* the
only trouble is that I haven't arranged with Katkov
about payment by the sheet—I wrote that I would
leave that matter to him.

I want to write something this year also for the
Roussky Slovo—not the novel, but a tale.   I won't
write the novel till I've got out of Siberia.   I must

put it off till then.   The motive of this book is most
excellent, the principal figure is new and has never
yet been done.   But as to-day in Russia such a figure
frequently emerges in actual life (so I conclude from
the new movements and ideas of which everyone
seems full), I feel sure that I shall succeed in enrich-
ing my novel, after my return, with fresh observations.[1]   One ought not to hurry, my friend ; one
must try to do nothing but what is good.   You write,
my dear fellow, that I am really very vain, and want
to step forth now with a peculiarly distinguished
work ; and that therefore I sit patiently on my eggs,
that the "distinguished work" may be hatched.
Well, suppose it really were the case : at any rate,
as I've now dropped the idea of bringing out the
novel at present, and am working at two stories,
which will both be only just tolerable, I don't think
there can be much talk of "hatching."   Where on
earth did you pick up the theory that a picture
should be painted "straight off," and so forth ?   When
did you come to that conclusion ?   Believe me, in all
things labour is necessary—gigantic labour.   Believe
me that a graceful, fleet poem of Pushkin's, consisting
of but a few lines, *is* so graceful and so fleet simply
because the poet has worked long at it, and altered
much.   That is solid fact.   Gogol wrote at his "Dead
Souls" for eight years.   Everything that he did
"straight off" was crude.   People say that in Shakespeare's MSS. there is not a single erasure.   That's
why there are so many monstrous errors of taste in
him.   If he had worked more, the whole would have
come off better.   You evidently confuse the inspiration, that is, the first instantaneous vision, or emotion

1 The "figure" is Raskolnikov, in "Crime and Punishment."

in the artist's soul (which is always present), with
the *work*. I, for example, write every scene down at
once, just as it first comes to me, and rejoice in it ;
then I work at it for months and years. I let it
inspire me, in that form, more than once (for I love it
thus) ; here I add, there I take away ; believe me
that the scene always gains by it. One must *have*
the inspiration ; without inspiration one can't of
course begin anything.

You write that big fees are now being paid in your
part of the world. Thus, Pissemsky got 200 or
250 roubles a sheet for his "Thousand Souls." In
such circumstances one could really live, and work at
ease. But do you really think Pissemsky's novel
excellent ? It is mediocre work—possibly a "*golden
mean*," but nevertheless mediocre. Come ! is there
one fresh thing in it—one thing of *his own*, that never
before was done ? All has been done before him, and
done by the most modern writers too, particularly by
Gogol. His are but ancient words to a new tune.
"Distinguished work " after foreign patterns—home
products from sketches by Benvenuto Cellini. It's
true I've read only the two first parts of the novel ;
papers reach us very late here. The end of the
second part is utterly improbable, and entirely bad.
Kalinovitch, who consciously betrays, is simply impossible. Kalinovitch, as the author had earlier
depicted him, would have *had* to offer a sacrifice,
propose marriage, intoxicate himself with his own
nobility, and be convinced that he was incapable of
any deception. Kalinovitch is so vain that he
couldn't possibly regard himself as a scoundrel. Of
course he would take his pleasure all the same, spend
a night with Nastenyka and then betray her ; but

only afterwards, under the pressure of actualities;
and he would assuredly solace himself even then, and
aver that he had acted nobly in this case also.   But a
Kalinovitch who consciously betrays, is repulsive and
impossible; that is to say, such a person is possible,
but he is not Kalinovitch.   Enough of this nonsense.
I am weary of waiting for my leave.

[Here follow plans for what Dostoevsky will do
when he gets his leave.]

XXIX

To his Brother Michael

SEMIPALATINSK,
MAY 9, 1859.

[At first he talks of his leave, which had been
granted so long ago as March 18, but of which
nothing was known in Semipalatinsk till May; and
of business matters.]

You always write me such tidings as, for example,
that Gontshazov has got 7,000 roubles for his novel,
and that Katkov (from whom I now demand 100
roubles a sheet) has offered Turgenev 4,000 roubles
for his " House of Gentlefolk "—which means 400
roubles a sheet.   (I have read Turgenev's novel at last.
It is extraordinarily good.)   My friend! I know very
well that I don't write as well as Turgenev; still
the difference is really not so great, and I hope
in time to write quite as well as he does.   Why
do *I*, then, in my need, allow myself to get only
100 roubles a sheet, while Turgenev, who has 2,000
serfs, gets 400 roubles?   I am poor, and so must write

DOSTOEVSKY AT SEMIPALATINSK
(1858), IN ENSIGN'S UNIFORM.

F. M. DOSTOEVSKY.

in greater haste and *for* money ; consequently I have to *spoil everything I do.*

[Here follow considerations upon the terms which Dostoevsky thinks of offering to Kachelyov, editor of the *Roussky Slovo.*]

I am now finishing a story for Katkov[1] ; it has got quite long—fourteen or fifteen sheets. I have already delivered three-quarters of it ; the rest I shall send in the beginning of June. Now listen, Micha! This story has of course great faults and is, above all, extravagantly long ; but I am perfectly certain that it has also the greatest merits and is my best work. I have been two years writing it (with an interruption in the middle, when I wrote "Uncle's Dream"). The beginning and the middle are decently worked out, but the end was written in great haste. Still I have put my whole soul, my flesh and blood, into it. I will not say that I have therein expressed my whole self : that would be nonsense. I have much more to say. And there is, in this story, far too little of the human, that is, the passionate, element (as exemplified, for instance, in "A House of Gentlefolk") ; but on the other hand it shows forth two colossal types, which I have been *working at and polishing* for five whole years ; they are (as I believe) faultlessly drawn ; wholly Russian types, and such as have been hitherto insufficiently studied in Russian literature. I know not whether Katkov will be able to appreciate the book, but if it is coldly received by the public, I shall really despair. On this novel I build my highest hopes, and, above all, that of the certainty of my literary vocation.

[Henceforth the topic again is money.]

---

[1] "Stepanchikovo Village."

XXX

To Frau Stackenschneider

[PETERSBURG],
May 3, 1860.

HONOURED AND DEAR FRAU ST.

I have now been back in Petersburg three
months, and have taken up my work again. The
whole visit to Moscow seems like a dream to me
now; here I am again amid the damp, the dirt, the
ice from Ladoga Lake,[1] the tedium, and so on.
Yes—back again, and I feel as if I were in a fever.
That's because of my novel.[2] I want it to come off.
I feel that there is poetry in it, and I know that on it
depends my whole literary career. I shall have to
work night and day for the next three months. But
what a reward awaits me, when I've finished! Rest,
a clear outlook on my surroundings, and the knowledge that I have done and attained what I wished.
Perhaps I shall give myself, as a treat, a few months'
travel; but first of all I shall in any event come again
to Moscow.

. . . Ambition is a good thing, but I think that
one may take it as one's aim only in things which
one has set one's-self to achieve, has made the reason
for one's existence. In anything else it's nonsense.
The only essential is to live with ease; and moreover
one must sympathize with one's fellow-creatures, and
strive to win their sympathy in return. And if,
indeed, one had no other determined aim, this would
by itself more than suffice.

[1] In the early part of the year the ice from Lake Ladoga comes
floating down the Neva.
[2] " Injury and Insult."

But I'm beginning to philosophize again. I have heard little or no news. Pissemsky is ill, suffering from rheumatism. I've been to see Apollon Maikov. He told me that Pissemsky rages, sulks, takes it very badly; that's no wonder; such sufferings are great torment. By-the-bye, didn't you know one Snitkin? He published some comic verses under the pseudonym of Ammos Schichkin. Only think: he fell ill suddenly, and died within six days. The Literary Relief Fund has undertaken to look after his family. It is very sad. But perhaps you didn't know anything of him. I had a talk with Krestovsky[1] lately. I like him very much. He wrote a poem the other day, and read it aloud to us with much pride. We told him with one voice that the poem was atrocious; it is our custom always to speak the truth. And what do you think? He wasn't in the least offended. He is such a dear, noble youth! I like him better and better, and on some drinking-bout or other I mean to drink brotherhood with him.[2] One often has such odd impressions! I always have this one—that Krestovsky must soon die. But whence it comes, I can't possibly say.

We are thinking of starting a serious literary enterprise. We are all very busy about it.[3] Perhaps it will come off. All these plans are but the first step, but at any rate they indicate vitality. I know very well what " the first step " means, and I love it. It is better than any leap.

[1] Vsevolod Krestovsky, a quite unimportant but highly popular novelist. He died about 1895.

[2] This is done with arms intertwined. (Translator's note.)

[3] The reference is to the journal *Vremya* (*The Times*).

I have a frightful character, but not always—only at times. That's my solace.

FYODOR DOSTOEVSKY.

XXXI
To Mme. V. D. Constantine[1]

PARIS,
September 1, 1862.

MY DEAR AND MUCH - HONOURED VARVARA DMITRYEVNA!

You have perhaps learnt from my letter to Pasha[2] that I arrived happy and well in Paris, and have settled down here, though I hardly think I shall stay long. I don't like Paris, though it's frightfully grand. There's a lot to see here, but when one undertakes the seeing, terrible boredom ensues. It would have been very different if I had come here as a student, to learn something: very different, for I should have had plenty to do, and should have *had* to see and hear a great deal; while for a tourist, who is merely observing customs, the French are disgusting, and the town as such is wholly unknown to me. The best things here are the wine and the fruit: the only things that in the long run don't pall on one. Of my private affairs I won't write you anything. "Letters are nonsense; only apothecaries write letters."[3] I will write only of a certain business matter. I have in fact a request to make of you, my dear Varvara Dmitryevna. You must know that on the way I stopped four days at Wiesbaden,

---

[1] Dostoevsky's sister-in-law; sister of Mme. Maria Dmitryevna.
[2] Pasha [Paul] Issayev, Dostoevsky's step-son.
[3] Quotation from Gogol's "Memoirs of a Madman."

and of course played roulette. And what do you think? I did not lose, but won; not, certainly, as much as I could have wished, no hundred thousand, but still a nice little sum.

N.B.: Tell this to no one, dear Varvara Dmitryevna. You *can't*, it is true, tell it to anyone, for you don't meet anyone; but I really mean Pasha; he is still a little goose, and would perhaps imagine that one can make a living out of play. He took it into his head lately to be a shop-boy, and earn money that way: "and so I needn't learn anything," he informed me. "*And so*" he needn't know that Papa frequents gaming-halls. Therefore tell him not a word about it. During those four days I watched the gamblers closely. Several hundred persons took part in the play, and only two knew really how to gamble—my word of honour! They were a Frenchwoman and an English Lord; *they* knew how, and lost nothing, indeed they nearly broke the bank. But please don't think that, in my joy at having won and not lost, I am swaggering, and imagining that *I* know the secret of play. I do know the secret, and it is extremely stupid and simple: it consists in controlling one's-self the whole time, and never getting excited at any phase of the game. That is all; in that way one can't possibly lose and *must* win. The whole point is that the man who knows this secret should have the power and capacity to turn it rightly to account. One may be ever so intelligent, one may have a character of pure iron, and yet one may come to grief. Even that philosopher Strachov would lose. Blessed therefore are they who do not gamble, who detest roulette and look upon it as the height of folly.

But to the point. I have, dear Varvara Dmitryevna, won 5,000 francs; or rather, I *had* won, at first,
10,400 francs, taken the money home, put it in my
wallet, and resolved to depart next day and not go
into the gaming-rooms again. But I did not hold
out, and played away half the money again. So only
5,000 francs are left. A part of these winnings I have
reserved to myself in case of accidents, and the rest I
am sending to Petersburg: half to my brother, that
he may put it by till my return, and the other half to
you, to give or send to Maria Dmitryevna.

[He then discusses how the money may best be
sent from abroad, and changed in Russia.]

XXXII
To N. N. Strachov[1]

ROME,
September 18 [30], 1863.

[Dostoevsky begins by begging Strachov to settle
his accounts at the office of the *Booklover's Library.*]

And Boborykin[2] may as well know what is known
already to the *Sovremennik* and the *Otetschestvennia
Zapiski*: that I never in my life have sold a work
(with the exception of "Poor Folk") for which I
have not been paid in advance. I am a proletarian
among the authors, and if anyone wants my work, he
must pay me for it beforehand. I myself condemn this

---

[1] Nikolay Nikolayevitch Strachov, critic and philosopher (1828-
96) was a close friend of Dostoevsky and Grigorovitch. He headed
an embittered political campaign against Nihilism and the material
tendencies of the 'sixties.

[2] Pyotr Boborykin, a still living popular novelist. At that time
he was editor of the *Booklover's Library*.

system. But I have established it once for all, and
will never abandon it. So now I'll go on :—

At the moment I have nothing ready. But I have
(what seems to me) a very good idea for a story.[1]
The greater part of it is already jotted down on
scraps of paper. I have even begun the actual
execution, but in the first place it's too hot here, and
in the second I don't want to spend more than a week
in Rome; how could anyone, staying only eight days
in a city like Rome, get any writing done? All the
going-about tires me extraordinarily. My story will
depict a typical figure, a Russian living abroad. You
know of course that last summer there was a great
deal of talk in our journals about the absentee
Russian. This will all be reflected in my story.
And the present state of our interior organizations
will also (as well as I can do it, of course) be woven
into the narrative. I depict a man of most simple
nature, a man who, while developed in many respects,
is yet in every way incomplete, who has lost all
faith, yet at the same time *does not dare to be
a sceptic*, who revolts against all authority and yet at
the same time fears it. He comforts himself with
the thought that in Russia there is nothing that he
can do, and therefore condemns in the harshest
manner those who would summon the absentee
Russians back to Russia. I can't tell it all here.
The character is very vivid (I can literally see it standing before me), and when once the story is finished it
will be worth reading. The real idea, though, lies in
his having wasted all his substance, energies, and
talents on roulette. He is a gambler, but no common
gambler, just as the " miserly knight " of Pushkin is

[1] " The Gambler."

no common miser. (I don't in the least mean to
compare myself with Pushkin. I only use the comparison for lucidity's sake.) He is in his way a poet,
yet he is ashamed of such poetry, for he feels profoundly its vulgarity, even though the *longing for
touch-and-go* ennobles him in his own eyes. The
whole story is concerned with his playing roulette for
full three years.

If my " Dead House "—as a picture of the prison,
which no one before me had thus psychologically
displayed—greatly interested the public, the new
story, as a psychological and faithful portrait of the
roulette-player, will interest them still more. Apart
from the fact that that kind of work is read
among us with the deepest interest, one must also
consider that the gambling in a foreign watering-
place is notorious, and the chief topic of the absentee
Russian ; this has, in addition to the rest, a certain
(though of course inferior) importance.

In short, I dare to hope that I shall succeed in
depicting all these most absorbing circumstances with
feeling, understanding, and not too long-windedly.
The story may be very good indeed. My " Dead
House " was really most interesting. And here
again shall be the picture of a hell, of the same kind
as that " Turkish bath in the prison." I want to
do this one too, and I shall take enormous pains
about it.

[Henceforth money-matters prevail.]

XXXIII

To A. P. Milyukov[1]

[Moscow],
June, 1866.

My dear and honoured friend Alexander
Petrovitch!

Katkov is taking the summer air at Petrovsky-
Park ; Lyubimov (the editor of the *Roussky Viestnik*)
also is taking the air. At the office one only now
and then comes across the moping secretary, from
whom one can extract nothing. I did, however,
succeed in the early days in catching Lyubimov. He
has had three chapters of my novel already set up.[2]
I proposed to him that I should write the fourth
chapter in less than no time ; the four would make
exactly half the conclusion of the second part (four
sheets) ; in the next number they could print four
more chapters—that is, to the end of the second part.
Lyubimov, however, almost interrupted me to say :
"I was waiting to tell you that now, in June and
July, we can print the novel in smaller portions—in
fact, we *must ;* one number, even, seeing it's the
summer season, might have no portion at all. We
should prefer to arrange that the whole second half
of the novel appears in the autumn, and the end in
the December number, for the effect of the novel
ought to help towards the new year's subscriptions."
It was therefore decided to pause for yet another
month. The four chapters (four sheets) will therefore not appear till the July number, and are already
in proof.

[1] See the Reminiscences of Milyukov, in the Appendix.
[2] " Crime and Punishment."

Later, however, it appeared that Lyubimov had yet another infamous back-thought : namely, that he won't print one of the chapters at all, and Katkov has approved of this his decision.[1]   I was infuriated with them both.   But they insist on their scheme !   About the chapter in question, I myself can't say at all : I wrote it in a positive inspiration, but it may be that it's really bad ; however, with them it's not a question of the literary value, but of nervousness about the *morality* of it.   In this respect I am in the right ; the chapter contains nothing immoral, *quite the contrary* indeed ; but they're of another opinion, and moreover see traces of *Nihilism* therein.   Lyubimov told me finally that I must write the chapter over again.   I undertook to do so, and the re-writing of this great chapter gave me at least as much labour and trouble as three new ones.   Nevertheless I have re-written, and delivered, it.   Unfortunately I haven't seen Lyubimov since, so I don't know whether they're satisfied with the new version, or will write it all over again themselves.   This actually happened to another chapter (of these four) : Lyubimov told me that he had struck out a great deal of it.   (That I didn't particularly mind, for they deleted a quite unimportant passage.)

I don't know how it will turn out, but the differences of opinion which this novel has brought to light between me and the office, begin to trouble me.

The novel for Stellovsky[2] I haven't yet begun,

---

[1] It is the ninth chapter of the second part of " Crime and Punishment "; the scene where Sonia and Raskolnikov together read the Gospel had given offence.   Dostoevsky was obliged to shorten the chapter.

[2] Publisher of the first edition of the " Collected Works " (1865-66).

but certainly shall begin.   I have a plan for a most
decent little novel; there will even be shadows of
actual characters in it.   The thought of Stellovsky
torments and disturbs me; it pursues me even in
dreams.

I'm telling you all this very cursorily and in great
haste, though my letter's long enough.   Answer me,
for God's sake.   Write to me about yourself, your
life, your views, and your health.   Write to me also
of our people; have you perhaps heard some news?
I must be silent about many things.   My best
regards to your Ludmilla Alexandrovna; remember
me to all your children, and greet all common
acquaintances from me.   Till next time, my kind
friend, I embrace you and remain your

FYODOR DOSTOEVSKY.

N.B.   I have not had any attacks up to the
present.   I drink schnaps.   How does it stand with
the cholera?

XXXIV

To Apollon Nikolayevitch Maikov

GENEVA,
August 16 [28], 1867.

So long have I kept silence, and not answered your
welcome letter, my dear and unforgettable friend
Apollon Nikolayevitch.   I call you *unforgettable
friend*, and feel deep in my heart that that description
is just; we are both such *old* and *accustomed* friends
that life, which sometimes parted us and even *separated*
us, not only has not succeeded in really " separating "
us, but has actually drawn us closer together.   You
write that you feel my absence to a certain extent;

much more do I feel yours. Quite apart from the
fact that every day shows me more clearly the likeness and sympathy between our thoughts and feelings,
I beg you to observe as well that *I*, since I lost you,
have come over into a strange land, where not only
are there no Russian faces, Russian books, Russian
thoughts and concerns, but no friendly faces of any
sort. I truly cannot understand how any Russian
living abroad, if he be a man of heart and intelligence,
can fail to notice this, and be made miserable by it.
Perhaps all these faces are friendly to one another ;
I can only say that I feel they're not friendly to us.
It really is so ! How *can* people endure this living
abroad ? By God, without home, *life is torture!*
I can understand going abroad for six months, or
even a year. But to travel, as I do, without knowing
or even guessing when one will get home again, is
very bad and grievous. The mere thought of it is
hard to bear. I need Russia for my work, *for my life*
(I speak of no life but *that*). I am like a fish out of
water; I lose all my energies, all my faculties. . . .
You know in what circumstances I left home, and
for what reason. There are two principal reasons :
in the first place, I had to save my health and even
my life. The attacks were recurring every eight days,
and it was unbearable to feel and *recognize* the destruc-
tion of my nerves and *brain*. I really was beginning
to lose my senses—that is a fact. I felt it ; the ruin
of my nerves often drove me to the very edge of
things. The second reason is that my creditors
would wait no longer, and on the day of my departure
several summonses were out against me. . . .

[He pursues the topic of his debts.]

. . . The burden was unbearable. I departed, with
death in my heart. I had no faith in foreign lands—
rather, I believed they might have a bad moral effect
upon me. I was wholly isolated, without resources,
and with a young creature[1] by my side, who was
naïvely delighted at sharing my wandering life ; but
I saw that that naïve delight arose partly from inexperience and youthful ardour, and this depressed and
tormented me. I was afraid that Anna Grigorovna
would find life with me a tedious thing. For up to
the present we have been literally *alone*. Of myself
I could hope little : my nature is morbid, and I
anticipated that she would have much to bear from
me. (N.B. Anna Grigorovna indeed proved herself
to be of a nature much stronger and deeper than I
had expected ; in many ways she has been my guardian angel ; at the same time, there is much that is
childish and immature in her, and very beautiful and
most necessary and natural it is, only I can hardly
respond to it. All this I saw vaguely before our
departure ; and although, as I said, Anna Grigorovna
is finer and stronger than I had guessed, I am not
even now free from all uneasiness.) Finally, our
insufficient means caused me much anxiety ; we had
only a very little money, and owed Katkov an
advance of three thousand (!) roubles. To be sure,
I intended to begin work immediately after our
departure. But what actually came to pass ? Up
to the present I have accomplished nothing, or
almost nothing, and want now to set seriously to
work at last. I must confess that I don't feel
sure I've really accomplished *nothing*, for I have
lived through so much, and *framed so much in my*

---

[1] His second wife, Anna Grigorovna, born Snitkin.

mind ; still, in *black and white* I have set down very
little as yet ; and only what stands written in black
and white is valid and money-making.

We left tedious Berlin as soon as we could (I could
only stop one day there, for the tiresome Germans
made me nervous and irascible, and I had to take
refuge in the Russian baths), and went to Dresden.
In Dresden we took lodgings and installed ourselves
for a time.

The effect was very singular ; instantly this question
presented itself to me : Why am I in Dresden, just
Dresden, and not in any other town ; and why on
earth had I to leave one place and go to another ?
The answer was most clear (my health, the debts,
etc.).   But worse is the clear perception that now
I don't in the least care where I may have to dwell.
In Dresden or another town—everywhere, in foreign
lands, I feel like a slice cut from the loaf.   I had
meant to set to work the very first day, but I felt
that I could not possibly work there, that all my
impressions were topsy-turvy.   What did I do ?   I
vegetated.   I read, wrote a few lines now and then,
nearly died of home-sickness, and, later, of heat.   The
days went monotonously by. . . .

I can't possibly tell you *all* my thoughts.   I collected
many impressions.   I read Russian newspapers and
solaced myself thus.   I felt eventually that so many
new ideas had been garnered up that I could write
a long article on Russia's relations to Western Europe,
and on the upper classes of Russian society.   I should,
indeed, have had plenty to say !   The Germans got
on my nerves ; and our Russian way of living, the
life of the upper classes, the faith in Europe and
civilization in which those upper classes are steeped—

all that got on my nerves also. The incident in Paris upset me frightfully.[1] Impressive, weren't they? the Paris lawyers who cried " Vive la Pologne !" Faugh, how nauseous, how stupid, how insipid ! I felt more than ever confirmed in my view that it is rather advantageous for us that Europe does not know us in the least, and has such a disgusting idea of us. And then the details of the proceedings against Beresovsky ! How ugly, how empty ; I can't imagine how they can ever recover from such twaddle, and get on to the next point !

Russia, seen from here, looks to a Russian much more plastic. On the one hand is the rare fact that our people have shown such unexpected independence and maturity in the initiation of reforms (as, for example, the judicial ones) ; on the other there is that news of the flogging of a merchant of the first guild in the Orenburg Government by the Chief of Police. One thing is clear: that the Russian people, thanks to its benefactor and his reforms, is at last in such a situation that it must of necessity accustom itself to affairs and self-criticism ; and that's the principal thing. By God, our age, in regard to reforms and changes, is almost as important as that of Peter the Great. How goes it with the railways? We must get down as quickly as possible to the south[2]; this is tremendously important. Before then, we must have *equitable tribunals everywhere:* how great will be the transformation! (I, over here, keep thinking of all these things, and my heart beats fast). I see hardly anyone here ; it is quite impossible, though, not to

[1] Beresovsky's attempt upon the life of Alexander II.

[2] Here Dostoevsky refers to Russia's efforts to get down to the Bosphorus and Constantinople.

come across somebody or other.   In Germany I met
a Russian who always lives abroad ; he goes to Russia
for about three weeks each year, and then returns to
Germany, where he has a wife and family ; they have
all become German through and through.   Among
other things I asked him : " Why actually did you
leave home ? "   He answered me hotly and curtly :
" Because here is civilization, and with us is barbarism."   This gentleman belongs to the Young
Progressives, but seems to keep himself aloof from
them all to some extent.   What snarling, peevish
curs all these absentees do become !

At last, Anna Grigorovna and I could no longer
bear our home-sickness in Dresden. . . .   We decided
to spend the winter somewhere in Switzerland or
Italy.   But we had no money at all.   What we had
brought with us was all spent.   I wrote to Katkov,
described my situation, and begged him for a further
advance of 500 roubles.   And what do you think: he
sent me the money !   What an excellent fellow he is !
So we came to Switzerland.   Now I am going to
confess to you my baseness and my shame.

My dear Apollon Nikolayevitch, I feel that I may
regard you as my judge.   You have heart and feeling,
as I have always, and of late freshly, been convinced ;
and therefore I have ever prized your judgment
highly.   I don't suffer in confessing my sins to you.
What I write you to-day is meant for you alone.
Deliver me not to the judgment of the mob.

When I was travelling in the neighbourhood of
Baden-Baden, I decided to turn aside and visit the
place.   I was tortured by a seductive thought :
10 louis-d'or to risk, and perhaps 2,000 francs to win ;
such a sum would suffice me for four months, even

with the expenses that I have in Petersburg. The
vile part of it is that in earlier years I *had* occasionally
won. But the *worst* is that I have an evil and exaggeratedly passionate nature. In all things I go to
the uttermost extreme ; my life long I have never
been acquainted with moderation.

The devil played his games with me at the beginning ; in three days I won, unusually easily,
4,000 francs. Now I'll show you how I worked
matters out : on the one hand, this easy gain—from
100 francs I had in three days made 4,000 ——— ; on
the other, my debts, my summonses, my heartfelt
anxiety and the impossibility of getting back to
Russia ; in the third place, and this is the principal
point, the play itself. If you only knew how it draws
one on ! No—I swear to you it was not the love of
winning alone, though I actually needed the money
for the money's sake. Anna Grigorovna implored me
to be contented with the 4,000 francs, and depart at
once. But that easy and probable possibility of
bettering my situation at one blow ! And the many
examples ! Apart from my own gains, I saw every
day how the other gamblers won from 20,000 to
30,000 francs (one never sees anyone lose). Why
should those others do better than I ? I need the
money more than they do. I risked again, and lost.
I lost not only what I had won, but also my own
money down to the last farthing ; I got feverishly
excited, and lost all the time. Then I began to pawn
my garments. Anna Grigorovna pawned her last,
her very last, possession. (That angel ! How she
consoled me, how she suffered in that cursed Baden,
in our two tiny rooms above the blacksmith's forge,
the only place we could afford !) At last I had had

enough; everything was gone. (How base are these
Germans! They are all usurers, rascals, and cheats!
When our landlady saw that we could not leave,
having no money, she raised our prices!) At last we
had to save ourselves somehow and flee from Baden.
I wrote again to Katkov and begged him for
500 roubles (I wrote nothing of the circumstances,
but as the letter came from Baden, he probably
guessed the state of affairs). And he sent me the
money! He did really! So now I have had altogether from the *Roussky Viestnik* 4,000 roubles in
advance.

Now to end my Baden adventures: we agonized
in that hell for seven weeks. Directly after my
arrival there, I met Gontscharov at the railway-
station. At first Ivan Alexandrovitch was cautious
before me. That State-Councillor—or State-Councillor that ought-to-be—was also occupied in gambling.
But when he realized that it could not be kept a
secret, and as I myself was playing with gross pub-
licity, he soon ceased to pretend to me. He played
with feverish excitement (though only for small
stakes). He played during the whole fortnight that
he spent in Baden, and lost, I think, quite a good
deal. But God give this good fellow health; when
I had lost everything (he had, however, seen me with
large sums in my hands), he gave me, at my request,
60 francs. Certainly he lectured me terribly at the
same time, because I had lost all, and not only half,
like him!

Gontscharov talked incessantly about Turgenev; I
kept putting off my visit to him—still, eventually I
had to call. I went about noon, and found him at
breakfast. I'll tell you frankly—I never really liked

that man. The worst of it is that since 1857,[1] at
Wiesbaden, I've owed him 50 dollars (which even
to-day I haven't yet paid back !). I can't stand the
aristocratic and pharisaical sort of way he embraces
one, and offers his cheek to be kissed. He puts on
monstrous airs; but my bitterest complaint against
him is his book " Smoke." He told me himself that
the leading idea, the point at issue, in that book, is
this : " If Russia were destroyed by an earthquake
and vanished from the globe, it would mean no loss
to humanity—it would not even be noticed." He
declared to me that that was his fundamental view of
Russia. I found him in irritable mood ; it was on
account of the failure of " Smoke." I must tell you
that at the time the full details of that failure were
unknown to me. I *had* heard by letter of Strachov's
article in the *O. Z.*, but I didn't know that they had
torn him to pieces in all the other papers as well, and
that in Moscow, at a club, I believe, people had
collected signatures to a protest against " Smoke."
He told me that himself. Frankly, I never could
have imagined that anyone could so naïvely and
clumsily display all the wounds in his vanity, as
Turgenev did that day ; and these people go about
boasting that they are atheists. He told me that he
was an uncompromising atheist. My God ! It is to
Deism that we owe the Saviour—that is to say, the
conception of a man so noble that one cannot grasp it
without a sense of awe—a conception of which one
cannot doubt that it represents the undying ideal of
mankind. And what do we owe to these gentry—
Turgenev, Herzen, Utin, Tchernychevsky ? In
place of that loftiest divine beauty on which they

---

[1] An error. He can refer only to the year 1862 or 1863.

spit, we behold in them such ugly vanity, such un-
ashamed susceptibility, such ludicrous arrogance, that
it is simply impossible to guess what it is that they
hope for, and who shall take them as guides. He
frightfully abused Russia and the Russians. But I
have noticed this : all those Liberals and Progressives
who derive chiefly from Bielinsky's school, find their
pleasure and satisfaction in abusing Russia. The
difference is that the adherents of Tchernychevsky
merely abuse, and in so many words desire that
Russia should disappear from the face of the earth
(*that*, first of all!). But the others declare, in the
same breath, that *they love Russia*. And yet they
hate everything that is native to the soil, they
delight in caricaturing it, and were one to oppose
them with some fact that they could not explain
away or caricature,—any fact with which they were
obliged to reckon—they would, I believe, be profoundly unhappy, annoyed, even distraught. And
I've noticed that Turgenev—and for that matter all
who live long abroad—have no conception of the true
facts (though they do read the newspapers), and have
so utterly lost all affection and understanding for
Russia that even those quite ordinary matters which
in Russia the very Nihilists no longer deny, but only
as it were caricature after their manner—*these* fellows
cannot so much as grasp. Amongst other things he
told me that we are bound to crawl in the dust before
the Germans, that there is but one universal and
irrefutable way—that of civilization, and that all
attempts to create an independent Russian culture
are but folly and pigheadedness. He said that he was
writing a long article against the Russophils and Slavo-

phils.   I advised him to order a telescope from Paris
for his better convenience. "What do you mean ?" he
asked.   " The distance is somewhat great," I replied ;
" direct the telescope on Russia, and then you will be
able to observe us ; otherwise you can't really see
anything at all."   He flew into a rage.   When I saw
him so angry, I said with well-simulated naïveté :
" Really I should never have supposed that all the
articles derogatory to your new novel could have discomposed you to this extent ; by God, the thing's not
worth getting so angry about.   Come, spit upon it all !"
" I'm not in the least discomposed.   What are you
thinking of ?" he answered, getting red.

I interrupted him, and turned the talk to personal
and domestic matters. Before going away, I brought
forth, as if quite casually and without any particular
object, all the hatred that these three months have
accumulated in me against the Germans.   " Do you
know what swindlers and rogues they are here ?
Verily, the common people are much more evil and
dishonest here than they are with us ; and that they
are stupider there can be no doubt.   You are always
talking of civilization ; with what has your ' civilization ' endowed the Germans, and wherein do they
surpass us ?"   He turned pale (it is no exaggeration),
and said : " In speaking thus, you insult me personally.   You know quite well that I have definitely
settled here, that I consider myself a German and
not a Russian, and am proud of it."   I answered :
" Although I have read your ' Smoke,' and have just
talked with you for a whole hour, I could never
have imagined that you would say such a thing.
Forgive me, therefore, if I *have* insulted you."

Then we took leave of one another very politely, and I promised myself that I would never again cross Turgenev's threshold. The next day, Turgenev came at exactly ten o'clock in the morning to my abode, and left his card with the landlady. But as I had told him the day before that I never saw anyone till noon, and that we usually slept till eleven, I naturally took his ten-o'clock call as a hint that he doesn't wish to see any more of me. During the whole seven weeks, I saw him only once more, at the railway-station. We looked at one another, but no greeting passed. The animosity with which I speak of Turgenev, and the insults we offered one another, will perhaps strike you unpleasantly. But by God, I can no other; he offended me too deeply with his amazing views. Personally, I really feel little affected, though his uppish manners are quite disagreeable enough in themselves; but I simply can't stand by and listen when a traitor who, if he chose, could be of service to his country, abuses Russia in the way he does. His tail-wagging to the Germans, and his hatred for the Russians, I had noticed already—four years ago. But his present rage and fury against Russia arises solely, *solely*, from the failure of "Smoke," and from the fact that Russia has dared refuse to hail him as a genius. It is nothing but vanity, and therefore all the more repulsive.

Hear now, my friend, what I have in view. Of course it was vile in me to gamble away so much. But I have lost a relatively small sum of my own actual money. Still, it would have lasted us for two months—in our present mode of living, even for four. I have already told you that I can't resist winning. If, right at the beginning, I had lost the ten louis-

d'or that I chose to stake, I should certainly have
played no more, and gone away at once.   But the
gain of 4,000 francs destroyed me.   The temptation
of winning more (which appeared so easy) and in
that way paying all my debts, and being able to
provide for myself and mine—Emilie Fyodorovna,
Pasha, and the others . . . it was too much for me,
I could not resist it.   But even this is no excuse, for
I was not alone.   I had with me a young, warm-
hearted, pretty creature who trusted me, whom I
should have protected and sheltered, and whom
consequently I ought not to have dragged down
with myself to destitution, by setting my entire,
though certainly not very great, possessions upon the
turn of a game.   My future appears to me very
dark; above all, I cannot, for the reasons I have
mentioned, return to Russia; and most heavily am I
oppressed by the question: What is to become of
those who depend on my help?   All these thoughts
murder me. . . .

You alone, my dear friend, are kind to me; you
are my Providence.   Help me in the future, too.
For in all my great and small matters, I shall call
upon your aid.

You well understand the basis of all my hopes: it
is clear that *only under one condition* can everything
be arranged so as to bring forth fruit—namely, *that
my novel really succeeds*.   To that I must devote all
my powers.   Ah, my dear fellow, how grave, how
unendurably grave it was for me, three years ago, to
yield to the crazy hope that I should be able to pay
all those debts, and therefore to sign the many bills
of exchange.   Whence shall I draw the needful
energy and vitality?   Experience indeed has shown

that I can make a success; but what are the conditions? These alone: that every one of my works so succeeds as to awaken the keenest public interest; else all goes crash. And is that really possible? Is there any use in reckoning on it? . . .

[The letter ends with a request for a loan and a further description of Dostoevsky's desperate situation.]

XXXV

To his Niece, Sofia Alexandrovna

GENEVA,
September 29 [*October* 11], 1867.

Good-day, my dear friend Sonetchka. Don't be cross with me for my far too long silence—nor with Anna Grigorovna. A. G. has had a letter to you ready for a week and more, but she will not send it with this, for she wants to add something to it. Frankly, I want to entice an answer from you. We are so frightfully bored here in Geneva that every letter you write to us will be reckoned as a good deed to you in Heaven. Moreover, you know yourself how very much I love you, and how deeply interested I am in everything that happens in your life. We arranged our trip very stupidly. We ought to have had more money, so that we could change our place of abode as often as we wished. We have had to turn our travels into a stay abroad, instead of a tour through Europe.

Life abroad, wherever it may be, is very tiresome. As it was very expensive and very dusty in Paris, and as the summer in Italy was very hot, and cholera was

cropping up there, we have spent this summer in
different parts of Germany, which we chose according
to the beauty of the scenery and the goodness of the
air. Everywhere it was tiresome, everywhere the
scenery was fine, and everywhere I had fairly good
health. I was most particularly glad that Anna
Grigorovna did not feel bored at all, though I am not
an over-agreeable companion, and we have lived six
months at a time together without friends or acquaintance. In that time we refreshed many of our old
memories, and I swear to you that we would have
enjoyed ourselves ten times better if we had spent the
summer, not in foreign lands, but at Lublin, near you.
Anna Grigorovna has developed a great talent for
travelling; wherever we went, she discovered everything that was worth seeing, and at once wrote down
her impressions; she has filled countless little note-
books and so on with her hieroglyphics; unfortunately she did not see half enough, even so. At last
the autumn arrived. Our money no longer sufficed
for a trip to Italy, and there were other hindrances
besides. We thought of Paris, and later regretted
much that we had not gone there, instead of to
Geneva. I had already, it is true, been three times
at Geneva, but had never stayed there long, and so
knew nothing of the climate of the town: the
weather changes at least three times a day, and I have
had my attacks again, just as in Petersburg. Nevertheless I must work, and must stop at least five
months at Geneva. I am very seriously attacking a
novel (which I shall give myself the pleasure of
dedicating to you, that is, Sonetchka, Sofia Alexandrovna Ivanovna, as I long since decided); I am
going to publish it in the *Roussky Viestnik*. I don't

know whether I shall bring it off; my God, if it weren't for my poverty, I should never have made up my mind to publish it now—that is, in these days of ours. The sky is so overcast. Napoleon has declared that already he perceives several black marks on his horizon. To settle the Mexican, the Italian, and, chiefest of all, the German questions, he will have to divert public attention by a war, and win the French to himself by the old method—a successful campaign. But though the French of to-day are probably not thus to be beguiled, a war is nevertheless very likely. You will already have seen this yourself (do you, by the way, read some newspapers? For God's sake, do! Nowadays they must be read, not only because it is the mode, but so as to trace the ever more decisively and strikingly evident connection of great and small events). But if war does break out, artistic wares will fall considerably in price. This is a very important contingency, which of itself makes me thoughtful. With us in Russia, indeed, there has lately been apparent, even without war, a great in-difference to artistic things. Most of all I dread mediocrity: a work should either be very good or very bad, but, for its life, not mediocre. Mediocrity that takes up thirty printed sheets is something quite unpardonable.

I beg you, dear, to write me as fully as possible about everything that has happened to you and yours in these six months. What have you—I mean you, yourself—been doing, and what are your plans? We shall have to make ours very much the same. My passport is good only for six months, but I shall have to stay here six months longer, or perhaps even more. It depends on purely business matters. And

yet I should like to get back to Russia, and that for
many reasons.   In the first place, I should then have
a fixed place of abode.   Moreover, after my return, I
should decidedly like to edit something in the shape
of a paper.[1]   (I think I have spoken before to you
of this; the form and scope of the undertaking I
now see quite clearly in my mind's eye.)   Now for
that, I must be at home, where I can hear everything
with my own ears and see it with my own eyes.   For
the rest, I'm glad that I now have some work on
hand; if I hadn't, I should die of *ennui*; whether,
when the novel is finished (which it may not be for a
long time), I shall begin anything else in these foreign
lands, I really don't know.   I simply can't understand
the Russian "tourists," who often stay here three
years.   A trip abroad may be useful, and even enjoy-
able, if it lasts about six months, and if one stays
nowhere longer than a fortnight and keeps continually
on the go.   And one might really get well on such
a trip.   But there are people who live here long
with their families, educate their children here, forget
the Russian language, and finally, when they are at
the end of their resources, return home, and set up to
instruct us, instead of learning from us.   Yes; here
they stay mouldering, and then need a whole year to
get used to things at home and fall into the right
groove again.   In particular a writer (unless he's a
scholar or a specialist) can't possibly stay long.   In
our craft, truth is the chief thing; but here one can
see only Swiss truth.

Geneva lies on the Lake of Geneva.   The lake is
wonderful, its shores are picturesque, but Geneva

---

[1] "The Diary of a Writer."   (This plan was carried out in
1873.)

itself is the essence of tedium.   It is an old Protestant
town, and yet one sees countless drunken people
everywhere.   When I arrived here, the Peace Congress was just beginning, to which Garibaldi himself
came.   He went away immediately afterwards.   It
was really incredible how these socialist and revolutionary gentlemen, whom hitherto I had known only
from books, sat and flung down lies from the platform
to their audience of five thousand!   It's quite
indescribable.   One can hardly realize, even for one's-
self, the absurdity, feebleness, futility, disunion, and
the depth of essential contradictoriness.   And it is
this rabble which is stirring up the whole unfortunate
working-class!   It's too deplorable.   That they may
attain to peace on earth, they want to root out the
Christian faith, annihilate the Great Powers and cut
them up into a lot of small ones, abolish capital,
declare that all property is common to all, and so
forth.   And all this is affirmed with no logical
demonstration whatever; what they learnt twenty
years ago, they are still babbling to-day.   Only when
fire and sword have exterminated everything, can, in
their belief, eternal peace ensue.   But enough of this.
I shall most certainly answer your letters, dear, by
return of post.

Your very loving
FYODOR DOSTOEVSKY

XXXVI

To Apollon Nikolayevitch Maikov

GENEVA,
October 9 [21], 1867.

[At first he talks of his want of money.]

As far as I *personally* am concerned, I don't care at all where I spend the next five months, for I intend to work for at least that time. But though that *is so*, Geneva is nevertheless detestable, and I deceived myself grossly in regard to it. My attacks recur every week here ; and also I sometimes have a peculiar, very troublesome fluttering of the heart. It is a horrible town, like Cayenne. There are storms that last for days, and even on the most normal days the weather changes three and four times. And this I have to endure—*I*, with my hæmorrhoids and epilepsy ! And then, it's so gloomy, so depressing ! And the people are so self-satisfied and boastful ! It is the mark of quite peculiar stupidity to be so self-satisfied. Everything is ugly here, utterly rotten, and expensive. The people are always drunk ! Even in London there are not so many rowdies and "drunks." Every single thing, every post in the street, they regard as beautiful and majestic. "Where is such-and-such a street ?" one asks. "*Voyez, monsieur, vous irez tout droit, et quand vous passerez près de cette majestueuse et élégante fontaine en bronze, vous prendrez,*" etc. The "*majestueuse et élégante fontaine*" is an insignificant and tasteless object in the rococo style ; but a Genevese must always boast, even if you only ask him the way. They've made a little garden out of a few bushes (there's not a single tree in it), about as big as two of the front gardens that one sees in Sadovaya Street in Moscow ; but they must needs photograph it, and sell the pictures as a view of "the English Garden at Geneva." The devil run away with the humbugs ! And all the while there lies, only two and a half hours from Geneva on the same lake, the town of Vevey, where, I am told, the climate in winter is very healthy and even pleasant. Who knows—perhaps we shall move over there, one of these days. Nothing depends *on me* now. Let come what come will.

Of my work I will write you nothing, for I have nothing to say about it as yet. Only one thing : I have to go at it hard, very hard indeed. In the intervals, my attacks rob me of all vitality, and after each one, I can't collect my thoughts for at least four days. And how well I was, at first, in Germany ! This confounded Geneva ! I don't know what on earth will become of us. And the novel is my one means of salvation. The worst of it is that it must *absolutely* come off. Nothing less will do. That's a *sine qua non*. But how *can* it, when all my capabilities are utterly crippled by my malady ! I still have my power of vision intact ; of late my work has shown me that. And nerves I have still. But I have lost all memory. In short, I must take this book by storm, fling myself on it head foremost, and stake all on the hazard of the die, come what may ! Enough of that.

I read the news about Kelsiyev[1] with much emo-

---

[1] V. Kelsiyev, a political émigré, and collaborator with Herzen. He came back to Russia penitent, and became a collaborator on the extremely conservative *Roussky Viestnik.*

tion. That's the right way, that's truth and reason! But be you very sure of this—that (of course excepting the Poles) all our Liberals of socialistic leanings will rage like wild beasts. It will thrill them to the marrow. They'll hate it worse than if all their noses had been cut off. What are they to say now, whom now shall they bespatter? The most they can do is to gnash their teeth; and everyone at home quite understands that. Have you ever yet heard a sensible idea from any of our Liberals? They can but gnash their teeth, at any time; and indeed it mightily impresses school-boys. Of Kelsiyev, it will now be maintained that he has denounced them all. By God, you'll see that I am right. But can anyone "denounce" them, I ask you? In the first place, they have themselves compromised themselves; in the second—who takes the slightest interest in them? They're not worth denouncing! . . .

[Again he writes of money and business matters.]

What will happen now in politics? In what will all our anticipations end? Napoleon seems to have something up his sleeve. Italy, Germany. . . . My heart stood still with joy when I read the news that the railway is to be opened as far as Kursk. Let it but come quickly, and then—long live Russia!

XXXVII
To his Stepson, P. A. Issayev

GENEVA,
October 10 [22], 1867.

Your letter, dear boy, uncommonly delighted me. If you thought that I should forget you after my marriage (for I observed that you really were of that

opinion, and I purposely did not set you right), you
were wholly mistaken.   It is quite the other way.
Know now that I care for you even more since my
marriage, and God be my witness that I suffer very
much through being able to help you so little.   I
have always considered you a cheerful, plucky boy,
and I retain that opinion.   A person with those
qualities must be happy in any position of life.   I
also think you very intelligent.   Only one thing is
against you: your lack of education.   But if you
really have no desire to learn something, at least hear
my advice: you must, in any case, be earnest about
your moral development, so far as that is capable of
going without education (but, for education, one
shall strive unto one's life's end).   On my departure,
I begged Apollon Nikolayevitch to be a friend to you,
and assist you with good counsel.   Pasha, he is the
rarest of rare men, mark that.   I have known him
now for twenty years.   He will always be able to
direct you wisely.   Above all things, you must be
frank and upright in your intercourse with him.   I
have known for some time that you have been
offered a place, and are still offered it.   I advise you
to take that place.   I believe that a position with a
police-magistrate *would* be incomparably more useful
for you.   You could in that way obtain a practical
acquaintance with judicial matters, you could develop
yourself, and accumulate much knowledge.   But I
have no confidence in you.   One has to work very
hard in such a post, and then it's very important to
know what sort of man you would be likely to go to.
If to a good sort, well and good; but if to a bad, as
bad as possible.   Moreover, a provincial town like
Ladoga is very dangerous at your age, particularly

such a dull and inferior sort of place. Of course, the
social relations in the railway-service *are* very bad.
But I am of opinion that even in the highest
Government-offices the social side is rotten-bad;
only there, more refined manners prevail. For this
reason, Petersburg would be better, for there one can
find suitable society. But anyhow, you must take
this place. As regards the danger of your falling
into evil ways, I *have* some confidence in you there.
You can't possibly have forgotten your dead father
and mother. Realize that I don't advise you to take
this place (nor on account of the salary either) because
in that way you will cease to be a charge on me.
Know that, though I have not a farthing to spare, I
shall support you to my life's end, whatever age you
may be. I give you this advice for the sake of work
alone, for work is the most important of all things.
Anna Grigorovna loves you as I do. Write me fully
about everything.

XXXVIII

To his Sister Vera, and his Brother-in-Law
Alexander Pavlovitch Ivanov

GENEVA,
January 1 [13], 1868.

MY DEAR AND PRECIOUS ALEXANDER PAVLOVITCH
AND VERA MICHAILOVNA!

First of all, I embrace you, congratulate you on
the New Year, and wish you of course most heartily
everything of the best! Yesterday Anna Grigorovna
surprised me with a quarter-bottle of champagne,
which, at exactly half-past ten o'clock in the evening,
when it was striking twelve in Moscow, she placed on

our tea-table; we clinked glasses, and drank to the
health of all our dear ones. Who are dearer to me (and
to Anna Grigorovna, her nearest relatives excepted)
than you and your children? Besides you, only
Fedya[1] and his family, and Pasha; there stand
written all my precious ones, for whom I care. I
have received both your letters, the last and the
November one; forgive my not having answered till
now. I love you always, and think of you no less
than hitherto. But I have been continually in such
a state of stress and dissatisfaction that I put off
answering to a better period; and indeed, of late, I
have (literally) not had a single free hour. I have
been working all the time—writing, and then destroy-
ing what I had written; not until the end of December was I able to send the first part of my novel[2] to
the *Roussky Viestnik*. They wanted it for the
January number, and I am afraid the MS. arrived
too late.

And now, for me, nearly everything depends on
this work: my existence, daily bread, and my whole
future. I have had huge advances of money from
the *Roussky Viestnik*—nearly 4,500 roubles; then, in
Petersburg, I still have bills to meet to the amount
of at least 3,000; and at the same time I must exist
somehow or other—and at such a period! Therefore
I stake all my hopes on the novel; I shall have to
work incessantly, scarcely rising from my desk, for
the next four months. I am so very much behind-
hand, because I have rejected nearly all that I've
written up to the present. The book will, by
the *Roussky Viestnik's* rates, bring me in about

---

[1] Dostoevsky's nephew, son of his brother Michael.
[2] "The Idiot."

6,000 roubles.   Now I've had 4,500 in advance;
consequently I have only 1,500 to get.   If it really
succeeds, I shall, in September, sell (as I am accustomed always to do) the second edition for about
3,000 roubles.   In that way I shall manage to live,
pay off, in September, about 1,500 roubles of my
debts, and come back to Russia.   Thus everything
depends on my work *now:* my whole future and my
whole present; and if the book is in any way good, I
shall get further credit from the *Viestnik* in September.   Now I'll tell you about our life and circumstances up to the present.

In that respect, it's all monotonous enough; while
we are in Geneva, every day resembles every other.   I
write, and Anna Grigorovna works at the outfit for
the little person whom we are expecting, or does
shorthand for me when I need her help.   She bears
her condition excellently (though lately she has not
been quite so well); our life suits her admirably, and
she only longs for her Mama.   Our seclusion is to
me personally of great value; without it I could not
have worked at all.   But, all the same, Geneva,
except for the view of Mont Blanc, the lake, and the
River Rhone that flows from it, is mightily tedious.
I knew that before; but circumstances arranged
themselves in such a way that in our situation we
could find no other abode for the winter than just
this Geneva, whither we came by chance in September.   In Paris, for instance, the winter is much colder,
and wood ten times dearer, as everything is.   We
really wanted to go to Italy—that is to Milan, of
course (not farther south), where the winter climate
is incomparably milder; while the town, with its
Cathedral, theatre, and galleries, is much more attrac-

tive.   But in the first place, all Europe, and particularly Italy, was at that very time threatened with
a campaign ; and for a woman with child to find
herself in the middle of a campaign would have
been far from pleasant.   Secondly, it was eminently
desirable that we should be able to render ourselves
intelligible to the doctor and the midwife, and we do
not know Italian.   Germany was out of our way, nor
did we much desire to return there.   Geneva is, at
any rate, a cultivated town with libraries, and many
doctors, etc., who all speak French.   We had not, to
be sure, guessed that it would be so dull here, nor
that there are periodical winds (called *bises*), which
come over the mountains, bringing with them the
chill of the eternal ice.   In our first abode we suffered
much ; the houses here are shockingly built ; instead
of stoves there are only fireplaces, and there are no
double windows.   So all day long one has to keep
burning wood in the fireplace (wood is very expensive here also, though Switzerland is the only land of
Western Europe where wood is really abundant)—
and one might as well be trying to warm the yard
outside.   In my room it was often only six and even
five degrees above zero ; in the others it sometimes
happened that the water in the jug froze at night.
But for the last month or so, we've been in a new
house.   Two of the rooms are very good, and one of
them is so warm that one can live and work comfort-
ably in it.   With us in Geneva the temperature never
fell below eight degrees ; in Florence it was ten
degrees *above*, and at Montpellier in France, on the
Mediterranean Sea, farther south than Geneva, it was
fifteen above.

I haven't written to Petersburg for a long time,

and I scarcely ever hear from them. I am much perturbed by the thought that Fedya and Pasha need money, which must be sent them as soon as may be. But I can't possibly expect any large sum from the *Roussky Viestnik* until I deliver the second part of the novel, which won't be, at earliest, for three weeks ; for I have already had too much money in advance, and have only worked off about 1,000 roubles; this worries me so that I often can't sleep at night. Fedya can't manage without extra help, and Pasha must have his money regularly. I live on the hundred roubles that the *Viestnik* sends me monthly. And soon I too shall need much more than that. At the end of February (by the Style here) Anna Grigorovna will be a mother, and for that occasion I must absolutely have money, and *a margin*—for one can't calculate with any certainty beforehand how much one will need. How goes it with you ? Your letters are real treats to me, and I wish I could go to Moscow just to see you all. But, once more, my future depends on my work. I beg you to write me most fully about yourselves and the children. By-the-bye, I was greatly vexed, Veryotchka, by your letter in November, saying that you want to get a Frenchwoman for your children. Why ? To what end ? On account of the accent ? From a French woman and even from a French tutor, one can't possibly (I know it by my own experience) acquire the French tongue in all its subtleties. One can acquire it only by firmly resolving to do so; and even then, *perfectly* to obtain the accent, one needs an extraordinarily strong will. I consider the " accent " superfluous. Believe me, dear Veryotchka, by the time your children are grown-up, French will no

longer be spoken in our drawing-rooms. Even to-day,
it often has a most absurd effect. It is a different
matter to be able to understand and read a language.
Then, if one's travelling, and it's necessary, one can
make shift to speak it ; but otherwise it's quite
enough to understand and read it. What is the
Frenchwoman going to talk to the children about ?
Nothing but tomfoolery ; and affected as she is, and
powerful as she'll be, she'll infect them with her
vulgar, corrupt, ridiculous, and imbecile code of
manners, and her distorted notions about religion
and society. It's a pleasure now to observe your
children. The tone in your house is unconstrained
and frank ; everything bears the stamp of happy,
tranquil family-life. The Frenchwoman will introduce a new and evil French element. While of the
expense I need not speak.

Yet another remark : If people want to acquire a
correct French accent nowadays, they must adopt
the guttural Parisian mode, which is very ugly and
offensive to the ear. This accent is modern, and has
been fashionable in Paris only within the last twenty-
five years at most. Our tutors and governesses don't
yet dare to introduce it among us. Therefore your
children would *not* acquire this " correct pronuncia-
tion." But I have written too much about the
governess. I am now about to take a rest of two
days, and then set to work again. The state of my
health has remarkably improved since the autumn.
Sometimes I don't have a single attack for seven
weeks at a stretch. And yet I am occupied in most
exacting brain-work. I can't understand how it has
come to pass, but I'm very glad of it.

Till next time, my dear and precious ones. I

kiss and embrace you, wish you heartily, as brother
and friend, all that is best, and beg you too not
to forget us.　My address is still Geneva.　Perhaps
at the end of April we may go over Mont Cenis into
Italy, to Milan and Lake Como.　That will be a
real Paradise !　Everything depends, however, on my
work.　Wish me success.

Your

FYODOR DOSTOEVSKY.

XXXIX

To his Niece Sofia Alexandrovna

GENEVA,
January 1 [13], 1868.

MY DEAR PRECIOUS SONETCHKA,

Despite your request I have not even yet
answered your letter, and give you herewith my
word of honour that henceforth I will write regularly
every month.　In my letter to Alexander Pavlovitch
I explained, as well as I could, the reason for my
silence.　All the time I was in such a bad temper
and such continuous anxiety, that I felt I needed to
shut myself into myself, and bear my woe in solitude.
In those days I should have found it hard to write to
you—what could I have said ?　Should I have talked
of my bad temper ?　(It would certainly have found
expression, anyhow, in my letter.)　But this nonsense is irrelevant.　My position was most difficult.
On my work hangs my whole future.　I have not
only had an advance of 4,500 roubles from the
Viestnik, but have also promised on my word of
honour, and reiterated that promise in every letter,

that the novel should really be written.   But directly
before dispatching the finished MS. to the office, I
found myself obliged to destroy the greater part of it,
for I was no longer pleased with it—and if one is
displeased with one's work, it can't possibly be good.
So I destroyed the greater part of what I had written.
Yet on this novel, and on the payment of my debts,
depended my whole present and future.   Three
weeks ago (December 18 by the Style here) I attacked
another novel, and am now working day and night.
The idea of the book is the old one which I always
have so greatly liked; but it is so difficult that
hitherto I never have had the courage to carry it out;
and if I'm setting to work at it now, it's only because
I'm in a desperate plight.   The basic idea is the
representation of a truly perfect and noble man.   And
this is more difficult than anything else in the world,
particularly nowadays.   All writers, not ours alone
but foreigners also, who have sought to represent
Absolute Beauty, were unequal to the task, for it is
an infinitely difficult one.   The beautiful is the ideal;
but ideals, with us as in civilized Europe, have long
been wavering.   There is in the world only one figure
of absolute beauty: Christ.   That infinitely lovely
figure is, as a matter of course, an infinite marvel
(the whole Gospel of St. John is full of this thought:
John sees the wonder of the Incarnation, the visible
apparition of the Beautiful).   I have gone too far in
my explanation.   I will only say further that of all
the noble figures in Christian literature, I reckon
Don Quixote as the most perfect.   But Don Quixote
is noble only by being at the same time comic.   And
Dickens's Pickwickians (they were certainly much
weaker than Don Quixote, but still it's a powerful

work) are comic, and this it is which gives them
their great value. The reader feels sympathy and
compassion with the Beautiful, derided and uncon-
scious of its own worth. The secret of humour consists precisely in this art of wakening the reader's
sympathy. Jean Valjean[1] is likewise a remarkable
attempt, but he awakens sympathy only by his
terrible fate and the injustice of society towards him.
I have not yet found anything similar to that, anything so *positive*, and therefore I fear that the book
may be a "positive" failure. Single details will
perhaps come out not badly. But I fear that the
novel may be tiresome. It is to be very extensive.
The first part I wrote in twenty-three days, and have
lately sent off. This first part has no action at all.
It is confessedly only a prologue. It is right that it
should not compromise the whole work in any way,
but it illuminates nothing, and poses no problem.
My sole aim is to awake at least such interest in the
reader as will make him read the second part. That
second part I am beginning to-day, and shall finish in
a month. (I have always worked as quickly as that.)
I believe that it will be stronger and more significant
than the first part. Well, dear, wish me luck! The
novel is called "The Idiot," and is dedicated to
you, Sofia Alexandrovna. My dear, I wish that the
book may turn out worthy of that dedication. At
any rate, I am not called upon to judge my own
work, least of all in the excited state in which I
now am.

My health is most satisfactory, and I can bear well
even the hardest work; but with regard to Anna
Grigorovna's condition, I am now anticipating a

---

[1] Hero of Hugo's "Les Misérables."

difficult time.   I shall work for four months longer,
and hope then to be able to go to Italy.   Solitude is
essential to me just now.   Fedya and Pasha make
me really sad.   I am writing to Fedya by this post.
Life abroad is on the whole very troublesome, and I
long terribly for Russia.   Anna Grigorovna and I live
quite solitary here.   My life passes thus : I get up
late, light the fire (it is fearfully cold), we drink
coffee, and then I go to work.   About four, I go to
a restaurant, where I dine for two francs (with wine).
Anna Grigorovna prefers to dine at home.   After
dinner I go to a café, drink coffee, and read the
Moskovskoie Viedomosti (*Moscow News*) and the *Golos*[1]
from A to Z.   For exercise I walk half-an-hour in
the streets, and then betake myself to home and work.
I light the fire, we drink coffee, and I set to again.
Anna Grigorovna declares that she's immensely happy.

Geneva is a dull, gloomy, Protestant, stupid town
with a frightful climate, but very well suited for work.

I don't suppose I shall be able to get back to Russia
at all before September—alas, my dear !   As soon as
I do, I shall hasten to embrace you.   I still dally
with the thought of starting a magazine after my
return.   But of course all depends upon the success
of my present novel.   Only think : I am working so
furiously, and yet I don't know whether the MS. will
arrive in time for the January number or not.   That
would be very unpleasant for me !

I embrace and kiss you.   Your ever friendly
inclined

FYODOR DOSTOEVSKY.

---

[1] *The Moscow Voice*, an important paper.

XL

To his Stepson, P. A. Issayev

GENEVA,
February 19 [*March* 3], 1868.

Don't reproach me and don't be angry with me,
my ever dear Pasha, because I send Emilie Fyodorovna[1] a hundred roubles, and you only fifty. You
are alone, my dear boy, and she is not alone. And
you wrote yourself, indeed, that she needed as much
as that. And then, she has to support her Fedya ;
he is at work, and I wish him luck. I love him
dearly. I would willingly give all I have, but I have
nothing. I must tell you that it is a great joy to me
that you have taken that place, and begun to work.
I respect you very much for it, Pasha. It was
noble of you ; the position is not distinguished, but
you are still young, and can wait. But remember
that you can always count on me. So long as I live,
I shall regard you as my dear son. I swore to your
mother, the night before she died, that I would never
forsake you. When you were still a little child, I
used to call you my son. How could I, then, forsake
you and forget you ? When I married again, you
threw out hints that your position would now be a
different one ; I never answered them, because the
idea wounded me deeply ; I may confess that to you
now. Know once for all that you will always be my
son, my eldest son ; and not duty bids me say so, but
my heart. If I have often scolded you, and been
cross to you, that was only my evil disposition ; I
love you as I have but seldom loved anyone. When

---

[1] His brother Michael's widow.

I come back to Petersburg some day, I shall do all I
can to find you a better place; I will also help you
with money as long as I live, and have anything at
all of my own. Your saying that you don't feel well
has alarmed me much. Write to me directly you
receive this, if only a few lines. Send the letter
unstamped; you must not have any unnecessary
expenses. My address is still the same. I set all
my hopes on the new novel. If it succeeds, I shall
sell the second edition, pay my debts, and return to
Russia. I may also get an advance from the paper.
But I fear that the novel will miss fire. I greatly
like the idea, but the execution——! The novel is
called "The Idiot"; the first part has already been
printed in the *Roussky Viestnik*. Perhaps you've read
it? The great thing is that it should come off—then
all will be well. I work day and night; our life is
monotonous. Geneva is a terribly dull town. I
froze through the whole winter; but now we are
having real spring weather. Ten degrees above—
Réaumur. My health is neither good nor bad. I
suffer from incessant poverty. We live on a few
groschen, and have pawned everything. Anna Grigorovna may be confined at any moment. I expect
it to happen to-night. I am in great anxiety, but
must work uninterruptedly. Judge for yourself
whether I can answer all your letters punctually.
Tell me fully about yourself. Take care of your
health.

XLI

To Apollon Nikolayevitch Maikov

GENEVA,
May 18 [30], 1868.

I thank you for your letter, my dear Apollon Nikolayevitch, and for not being angry with me and so breaking off our correspondence. I was always convinced, in the depths of my soul, that Apollon Nikolayevitch would never do such a thing as that.

My Sonia is dead; we buried her three days ago. Two hours before her death, I did not know that she was to die. The doctor told us, three hours before she died, that things were going better and she would live. She was only a week ill; she died of inflammation of the lungs.

Ah, my dear Apollon Nikolayevitch, my love for my first child was probably most comical; I daresay I expressed it most comically in my letters to all who congratulated me. I have doubtless been ridiculous in everybody's eyes, but to you, to *you*, I am not ashamed to say anything. The poor little darling creature, scarcely three months old, had already, for me, individuality and character. She was just beginning to know and love me, and always smiled when I came near. And now they tell me, to console me, that I shall surely have other children. But where is Sonia? where is the little creature for whom I would, believe me, gladly have suffered death upon the cross, if *she* could have remained alive? I'll speak of it no more. My wife is crying. The day after to-morrow we shall say our last good-bye to the little grave, and go away somewhere. Anna

Nikolayevna[1] is staying with us; she arrived here
only a week before the little one died.

For the last fortnight, since Sonia's illness, I have
not been able to work. I have written a letter of
apology to Katkov, and in the May number of the
Roussky Viestnik, again only three chapters can appear.
But I hope from now to be able to work day and
night, so that from the June number onward the
novel will appear with some degree of regularity.

I thank you for consenting to be godfather to the
little one. She was baptized a week before her
death. . . .

[The second half of the letter is on business only.]

XLII

To Apollon Nikolayevitch Maikov

VEVEY,
June 10 [22], 1868.

MY DEAR FRIEND APOLLON NIKOLAYEVITCH,

I know and believe that your sympathy is real
and true. But I have never yet been so profoundly
unhappy as of late. I don't intend to describe my
state to you, but the more time goes by, the more
painful does remembrance become, and the more
clearly does my dead Sonia's image stand before me.
There are moments in which I can hardly bear it.
She already knew me; when I was leaving the house
on the day she died, just to read the papers, and
without the least idea that she would be dead in two
hours, she followed so attentively all my movements,
and looked at me with such eyes that even at this
moment I can see them, and the memory grows

---

[1] His wife's mother.

livelier every day. I shall never forget her, my grief
will never come to an end. And if I ever should
have another child, I don't know, truly, how I shall be
able to love it—I don't know where the love could
come from. I want only Sonia. I can't realize in
the least that she is no more, and that I am never to
see her again. . . .

[He speaks of his wife's condition and of business
matters.]

I have grown quite stupid from sheer hard work,
and my head feels as if it were in pieces. I await
your letters always as one awaits Heaven. What is
there more precious than a voice from Russia, the
voice of my friend? I have nothing to tell you, no
news of any kind, I get duller and stupider every
day that I'm here, and yet I daren't do anything until
the novel's finished. Then, however, I intend in any
event to go back to Russia. To get the book done,
I must sit at my desk for at least eight hours daily.
I have now half worked off my debt to Katkov. I
shall work off the rest. Write to me, my friend—
write, for Christ's sake. . . .

In the four chapters that you will read in the June
number (perhaps there may be only three, for the
fourth probably arrived too late), I have depicted
some types of the modern Positivist among the highly
"extreme" young men. I know that I have presented
them truthfully (for I understand the gentry from
experience ; no one but me has thus studied and
observed them), and I know too that everyone will
abuse me and say: " Nonsensical, naïve, stupid, and
false."

XLIII

To Apollon Nikolayevitch Maikov

MILAN,
October 7 [19], 1868.

Above all, I must declare that I never have been
in the least degree offended with you, and I say it
sincerely and honestly; on the contrary—I supposed
that you were angry with me for some reason or
another.   In the first place, you had ceased to write
to me; though every one of your letters is to me,
here, a great event—a breath from Russia, a real
festival.   But how could you ever have thought that
I considered myself offended by anything you may
have written?   No; my heart is not like that.   And
moreover, think of this: twenty-two years ago (it
was at Bielinsky's, do you remember?) I made your
acquaintance.   Since then life has properly rattled
me about, and sometimes given me amazing surprises;
and in short and in fine I have at the present moment
no one but you: you are the only man on whose
heart and disposition I rely, whom I love, and whose
thoughts and convictions I share.   How then should
I not love you, almost as much as I loved my brother
who is dead?   Your letters have always rejoiced and
encouraged me, for I was in dejected mood.   My
work, more than anything else, has frightfully weak-
ened and broken me.   For almost a year now I have
written three and a half printed sheets every month.
That is very stiff.   Also I miss the Russian way of
life; its impressions were always essential to my
work.   Finally, though you praise the idea of my
novel, the execution has not hitherto been distin-

guished. I am chiefly distressed by the thought
that if I had got the novel written in a year, and
then had had two or three months to devote to re-
writing and re-touching, it would have been quite a
different thing; I can answer for it. Now, when I
can take a bird's-eye view, as it were, of the whole,
I see that very clearly. . . .

I have become totally alienated from your way of
life, though my whole heart is with you; that is why
your letters are like heavenly manna to me. The
tidings of the new paper[1] greatly rejoiced me. . . .
What more can Nikolay Nikolayevitch[2] now desire?
The chief point is that he should be absolute master
of the paper. It is very desirable that it be edited
in the *Russian spirit*, as we both conceive it, if it
is not to become purely Slavophil. I hold, my friend,
that it is no part of our duty to woo the Slavs too
ardently. They must come to us of their own accord.
After the Pan-Slavist Congress at Moscow, some
individual Slavs made insolent mock of the Russians,
because they had taken on themselves to lead others,
and even aspired to dominate *them*, while they
themselves had so little national consciousness, and
so on. Believe me: many Slavs, for instance those
in Prague, judge us from a frankly Western, from a
French or German, point of view; I daresay they
wonder that our Slavophils trouble themselves so
little about the generally accepted formulas of West-
European civilization. Thus we have no motive at
all for running after them and paying court. It is a
different thing for us merely to study them; we
could then help them in time of need; but we should

[1] The allusion is to *Sarya* (*Morning Red*).
[2] Strachov.

not pursue them with fraternal sentiment, although we must very assuredly regard them as brothers and treat them so. I hope too that Strachov will give the paper a definite political tone, to say nothing at all of national consciousness. National consciousness is our weak spot; it lacks more than anything else. In every case, Strachov will make a brilliant thing of it, and I look forward to the great delight that his articles will afford me; I have read nothing of his since the failure of the *Epoch*. . . .

The book about which you write I had shortly before read,[1] and I must confess that it enraged me terribly. I can imagine nothing more impudent. Of course one should spit upon such stuff, and so I was ready to do at first. But I am oppressed by the thought that if I don't protest against it, I shall thus seem, as it were, to acknowledge the vile fabrication. Only, where is one to protest? In the *Nord*? But I can't write French well, and I should like to proceed with all tact. I have an idea of going to Florence, and there getting advice from the Russian Consulate. Of course that is not the only reason why I wish to go to Florence. . . .

XLIV

To his Niece Sofia Alexandrovna

MILAN,
October 26 [November 7], 1868

MY DEAR GOOD FRIEND SONETCHKA,

It is a very long time since I have written to you. I can say only one thing in excuse: I am still

---

[1] He is speaking of the novel "Les Secrets du Palais des Tsars," which deals with the Court of Nicholas I. In this book Dostoevsky and his wife appear.

busy with my novel. Believe me, dear, I literally
toil day and night; if I am not precisely writing, I
am walking up and down the room, smoking and
thinking of my work. I can scarcely myself believe
that I can't find a free hour in which to write to you.
But it really is so. Of myself and my life I can give
you the following information: I live on the best of
friendly terms with my wife. She is patient, and
my interests are more important to her than aught
else; but I see that she is pining for her friends
and relations in Russia. This often grieves me, but
my position is still so perplexed that for the next
few months we dare not make any plans at all.
My affairs have turned out sadly worse than I had
calculated.

In two months, you see, the year will be at an end,
but of the four parts of my novel only three are
finished; the fourth and longest I have not even
begun. And as it is quite impossible (working uninterruptedly through the whole year) to write more
than three and a half sheets a month (I say this from
actual experience), I shall be in arrears by six sheets
—that is, the end of the novel cannot appear in the
December number of the *Roussky Viestnik*. This
puts me in a most awkward and painful position; in
the first place, I cause the staff much inconvenience,
and even loss, for they will have to give their subscribers the conclusion of the novel as a supplement
(which, quite apart from anything else, is attended
with great expense); in the second place, I myself
lose thereby 900 roubles, for I proposed to the staff
that I should indemnify them by claiming no fee for
the six sheets by which I am in arrears. Finally, this
fourth part, and particularly its conclusion, are the

most important things in the whole book, which was, strictly speaking, conceived and written for its conclusion alone.

Of our personal life I'll tell you as follows. After we had buried Sonia in Geneva, we went, as you already know, to Vevey. Anna Grigorovna's mother came to her, and stayed with us a long time. In tiny, picturesque Vevey we lived like hermits, our only pastime being many mountain-walks. Of the beauty of the scenery I'll say nothing at all; it's like a dream; yet Vevey is most enervating: all the doctors in the world know this, but I did not.

I suffered much from epileptic and other nervous attacks. My wife was ill too. So we crossed the Simplon (the most ardent imagination could not depict the beauty of the Simplon Pass) into Italy, and settled down in Milan; our means prevented us from going farther. (During the last year and a half I have had so many advances from the *Roussky Viestnik* that I must now work at full pressure to get matters square; indeed, they still send me regularly comparatively large sums, yet I often find it very difficult to manage; and for a long time I've sent nothing to Petersburg, either to Pasha or Emilie Fyodorovna, which greatly troubles me.)

In Milan it certainly rains a good deal, but the climate suits me extraordinarily well. Yet it is said that fits are highly prevalent at Milan; perhaps I shall be spared one, nevertheless. Living in Milan is very expensive. It is a big, important town, but not very picturesque, and somewhat un-Italian. In the neighbourhood, that is, half-an-hour's railway journey from Milan, lies the exquisite Lake of Como,

but I have not yet been there this time. The only
"sight" in the town is the famous Duomo; it is of
marble, gigantic, Gothic, filigree-like, fantastic as a
dream. Its interior is amazingly fine. At the end
of November, I mean to move to Florence, for there
are Russian papers there, and perhaps living may be
cheaper. On the way I shall make a *détour* to Venice
(so as to show it to my wife), which will cost me about
a hundred francs.

Now I have given you in few words a full account
of myself. I am very heavy-hearted; homesick, and
uncertain of my position; my debts, etc., deject me
terribly. And besides I have been so alienated from
Russian life that I find it difficult, lacking fresh
Russian impressions as I do, to write anything at all:
only think—for six months I haven't seen a single
Russian newspaper. And I still have the fourth part
of my novel to do, and it will take about four months
more. Enough of me. Write fully of all your
affairs, of your external circumstances, and of your
state of mind. Embrace your Mama from me; I
often think of her, and pray for her every day. I
frequently recall our past days together. Kiss your
Missenika for me. Tell me your right address.
Write to me at Milan, *poste restante.*

Even if I should have left Milan, and be in
Florence or Venice (which is recommended me for
the winter), I shall get your letters addressed to
Milan; before my departure I shall give my new
address to the post-office here. As soon as I go to
another town, I'll let you know without delay. My
wife sends greeting and kisses. We both long for our
home. I have been told that after New Year, a new
journal is to appear in Petersburg. The publisher is

Kachpirev ; the editor—my friend Strachov. They have asked me to contribute. The undertaking seems to be quite serious and very promising. Maikov writes of it in great delight.

Do read, in the September number of the *Roussky Viestnik*, the article on the British Association.

I kiss and embrace you, I press you to my heart.

Your friend and brother,

FYODOR DOSTOEVSKY.

XLV

To Apollon Nikolayevitch Maikov

FLORENCE,
December 11 [23], 1868.

I have had a letter from Strachov too ; he tells me a lot of literary news. Particularly do I rejoice to hear of Danilevsky's article, " Europe and Russia,"[1] which Strachov says is splendid. I must confess that I have heard nothing of Danilevsky since the year 1849, though I've often thought of him. What a frenzied Fourierist he was at one time ; and now that same Fourierist has turned himself back into a Russian who loves his native soil and customs ! Thus may one know the people who really matter ! . . .

But, on the other hand, I'll never agree with the

---

[1] The articles by Danilevsky, which appeared in *Sarya*, were afterwards collected under the title of " Russia and Europe." Danilevsky aimed at giving a scientific basis to the Slavophil Utopias, and taught, among other things, that Russia must place herself at the head of a Pan-Slavist Federation, whose centre should be in Constantinople, unconquered yet, but to be conquered.

view of the dead Apollon Grigoryev, that Bielinsky
also would have ended by becoming a Slavophil.
No ; with Bielinsky that was quite out of the
question.　He was, in his day, a remarkable writer,
but could not possibly have developed any further.
Rather, he would have ended as adjutant to some
leader of the Women's Rights movement over here,
and have forgotten his Russian while learning no
German.　Do you know what the new Russians are
like ?　Well, for example, look at the moujik, the
" sectarian " of the time of Paul the Prussian,[1] about
whom there's an article in the June number of the
Roussky Viestnik.　If he's not precisely typical of the
coming Russian, he is undoubtedly *one* of the Russians
of the future.

*　　　　*　　　　*

Those cursed creditors will kill me to a certainty.
It was stupid of me to run away to foreign lands ;
assuredly 'twere better to have stayed at home and
let myself be put in the debtor's prison.　If I could
only treat with them from here !　But that can't be,
for my personal presence is indispensable.　I speak of
this, because at the moment I am meditating two and
even three publishing ventures which will demand the
labour of an ox to carry out, but must inevitably
bring in money.　I have often had luck with similar
projects.

Now here's what I propose :

1.　A long novel entitled " Atheism " (but for God's
sake, let this be entirely between ourselves) ; before I
attack it, I shall have to read a whole library of
atheistic works by Catholic and Orthodox-Greek

---

[1] Paul I., so called because of his love for all things German.

writers. Even in the most favourable circumstances, it can't be ready for two years. I have my principal figure ready in my mind. A Russian of our class, getting on in years, not particularly cultured, though not uncultured either, and of a certain degree of social importance, loses *quite suddenly*, in ripe age, his belief in God. His whole life long he has been wholly taken up by his work, has never dreamed of escaping from the rut, and up to his forty-fifth year, has distinguished himself in no wise. (The working-out will be pure psychology : profound in feeling, human, and thoroughly Russian.) The loss of faith has a colossal effect on him ; (the treatment of the story, and the environment, are both largely conceived). He tries to attach himself to the younger generation —the atheists, Slavs, Occidentalists, the Russian Sectarians and Anchorites, the mystics : amongst others he comes across a Polish Jesuit ; thence he descends to the abysses of the Chlysty-sect [1] ; and finds at last salvation in Russian soil, the Russian Saviour, and the Russian God. (For heaven's sake don't speak of this to anyone ; when I have written this last novel, I shall be ready to die, for I shall have uttered therein my whole heart's burden.) My dear friend, I have a totally different conception of truth and realism from that of our " realists " and critics. My God ! If one could but tell categorically all that we Russians have gone through during the last ten years in the way of spiritual development, all the realists would shriek that it was pure fantasy ! And yet it would be pure realism ! It *is* the one true, deep realism ; theirs is altogether too superficial. Is

---

[1] A flagellant sect still widely spread over Russia.

not the figure of Lyubim Torzov,[1] for instance, at bottom hideously unmeaning? Yet it's the boldest thing they've produced. And they call *that* profound realism! With such realism, one couldn't show so much as the hundredth part of the true facts. But our idealists have actually *predicted* many of the actual facts—really, that has been done. My dear fellow, don't laugh at my conceit; for I'm like Paul: " Nobody praises me, so I'll praise myself."

In the meantime I've got to live somehow. I don't mean to hurry my "Atheism" on to the market (I have such lots to say therein about Catholicism and Jesuitry, as compared with Orthodoxy). Moreover, I have an idea for a tolerably lengthy novel of about twelve sheets; it strikes me as most attractive. And I've another plan besides. Which shall I decide on, and to whom shall I offer my work? To the *Sarya*? But I always demand payment in advance; and perhaps on the *Sarya* they won't agree to that? . . .

[Here follow some purely business details.]

XLVI

To his Niece Sofia Alexandrovna

FLORENCE,
January 25 [February 6], 1869.

MY DEAR, GOOD, AND VALUED FRIEND SONETCHKA,
    I did not at once answer your last letter (undated), and nearly died of conscience - pangs therefor, because I love you very much. But it was not my fault, and it shall be different in future.

---

[1] Hero of a drama by Ostrovsky.

Regularity in our correspondence henceforth depends
wholly on you ; I shall from now onward answer each
of your letters the same day I receive it ; but as every
letter from Russia is now an event to me, and deeply
moves me (*yours* always in the most delightful sense),
do write, if you love me, as often as you possibly can.
I have not answered you for so long, because I put
off all business and even the most important letters
until I had finished the novel. Now it is done at last.
I worked at the concluding chapters by day and by
night, in the deepest anxiety and amid great torment
of mind. A month ago I wrote to the *Roussky
Viestnik*, asking them to postpone the appearance of
the December number for a little while, and so make
it possible for me to bring out the conclusion of my
book this year. I swore that I would deliver the last
lines by the 15th of January (by our Style). But
what happened ? I had two attacks, and therefore
was obliged to overstep by ten days the term which
I had myself fixed. They can only to-day (January 25)
have received the two last chapters. You can easily
imagine how much perturbed I have been by the
thought that they might lose patience, and, as they
had not received the end by the 15th, might let the
number appear without the novel ! That would be
terrible for me. In any case, they must be infuriated ;
I was in dire need and had to write to Katkov for
money.

The climate of Florence is perhaps even more
unfavourable to my health than that of Milan or
Vevey ; the epileptic attacks return more frequently.
Two, with an interval of six days, have brought about
this delay of ten days. Besides, it rains too much in
Florence ; though in fine weather it is real Paradise

here. One can imagine nothing lovelier than this
sky, this air, and this light. For a fortnight it was
somewhat cool, and as the houses here are poorly
equipped, we froze during that fortnight like mice in
a cellar. But now I have my work behind me, and
am free; this work, which took a year, carried me
away so completely that I have not yet been able to
collect my thoughts. The future is to me an enigma;
I don't even yet know what I shall decide to do.
However, I shall have to make up my mind to something. In three months, we shall have been exactly
two years abroad. In my opinion, it is worse than
deportation to Siberia. I mean that quite seriously;
I'm not exaggerating. I cannot understand the
Russians abroad. Even though there *is* a wonderful
sky here, and though there are—as, for example,
in Florence—literally unimaginable and incredible
marvels of art, there are lacking many advantages
which even in Siberia, as soon as I left the prison,
made themselves evident to me : I mean, especially,
home and the Russians, without which and whom
I cannot live. Perhaps you may experience this
yourself one day, and then you'll see that I don't
exaggerate in the least. And yet my immediate
future is still hidden from me. My original positive
plan has for the moment broken down. (I say
positive, but naturally all my plans, like those of any
man who possesses no capital and lives only by his
own toil, are associated with risks, and dependent on
many attendant circumstances.) I hope that I shall
succeed in bettering my finances by the second edition
of the novel, and then returning to Russia ; but I'm
dissatisfied with the book, for I haven't said a tenth
part of what I wanted to say. Nevertheless, I don't

repudiate it, and to this day I love the plan that miscarried.

But in fact the book is not showy enough for the public taste ; the second edition will therefore, even if it comes off at all, bring in so little that I can't reckon on it for any new arrangements. While I'm here in this foreign land, besides, I know nothing of what reception the book had in Russia. Just at first I was sent some cuttings, full of ecstatic praise. But lately—never a word. The worst of it is that I don't know anything, either, about the views of the *Roussky Viestnik* people. Whenever I've asked them for money, they've sent it by return of post, from which I am inclined to draw a favourable conclusion. But I may be mistaken. Now Maikov and Strachov write from Petersburg that a new journal, *Sarya*, has been started, with Strachov as editor ; they sent me the first number, and begged for my collaboration. I promised it, but am hindered by my long connection with the *Roussky Viestnik* (it is always better to stay with the same paper), and by the fact that Katkov gave me an advance of 3,000 roubles before I came abroad. And I owe the editorial staff a good deal besides, for (together with the first three thousand) I have gradually borrowed in all about seven thousand roubles ; so that on that ground alone I can at present work for no other paper but the *Roussky Viestnik*.

On their answer to my request for more money all now depends. But even if they answer favourably, my position will remain most uncertain. I must at all costs get back to Russia ; for here I am losing all power to write, not having the, to me, essential material at hand—that is to say, Russian actualities (from which I draw my ideas) and Russian people.

Every moment I am obliged to look up something, or make inquiries about something, and know not where to turn for it. I am now dallying with the idea of a gigantic novel, which in any event, even should it miscarry with me, *must* be very effective by reason of its theme alone. That theme is—*Atheism* (it is not an indictment of the now prevalent convictions, but something quite different: a real story). What it has to do is to take the reader captive *even against his will*. Of course I shall have to study hard for it. Two or three important characters I have already got into extraordinary perspective, among others a Catholic enthusiast and priest (something like St. François Xavier). But I can't possibly write it here. I should most assuredly be able to sell the second edition of this work, and make much money thereby; but when? Not before two years. (Don't tell anyone about this idea.) In the meantime I must write something else, for daily bread. All this is most depressing. *Some* change must absolutely take place in my situation; but from what quarter is it to arrive?

You are right, my dear, when you say that I should be able to make money much more easily and quickly in Russia. And as a matter of fact I am now meditating two ideas for publications: one would demand much work and would entirely preclude all idea of simultaneous occupation with a novel, but might bring in much money (of that I have no doubt). The other is pure compilation and almost mechanical; it is an idea for an *annually*-appearing large and universally useful volume of about sixty sheets of small print, which would be widely bought and would come out every January; this idea I won't as yet disclose,

for it is too " safe " and too valuable ; the profits are
beyond doubt ; my work would be purely editorial.[1]
All the same it would require some ideas, and much
special knowledge.   And *this* work would not prevent
me from doing a novel at the same time.   I shall
need collaborators therein, and shall think of you
first of all (I shall need translators too), and of course
on the understanding that profits shall be shared in
proportion to the work done ; you will earn ten times
as much as you now get for your work.

I can say without boasting that I've already in the
course of my life had many a good literary idea.   I
have suggested them to different editors, and to
Krayevsky also and my dead brother ; each one that
has been carried out has proved highly lucrative.   So
I am building on these latest notions.   But the chief
thing is this next big novel.   If I don't write it, it
will torment me to death.   But I can't write it here.
And neither can I return to Russia until I have paid
at least 4,000 roubles of my debts, and have besides
in my possession 3,000 roubles (so as to be able to
exist through the first year)—thus, seven thousand
altogether.

But enough of me and my tiresome affairs !   One
way or another, some sort of an end must come, else
I shall die of it all. . . .

Your ever loving
FYODOR DOSTOEVSKY.

P.S.   My address is Florence, *poste restante.*   I
hear that an enormous lot of letters get lost.

---

[1] This is his plan for " The Diary of a Writer."

XLVII

To Nikolay Nikolayevitch Strachov

FLORENCE,
February 26 [*March* 10], 1869.

. . . And have you observed the following peculiarity of our Russian criticism? Every outstanding critic (such as Bielinsky, Grigoryev) first presented himself to the public under the protection, so to speak, of some outstanding writer — and thenceforward devoted himself wholly to the interpretation of that writer, nor ever expressed his ideas save in the form of a commentary upon that writer's works. The critics made no concealment of this, and indeed it appeared to be taken as a matter-of-course. I mean to say that our critics can only express their own ideas when they step forth arm-in-arm with some writer who attracts them. Thus, Bielinsky, when he passed our whole literature under review, and even when he wrote his articles on Pushkin, could only do so by leaning on Gogol, to whom he had paid honour in his youth. Grigoryev has relied on his interpretations of Ostrovsky, in championing whom he made his début. And *you* have, as long as I've known you, had a boundless and instant sympathy for Leo Tolstoy. When I read your article in the *Sarya*, I felt, to be sure, an impression of its being wholly *necessary*, of your being *obliged* to begin with Leo Tolstoy, and *an analysis of his last work*,[1] before you could utter your own idea. In the *Golos*, a feuilletonist declares that you share Tolstoy's *historical fatalism*. That idiotic phrase leaves things precisely

---

[1] "War and Peace."

where they were; do tell me how people manage to
come upon such amazing notions and expressions!
What may *historical fatalism* mean? Why this
eternal jargon, and why do simple-minded men who
can only see as far as the end of their noses, so deepen
and darken counsel that no one can make out what
they're driving at? It was evident that that feuilletonist had something that he wanted to say; he had
read your article, beyond doubt. What you say in
the passage referring to the battle of Borodino,
expresses the profoundest essence of the Tolstoyan
idea, and of your own reflections thereon. I don't
think you could possibly have spoken with more
lucidity. The national Russian idea stands almost
nakedly forth in that passage. Precisely *it* is what
people have failed to comprehend, and therefore have
designated as fatalism. As regards other details of
the article, I must await the sequel (which I haven't
yet received). At any rate your thoughts are lucid,
logical, definitely conceived, and most admirably
expressed. Certain details, though, I don't entirely
agree in. We could treat these questions quite
otherwise, were we talking to one another, instead of
writing. In any case, I regard you as the only
representative of our criticism with whom the future
will reckon. . . .

I thank you, my kind and much-esteemed Nikolay
Nikolayevitch, for the great interest that you show in
me. My health is as satisfactory as hitherto, and the
attacks are even less violent than in Petersburg.
Lately (that is, till about six weeks ago), I have been
much occupied with the end of my " Idiot." Do
write and give me the opinion you promised on the
book; I await it eagerly. I have my own idea about

art, and it is this: What most people regard as
fantastic and lacking in universality, *I* hold to be the
inmost essence of truth.   Arid observation of every-
day trivialities I have long ceased to regard as realism
—it is quite the reverse.   In any newspaper one takes
up, one comes across reports of wholly authentic
facts, which nevertheless strike one as extraordinary.
Our writers regard them as fantastic, and take no
account of them; and yet they are the truth, for
they are facts.   But who troubles to observe, record,
describe, them?   They happen every day and every
moment, therefore they are not " exceptional." . . .

The Russians are often unjustly reproached with
beginning all sorts of things, making great plans—but
never carrying out even the most trivial of them.
This view is obsolete and shallow, and false besides.
It is a slander on the Russian national character; and
even in Bielinsky's time it was prevalent.   How paltry
and petty is such a way of driving home actualities!
Always the same old story!   In this way, we shall
let all true actuality slip through our fingers.   And
who will really delineate the facts, will steep himself
in them?   Of Turgenev's novel I don't wish even to
speak; the devil knows what it may mean!   But is
not my fantastic " Idiot," the very dailiest truth?
Precisely such characters *must* exist in those strata of
our society which have divorced themselves from the
soil—which actually are becoming fantastic.   But I'll
talk of it no more!   In my book much was written
in haste, much is too drawn-out, much has miscarried;
but much, too, is extremely good.   I am not defend-
ing the novel, but the idea.   Do tell me your view
of it; and, of course, quite frankly.   The more you

find fault with me, the higher shall I rate your honesty. . . .

[Thenceforth he writes of the journal *Sarya*, and the articles which have been published therein.]

XLVIII

To his Niece Sofia Alexandrovna

FLORENCE,
March 8 [20], 1869.

You have, as I begged you, answered all my letters regularly by return, my dear and precious friend Sonetchka. But I have broken my word, and made you wait more than a fortnight for my answers. This time I can't even excuse myself by pressure of work, for all my jobs have long been ready and delivered. I can explain my silence only by the depressed state of mind in which I have been.

The *Roussky Viestnik* did not answer my request for money for *seven weeks* (so that I had to wait through all Lent); only to-day have I received the money, though I had depicted my desperate situation to the people there more than two months ago. They write, with *many* apologies, that they have not been able to send me the money any sooner, because, as always at the beginning of the year, they were confronted with a terrible lot of work that could not be postponed, and with the accounts. And it is a fact that about New Year one never can get anything out of them; it was wont to be so in earlier days, and I can still remember how in the years 1866 and 1867 they made me wait whole months for an answer, just as now. So we've had anything but an easy time of it—we

were even in actual distress. If we had not been
able to borrow two hundred francs from an acquaintance, and to get a further hundred from other sources,
we might easily have died of hunger in this foreign
town. But what worried us most was the constant
suspense and uncertainty. In such circumstances, I
could not possibly write to anyone, not even you, my
dear. Evidently the staff, as I gather from their
letter, wish to retain me as a contributor; otherwise
they would not have granted me a further advance.
Indeed I can't complain of Katkov, and am even
grateful to him for the many advances he has made
me. Journals are impoverished nowadays, and
don't usually give any advances; but in the very beginning, before I even began to write the novel, I had
4,000 roubles from these people. For that reason I
must not be either angry or disloyal. . . . I must
strive even harder than hitherto to make myself useful to them. You write that people declare the
magazine has lost ground. Is that really possible?
I can't at all believe it; of course not because *I* am a
contributor, but because the paper is, in my opinion,
the best in Russia, and strikes a really consistent note.
To be sure, it is a little dry; and the literary side is
not always up to the mark (but not oftener than in
the other magazines; all the best works of modern
literature have appeared therein: " War and Peace,"
" Fathers and Sons," etc., to say nothing of more distant years; and the public knows that well); critical
articles are rare (but often very remarkable, particularly when it is not a question of so-called fine
literature); but then there appear annually, as every
subscriber knows, three or four strikingly able, apt,
individual, and in these days most necessary articles,

such as one finds nowhere else. The public knows
that, too. Therefore I believe that the paper, even
if it *is* dry and addressed to a particular section of
the public, cannot possibly lose ground.

In the year 1867, Katkov told me, in the presence
of Lyubimov and the editorial secretary, that the paper
had five hundred more subscribers than the year before,
which was to be attributed entirely to the success
of my "Raskolnikov." [1]   I hardly think that "The
Idiot" will have obtained fresh subscribers for the
paper; therefore I am doubly glad that, despite the
manifest failure of the story, they still depend on me.
The editors beg me to excuse them for being unable
to bring out the conclusion in the December number,
and propose to send it to subscribers as a supplement.
This is quite peculiarly painful for me.   Have *you*
had the conclusion?   Do write and tell me.   I get
the *Roussky Viestnik* here, however; perhaps the
supplement will come with the February number.

From Petersburg I am told quite frankly that
"The Idiot" has certainly many shortcomings, and is
generally regarded as a falling off; but nevertheless
has been followed with great interest by those who
read at all.   And that is really the utmost I aimed at.
As to the shortcomings, I perfectly discern them myself; I am so vexed by my errors that I should like
to have written a criticism of the book.   Strachov
means to send me his article on "The Idiot"; I
know that he is not among my partisans.

I clearly perceive that I am writing only about
myself to-day; but as I am now in that vein, I'll go
on, and I beg you to hear me patiently.   On all these
literary matters depend now my whole future, and

---

[1] "Crime and Punishment."

my return to Russia.   My dearest wish is to embrace
you all, and ever to remain with you ; perhaps it will
really come true some day !   I needn't emphasize the
fact, dear friend (and you will be sure to understand
me), that my whole literary activity has embodied for
me but one definite ideal value, but one aim, but one
hope—and that I do not strive for fame and money,
but only and solely for the synthesis of my imagina-
tive and literary ideals, which means that before I die
I desire to speak out, in some work that shall as far
as possible express the whole of what I think.

At the moment I am meditating a novel.   It will
be called " Atheism "; I think that I shall succeed in
saying all that I wish to say.   But think, my dear :
I cannot possibly write here.   I must absolutely be in
Russia, I must see and hear everything, I must take
my own part in Russian life ; and besides, the work
would take at least two years.   I can't do it here, and
must therefore write something else in the meantime.

On this account, life abroad becomes more unbearable to me every day.   You must know that I should
have 6,000, or at the very least 5,000, roubles before
I can think of returning to Russia.   I reckoned
originally on the success of " The Idiot."   If it had
been equal to that of " Raskolnikov," I should have
had those 5,000 roubles.   Now I must set all my
hopes on the future.   God knows when I shall be
able to return.   But return I must.

You write of Turgenev and the Germans.   Turgenev, however, has lost all his talent in this foreign
sojourn, as already the *Golos* has declared.   Certainly
no such danger threatens me as that of succumbing
to Germanic influence, for I do not like the Germans.
But I must contrive to live in Russia, for here I shall

lose the last vestiges of my talent and my powers.
I feel that, in all my being.   Therefore I must talk
to you still more about those literary matters upon
which depend my present, my future, and my return
to Russia.   So I continue.

The *Sarya* sent me, through Strachov, a second
letter with an official request to contribute.   This
invitation comes from Strachov, from the editor
Kachpirev, and some other contributors whom I do
not personally know (Gradovsky is not among them);
Danilevsky also (whom I have not seen for twenty
years) is of the number—this is not the novelist
Danilevsky, but another very remarkable man of the
same name.   I perceive that a set of new coadjutors
of great distinction, and of thoroughly Russian and
national tendency, have clustered round this journal.
The first number impressed me deeply with its very
frank and outspoken tone, but especially the two long
articles by Strachov and Danilevsky.   You must be
sure to read Strachov's.   It is quite certain that you
have never read any critical writing that can compare
with it.   Danilevsky's article, " Europe and Russia,"
is to be very long and run through several numbers.
This Danilevsky is a most unusual phenomenon.
Once upon a time he was a Socialist and Fourierist;
twenty years ago, even, when he was involved in our
affair, he struck me as most remarkable; from his
banishment he returned a thorough Russian and
Nationalist.   This article (which I very particularly
recommend to you) is his maiden effort.   The paper
seems to me, in general, to have a great future
before it; but will the contributors continue to pull
together ?   Again, Strachov, the real editor, strikes
me as little fitted for a continuous task.   But I

may be mistaken. I answered the invitation to collaborate thus : I was most willing (I said) to contribute to the paper ; but as my situation obliged me always to demand payment in advance, which, moreover, Katkov had always allowed me to do, I now begged for an advance of a thousand roubles. (It is not too much : what am I to live on while I'm doing the work ? I can't possibly ask Katkov for money, while I'm working for another paper.) I sent this letter some days ago, and am now awaiting the answer. All I know is this : if they have money, they'll send it me at once ; but I must reckon with the possibility that they have none, for I know from experience what difficulties a new journal has to encounter in its first year. Even if they do send me the thousand roubles, that will be no particular advantage to me. From Katkov I could have got quite as much, even a great deal more. The only advantage would be that I should at once have a large sum of money (which I urgently need) to dispose of ; I could then lay aside 400 roubles for Pasha and Emilie Fyodorovna, and besides that pay a peculiarly worrying debt that I owe in Petersburg : it is a debt of honour without any promissory note. It's only on account of this debt that I've asked for the advance.

Again, I think it would be to my advantage to appear successfully before the public in another paper ; for then the *Roussky Viestnik* would esteem me more highly still. I fear only that the *Viestnik* people may be offended, although I never promised them an *exclusive* collaboration, and consequently have a right to work for other papers. But I don't quite like the fact that I still owe the *R. V.* about 2,000 roubles, for I've gradually obtained from them as much as 7,000 roubles. It's just on that ground that they may take it ill of me. But three months ago, I wrote and told them that the novel I had promised them could not appear this year, but only in the course of next (1870). For the *Sarya* I want to write a story which would take about four months to do, and to which I propose to devote the hours that I had reserved to myself for walks and recreation after my fourteen months of labour. But I am afraid that the affair will get talked about, and that this may injure me with the *Roussky Viestnik.* . . .

Wholly yours,

FYODOR DOSTOEVSKY.

XLIX

To Nikolay Nikolayevitch Strachov

FLORENCE,
March 18 [30], 1869.

. . . Danilevsky's article seems to me more and more important and valuable. It will assuredly be for many a day the " Household Companion " of every Russian. Quite apart from its content, the clear language, the " popular," lucid manner of presentation, joined to his uncompromising knowledge of his subject—all combines for success. How I should like to talk with you about this article—with you, precisely *you*, Nikolay Nikolayevitch. I should have so much to say to you on the subject! The article is so in harmony with my own views and convictions that here and there I stand amazed at the identity of our conclusions ; as long as two years ago, I began to jot down certain of my reflections, for I had proposed to write an article with a very similar title, and with the same tendency and the same conclusions. How great was my joy and amazement when I beheld this plan, which I had hoped to carry out in the future, already carried out, and that so harmoniously and logically, and with such knowledge as I, with the best will in the world, could never have brought to the task. I await so eagerly the continuation of that article that I daily hurry to the post, and am always making elaborate calculations as to when the next number of the *Sarya* will be likely to arrive. My impatience is the greater because I have some misgivings about the final summing-up ; I am not quite sure that Danilevsky will dwell *with sufficient emphasis* upon what is the inmost essence, and the ultimate destiny, of the Russian nation : namely, that Russia must reveal to the world her own Russian Christ, whom as yet the peoples know not, and who is rooted in our native Orthodox faith. *There* lies, as I believe, the inmost essence of our vast impending contribution to civilization, whereby we shall awaken the European peoples ; there lies the inmost core of our exuberant and intense existence that is to be. I cannot in the least express it in these few words ; indeed I regret that I have touched on it at all. I will only say this much more : after our paltry, hypocritical, angry, one-sided, and barren attitude of negation, such a journal as yours, with its grave, its thoroughly Russian, its statesmanlike and vital, tone, must undoubtedly have a great success.

[Dostoevsky goes on to praise an article by Strachov, and then enlarges on the purely business details of his proposed collaboration on the *Sarya*.]

L

To his Niece Sofia Alexandrovna

DRESDEN,
August 29 [September 10], 1869.

At last I have arrived at writing to you, my dear and only woman-friend Sonetchka. What can you have thought of my long silence? . . . I'll tell you in a few words all that is worth knowing about myself; I am only writing to link up our broken chain of communication. But I will say besides that my thoughts of you and yours have not been broken. Anya and I always talk of you, whenever we think of our Russian home, and that is many times a day.

I remained stuck so long at Florence only because I had not the money to leave it. The staff of the *Roussky Viestnik* left my urgent request for money unanswered for more than three months (I have— but this between ourselves!—grounds for supposing that they had no money in the till, and that that was the only reason why they did not answer for so long). At last they sent me (five weeks ago) seven hundred roubles to Florence. Well, dear friend, call upon your whole powers of imagination, and try to depict for yourself what we in Florence, during the whole of June and July, and half of August, were going through! In my whole life I've never experienced anything like it! The guide-books may say that Florence, by reason of its position, is the coldest town in winter of all Italy (they mean the actual Italy—that is to say, the whole peninsula); but in summer, it is the *hottest* town in the whole peninsula,

and even in the whole Mediterranean region—only
some parts of Sicily and Algiers can touch Florence
for heat.   Well, and so it was as hot as hell, and we
bore it like true Russians, who notoriously can bear
anything.   I may add that for the last six weeks of
our stay there, we were very hard-up.   We had not,
it is true, to suffer actual privation in any respect,
nor did we deny ourselves anything, but our abode
was thoroughly uncomfortable.   We had been obliged,
for unforeseen reasons, to leave the house where we
had spent the winter ; while we were waiting for that
money, we went to a family with whom we are
friendly, and rented provisionally a tiny dwelling.
But as the money delayed to come, we had to stay
in that hole (where we caught two beastly tarantulas)
three whole months.

Our windows gave on a market-square with arcades
and splendid granite-pillars ; in the square was a
municipal fountain in the form of a gigantic bronze
boar from whose throat the water flowed (it is a
classic masterpiece of rare beauty).   Well, now reflect
that all those arcades and the masses of stone by
which the whole square is surrounded, drank in and
accumulated all the heat of the sun, and got as
scorching as a stove-pipe in a vapour-bath—and that
was the atmosphere we had to live in.   The real
heat, that is, the real hell-heat, we had to groan
under for six weeks (earlier, it was just in a sort of
way endurable) ; it was nearly always 34 and 35 degrees
Réaumur in the shade.   You must know that the
air, despite this heat and drought (it never once
rained), was wonderfully light ; the green in the
gardens (of which there are astonishingly few in
Florence ; one sees hardly anything but stones)—the

green neither withered nor faded, but seemed brighter
and fresher every day; the flowers and lemon-trees
had apparently only waited for the heat; but what
astonished me most—me, who was imprisoned in
Florence by untoward circumstance—was that the
itinerant foreigners (who are nearly all very rich)
mostly remained in Florence; new ones even arrived
every day. Usually the tourists of all Europe throng,
at the beginning of the hot weather, to the German
spas. When I saw in the streets well-dressed
Englishwomen and even Frenchwomen, I could not
conceive why these people, *who had money to get
away with*, could voluntarily stay in such a hell. I
was sorriest of all for poor Anya. The poor thing
was then in her seventh or eighth month, and so
suffered dreadfully from the heat. Moreover, the
population of Florence spends the whole night on
its feet, and there's a terrible deal of singing. Of
course we had our windows open at night; then
about five o'clock in the morning, the people began
to racket in the market, and the donkeys to bray, so
that we never could close an eye.

The distance from Florence to Prague (by Venice
and then by boat to Trieste; there's no other way) is
more than a thousand versts; I was therefore very
anxious about Anya; but the renowned Dr. Sapetti
of Florence examined her and said that she could
undertake the journey without any risk. He was
right too, and the journey went off well. On the
way we stopped two days in Venice; when Anya
saw the Piazza of St. Mark's and the palaces, she
almost screamed with delight. In St. Mark's (the
church is a wonderful, incomparable building !) she
lost her carved fan which I had bought her in

Switzerland, and which was particularly dear to her;
she has so few trinkets, you see. My God, how she
did cry over it! We liked Vienna very much too;
Vienna is decidedly more beautiful than Paris. In
Prague we spent three days looking for a place of
abode, but found none. One can, in fact, only get
unfurnished rooms there, as in Petersburg or Moscow;
then one has to get one's own furniture, and a servant-
maid, and set up house, and so forth. Nothing else is
to be had. Our means did not permit of it, and
therefore we left Prague.

Now we have been three months in Dresden;
Anya's confinement may happen at any moment.
For the present we are not doing so badly; but I am
badly " sold," for it seems now that the hot, dry air in
Florence was extraordinarily beneficial to my health,
and even more so to my nerves (nor had Anya anything to complain of, rather the contrary). It was
precisely on the *hottest* days that the epilepsy was
least perceptible, and my attacks in Florence were
much slighter than anywhere else. But here I'm
always ill (perhaps it may be only the effect of the
journey). I don't know if I've caught cold, or if the
feverish attacks come from the nerves. These last
three weeks I have had two; both very vicious ones.
Yet the weather is glorious. I ascribe it all to the
fact of coming suddenly from the Italian to the
German climate. I have fever at the actual moment,
and think that in this climate I shall write feverishly
—that is, incoherently.

Now I have given you a lot of information about
myself. Of course it is only the hundredth part;
besides illness, many things oppress me, of which I
can give no idea at all. Here is an example: I must

absolutely deliver the beginning of my novel in time
for the January number of the *Roussky Viestnik* (to
be sure I am bound to admit that they do not press
me in any way; they behave remarkably well to me
and never refuse advances, though I already owe
them a very great deal; but I am tormented by
pangs of conscience, and so feel just the same as if
they *did* press me).　Moreover, I took an advance of
300 roubles from the *Sarya* early in the year, and
that with a promise to send them this very year a
story of at least three sheets.　At the present moment
I have not begun either the one or the other of these
tasks; at Florence I could not work on account
of the heat.　When I undertook the obligation, I
reckoned on going from Florence to Germany early
in the new year, and there setting to work at once.
But what can I do when people make me wait three
months for money, and thus remove from me the
possibility of doing anything at all?　Anya will, in
about ten days, present me with a child, probably a
boy, and this will further delay my endeavours.　She
will certainly have to keep her bed for three weeks,
and so will not be able either to do shorthand or to
copy for me.　Of my own health, I need not speak.
And then the work itself!　Must I, to carry out my
commissions punctually, tumble over my own feet, as
it were, and so spoil all?　I am now utterly possessed
by one idea; yet I dare not take any steps to carry it
out, for I am not sufficiently prepared to do so—I
still have much to ponder, and I must collect material.
Thus I have to force myself to write, meanwhile, some
new stories.　And to me that is terrible.　What lies
before me, and how I shall arrange my affairs, is to
me an enigma! . . .

Till the next time, my dear friend. Write me a great deal about yourself. And above all as many facts as possible.

I embrace you.

Your ever devoted
FYODOR DOSTOEVSKY.

LI

To Apollon Nikolayevitch Maikov

DRESDEN,
October 16 [28], 1869.

[The greater part of the letter deals with a business misunderstanding with the staff of the *Sarya*.]

What am I to do now ? When shall I get my money *now ?* Why does he [Kachpirev, the editor of the *Sarya*] wait for my telegram, and request me to return to him the letter of exchange ("then I shall send you the money in the course of post," he said) instead of sending me now, directly, the second instalment of seventy-five roubles, which was due ten days ago ? Does he think that the letter in which I described my destitute condition was a piece of fine writing and nothing more ? How can I work, when I am hungry, and had to pawn my very pantaloons to get the two thalers for the telegram ? The devil take me and my hunger ! But she, my wife, who now is suckling her infant, *she* had to go herself to the pawn-shop and pledge her last warm woollen garment ! And it has been snowing here for the last two days (I am not lying : look at the newspapers !) How easily may she catch cold ! Isn't he capable of understanding, then, that I am *ashamed* of telling him all these things ? And it's nothing like the whole of them

either ; there are other things of which I'm *ashamed*:
we haven't yet paid either the midwife or the landlady ; and all these vexations must fall upon her
precisely in the first month after her accouchement !
Doesn't he see that it's not only me, but *my wife*,
whom he insults, by taking my letter so frivolously,
for I told him of my wife's great need.   Indeed he
has grossly insulted me !

Perhaps he may say: "Confound him and his
poverty !   He must *plead*, and not *demand*, for I am
not bound to pay him his fee in advance."   Can't he
understand that by his favourable answer to my first
letter he did bind *me !*   Why did I turn to him with
my request for 200 roubles, and not to Katkov?
Only and solely because I believed that I should get
the money sooner from him than from Katkov (whom
I did not wish to trouble) ; if I *had* written to Katkov
then, the money would have been in my hands at
least a week ago !   But I did *not*.   Why ?   Because
he [Kachpirev] had *bound* me by his answer.   Consequently he has no right to say that he confounds me
and my poverty, and that it's an impertinence in
me to urge him to make haste.

But of course he *will* say that he has nothing to do
with it, and that I'm impertinent.   Of course he'll say
he has done all that lay in his power, that he sent off
the letter of exchange in the course of post, that he is
nowise to blame, that there is a misunderstanding,
and so forth.   And by God, he really believes that
he's right !   Can he not see, then, that it's *unforgiv-
able* to leave my despairing letter, in which I told him
that through his negligence I had been so long penniless—to leave it unanswered for *twelve* days.   Yes,
for twelve days, I am not telling a lie ; I still have

the envelope with the post-mark intact.   It's unheard
of—not to reply for *six days* to a telegram, that he
himself *made me send*, when a letter would have taken
only four days !   Such negligence is unpardonable,
insulting !   It is a personal offence.   For I had told
him about my wife and her accouchement.   He had
bound himself to me in advance, by making it seem
superfluous that I should apply to Katkov : it *is* a
serious personal offence !

He requests me to explain by telegram what my
first telegram meant, and adds : " Of course at my
expense " !   Doesn't he know, then, that an unstamped
telegram is accepted nowhere, and that consequently I
must have two thalers before I can send one ?   After
all my letters, is he unable to divine that it's possible
I may not have those two thalers ?   It is the thought-
lessness of a man who cares nothing for his fellow's
perplexity.   And then they demand of me lucid art,
effortless and untroubled poetry, and point me to
Turgenev and Gontscharov !   If they but knew the
conditions under which *I* have to work ! . . .

LII

To Apollon Nikolayevitch Maikov

DRESDEN,
February 12 [24], 1870.

My attacks, after a long respite, are now coming
on me terribly again, and disturb me in my work.
I have a big idea in hand[1]; I don't mean that the
execution is big, but the idea *as such*.   It is somewhat
in the kind of " Raskolnikov " [" Crime and Punishment "], but is still closer to actuality, and deals with

---

[1] " The Possessed."

the most weighty question of our time. I shall be
ready with it in the autumn ; and that without over-
hurrying. I shall make an effort to bring out the
book directly—that is, in the autumn too ; if I can't,
it won't matter. I hope to earn at least as much
money with it as I did with " Raskolnikov "; and so
look forward to having all my affairs in order by the
end of the year, and returning to Russia. Only the
theme is almost too intense and thrilling. I have
never yet worked so easily and with such enjoyment.
But enough. I must be positively slaying you with
my interminable letters ! . . .

[The greater part of the letter refers to his relations
with the publisher Stellovsky, and with the staff of
the *Sarya*.]

LIII

To Nikolay Nikolayevitch Strachov

DRESDEN,
February 26 [*March* 10], 1870.

MUCH-ESTEEMED NIKOLAY NIKOLAYEVITCH,
I hasten to thank you for your letter and your
interest in me. In foreign lands, the letters of our
old friends are peculiarly precious to us. Maikov
apparently means to write to me no more. With the
deepest interest I have read the kindly lines which
you devote to my story.[1] What you say is agreeable
and flattering to me ; just like you, I have an earnest
desire to please my readers. Kachpirev is satisfied,
too ; he has written two letters in that sense. It all
rejoices me extraordinarily ; I take particular pleasure

[1] " The Eternal Widow," which appeared in the *Sarya* (1870,
Nos. 1 and 2).

in what you tell me about the *Sarya ;* it is certainly
very gratifying that the existence of the journal is
assured. As far as its tendency is concerned, I am
in entire agreement with it ; consequently its success
is my success. The paper reminds me in many
respects of the *Vremya*—of our youthful days.

[Here follow some remarks upon the journal, and
on the feasibility of Dostoevsky's further collaboration
on the *Sarya*.]

I will tell you honestly : I have never yet sought
a theme for the money's sake, nor even from a sense
of duty, so as to have a promised work ready by the
appointed time. I have undertaken commissions only
when I already had a theme ready in my head, one
that I really desired to work out, and the working-
out of which I considered necessary. Such a theme
I have now. I won't enlarge upon that ; I will only
say that I have never had a better or a more original
idea.[1] I may say this without incurring the reproach
of lack of modesty, because I speak only of the idea,
not of the execution of it. *That* lies in God's hand ;
I may indeed spoil all, as I have so often done ; still,
an inward voice assures me that inspiration will not
fail in the execution, either. Anyhow I can answer
for the novelty of the idea, and the originality of the
manner, and I am, at the present moment, fire and
flame. It is to be a novel in two parts of at least
twelve, and at most fifteen, sheets (so I see it at this
stage).

[There follow considerations of the feasibility of
bringing out the new novel in the *Sarya*.]

[1] He here again refers to the still projected novel " Atheism
(see letters to Maikov of December 11, 1868,and March 25, 1870)

So I await your answer; and make you, besides, one great and urgent request: Send me if possible, putting it down against my forthcoming resources (as you once sent me Tolstoy's "War and Peace") Stankevitch's book upon Granovsky. You will do me thereby a great service, which I shall never forget. I want the book as urgently as I want air to breathe, and that as soon as possible; I need it as material for my work[1]; without that book I can do nothing. Don't forget it, for Christ's sake; send it me, no matter how you manage it. . . .

LIV

To Nikolay Nikolayevitch Strachov

DRESDEN,
March 24 [*April* 5], 1870.

I hasten, much-esteemed Nikolay Nikolayevitch, to answer your letter, and I shall come at once to myself. I want to tell you, decisively and frankly, that, after the closest consideration, I cannot possibly promise to have the novel ready so soon as the autumn. It appears to me quite impracticable; and I should like to beg the staff not to press me, for I want to do my work quite as carefully and neatly as certain gentlemen (that is, the Great Ones) do theirs. All I will guarantee is that the novel shall be ready in the January of the coming year. This work is more to me than aught else. The idea is more precious to me than any of my other ideas, and I want to do it well. . . . I also set great hopes on the novel which

[1] Dostoevsky gave the character of Stepan Trophimovitch Verchovensky in "The Possessed" some of the traits of Granovsky.

FACSIMILE OF "THE POSSESSED," PART III.: BEGINNING OF
CHAPTER I.

DOSTOEVSKY, PETERSBURG, 1876.

I am now writing[1] for the *Roussky Viestnik ;* I don't
mean as a work of art, but because of its tendencies ;
I mean to utter certain thoughts, whether all the
artistic side of it goes to the dogs or not. The
thoughts that have gathered themselves together in
my head and my heart are pressing me on ; even if
it turns into a mere pamphlet, I shall say all that I
have in my heart. I hope for success. For that
matter, who ever sets himself to a task without
so hoping ? This work for the *Roussky Viestnik*
I shall soon have finished, and then I can turn with
gusto to *the* novel.

I have been meditating the idea of this novel for
three years ; till now I have not been able to make up
my mind to attack it in these foreign lands ; I wanted
not to begin till I was in Russia. But during these
three years, the whole conception has matured within
me, and I think that I *can* begin the first part (which
I intend for the *Sarya*) even here, for the action of
that part is concerned with many years ago. You
need not be uneasy when I speak of a " first part."
The idea demands great length ; at least as great as in
the Tolstoyan novels.   It will really be a cycle of five
distinct stories ; these will be so independent of one
another that any one of them (except the two that
come midway) could perfectly well be published in
different journals as completely separate works. The
general title is to be : " The Life-Story of a Great
Sinner,"[2] and each separate tale will have its own
title as well. Each division (that is, each single
story) will be about fifteen sheets at most in length.

[1] " The Possessed."

[2] This, like " Atheism," is the original idea, never completely
carried out, of " The Brothers Karamazov."

To write the second story, I *must* be in Russia; the
action of that part takes place in a Russian monastery;
although I know the Russian monasteries well, I
must nevertheless come back to Russia. I should
like to have said much more about it to you, but
what can one say in a letter? I repeat, however,
that I can't possibly promise the novel for this year;
don't press me, and you will get a conscientious,
perhaps even a really good, work (at all events I have
set myself this idea as the goal of my literary future,
for I can't at all hope to live and work more than six
or seven years longer).

I have read the March number of the *Sarya* with
great enjoyment. I await impatiently the continuation of your article, so that I may grasp it in its
entirety. It seems to me that your point is to show
Herzen as an Occidentalist, and in general to speak
of the Occident in contradistinction to Russia; am
I right? You chose your point of departure very
cleverly; Herzen is a pessimist; but do you *really*
hold his doubts (" Who is guilty?" " Krupov," and
the rest) to be insoluble? It seems to me that you
evade that question, in order to give your fundamental idea more value. Anyhow I await most
eagerly the continuation of the article; the theme is
positively *too* exciting and actual. What will come
of it, if you really adduce the proof that Herzen,
earlier than many others, pointed to the decadence
of the West? What will the Occidentalists of the
Granovsky period say to that? To be sure, I don't
know if that is what you really are working up to;
it is only a presentiment of mine. Don't you, moreover, think (although it has nothing to do with the
theme of your article) that there is another stand-

point from which to judge the character and activities of Herzen—namely that he ever and always was first of all a *writer*?   The writer in him prevails ever and always, in everything that he does. The agitator is a writer, the politician a writer, the Socialist a writer, the philosopher, to the last degree, a writer! This peculiarity of his nature is, I think, explanatory of much in his work; even to his levity and his love of punning when he is treating the most serious moral and philosophical questions (which, by-the-bye, is not a little repellent in him).

[He then speaks of Strachov's polemical articles, which Dostoevsky thinks too mild: " The Nihilists and Occidentalists deserve the knout."]

You maintain, among other things, that Tolstoy is equal to any of our greatest writers; with that passage in your letter I cannot possibly say that I agree.   It is a thing that ought not to be affirmed ! Pushkin and Lomonossov were geniuses. A writer who steps forward with the " Negro of Peter the Great " and " Bielkin " comes bringing a message of genius, a new message, that nobody before him has anywhere whatever delivered.   But when such an one comes with " War and Peace," he comes *after* that new message which had been already delivered by Pushkin; and *this stands fast*, however far Tolstoy may go in the development of that message already delivered before him by another genius.   I hold this to be very important.   But I can't explain myself at all fully in these few lines. . . .

LV

To Apollon Nikolayevitch Maikov

DRESDEN,
March 25 [April 6], 1870.

[The first half of the letter deals with business matters.]

The job for the *Roussky Viestnik* will not particularly tax me ; but I have promised the *Sarya* a real piece of work, and I want *really* to do it. This latter has been maturing in my brain for two years past. It is the same idea about which I have already once written to you. This will be my last novel ; it will be as long as " War and Peace." I know from our one-time talks that you will approve the idea. The novel will consist of five longish tales (each of fifteen sheets ; in these two years my plan has fully ripened). The tales are complete in themselves, so that one could even sell them separately. The first I intend for Kachpirev ; its action lies in the 'forties. (The title of the whole book will be " The Life-Story of a Great Sinner," but each part will have its own title as well.) The fundamental idea, which will run through each of the parts, is one that has tormented me, consciously and unconsciously, all my life long : it is the question of the existence of God. The hero is now an atheist, now a believer, now a fanatic and sectarian, and then again an atheist. The second story will have for its setting a monastery. On this second story I base all my hopes. Perhaps people will admit at last that I can write something but pure nonsense. (I will confide to you alone, Apollon Nikolayevitch, that in this second story the principal character is to be taken from Tikhon Zadonsky; of course under another name, but also as a Bishop who has withdrawn to a monastery for repose.) A thirteen-yeared boy, who has been concerned in a serious crime, a lad intellectually mature, but utterly corrupt (I know the type), and the future hero of the novel as a whole—has been sent by his parents to the monastery to be there brought up. The little wolf, the little Nihilist, there comes in contact with Tikhon. In the same monastery is to be found Tchaadayev [1] (also of course under another name). Why should not Tchaadayev have spent a year in a monastery? Let us suppose that Tchaadayev, after that first article which caused him to be weekly examined by physicians as to his state of mind, had been unable to refrain from publishing a second article somewhere abroad (say, in France); it is quite conceivable; and for *this* article he gets banished for a year to a monastery. But he is allowed to receive visitors there—for example, Bielinsky, Granovsky, even Pushkin, and others. (Of course it is not to be the actual Tchaadayev; I only want to display the type.) At the monastery there is also a Paul the Prussian, a Golubov, and a Monk Parfeny. (I know the *milieu* through and through; I have been familiar with the Russian monasteries from childhood.) But the principal figures are to be Tikhon and the boy. For God's sake, don't tell anyone what this second part is to be about. Usually I never tell anybody about my work beforehand; only to you would I whisper it; whatever others may think of the value

---

[1] Pyotr Yakovlevitch Tchaadayev (1796-1856), a philosopher, author of "Philosophical Letters," after the publication of which he was declared by Nicholas I. to be mad.

of my plan, to me it is worth more than aught else.
Don't talk to anybody about Tikhon. I have told
Strachov about the monastery idea, but said no word
about the figure of Tikhon. Perhaps I shall succeed
in creating a majestic, authentic saint. Mine is to be
quite different from Kostanchoglov,[1] and also from
the German in Gontscharov's "Oblomov." I shall
probably not *create* at all, but present the real Tikhon,
who has long been shrined in my heart. But even a
close, faithful delineation I should regard it as a great
achievement to succeed in. Don't talk to anyone
about it. Now, to write this second part of the novel,
which goes on in the monastery, I must absolutely
be in Russia. Ah, if I could but bring it off! The
first part deals with the childhood of my hero. Of
course there are other characters besides children ;
it is a real novel. This first part, fortunately, I *can*
write even here ; I shall offer it to the *Sarya*. Will
they not refuse it, though ? But a thousand roubles
is no very excessive fee. . . .

Nihilism isn't worth talking about. Only wait
until this scum that has cut itself adrift from Russia,
is quite played-out. And, do you know, I really
think that many of the young scoundrels, decadent
boys that they are, will sooner or later turn over
a new leaf, and be metamorphosed into decent,
thorough-going Russians? And the rest may go
rot. But even *they* will finally hold their tongues,
for sheer impotence. What scoundrels they are,
though ! . . .

[1] In Gogol's "Dead Souls."

LVI

To his Sister Vera, and his Niece Sofia Alexandrovna

DRESDEN,
May 7 [19], 1870.

MY DEAR FRIENDS SONETCHKA AND VEROTCHKA,

I have not written to you for much too long a period; the reason is not my laziness, but lies in my many recent anxieties and my generally depressed condition of mind.

We are still living in Dresden, and are at present comfortable enough. Little Lyuba is a dear and most healthy child. As we have already lost a child, we are very anxious about this one. Anya is nursing, and it is clear that she finds it more and more trying to her every day. She has grown very thin and weak, and is consumed with home-sickness. I too long frightfully for Russia, and from that longing arises my constant enervation. My affairs are in the worst conceivable condition. We certainly have quite enough to live on, but we cannot even think of returning to Russia. Nevertheless, I must get back somehow, for life here is to me quite unbearable. To go from here to Petersburg, we should have to make a move before October; later it will be too cold, and the little one might easily catch a chill. Moreover, to pay our debts here before we leave, we should need at least three hundred roubles; besides that, the travelling expenses for our whole family and for the instalment in Petersburg: the whole amounts to no small sum. But this is not all; the principal thing is the creditors. I owe them, with the interest, nearly

6,000 roubles. Less than a third—that is, 2,000 roubles—I cannot offer them, if they are to consent to wait a year for the rest. But they would not agree to do that, even if I paid this third. They are all furious with me, and would certainly come down without mercy, in order to punish me. So you can reckon for yourself what a sum I must have to settle all, and be able to come back : that is, from three to four thousand roubles at least. Where am I to get such an amount ? The one thing I can build on is my literary labour. Three years ago, when I left Russia, I cherished the same hopes. I had just had great success with a novel, and it is therefore comprehensible that I should still be filled with the hope of writing another which will enable me to get rid of all my debts in a year or so. But at *that* time I paid three creditors seven thousand roubles all of a sudden, and this enraged the others, who came down on me, demanding to know why I had satisfied those three creditors, and not the rest as well. They indicted me, and I took to my heels, but in the hope that I should manage to write another novel in a year and pay off all my debts. That hope was mistaken. The novel has been a failure, and in addition there has happened something that I could not have foreseen : namely, that through being obliged to live away from Russia for so long, I am losing the capacity to write decently at all, and so could hope nothing from a fresh attempt at a novel. (These difficulties are less of an intellectual than a material nature : for example, while I live abroad I can have no personal outlook upon the most ordinary events of our period.) I have a plan for a new novel, the success of which I consider an absolute certainty ; but I *cannot* decide to

write it here, and am obliged to postpone it.   For the
moment I am writing a very odd story[1] for the
Roussky Viestnik ; I have to work off an advance
from them.

You remember, I daresay, my dear Sonetchka,
what you wrote with regard to the novel which I
did over here : that you wondered how I could undertake and bind myself to get such a work done in a
fixed space of time.   But the work which I am now
writing for the *Roussky Viestnik* is a good deal more
arduous still.   I have to cram into twenty-five sheets
material which ought to take at least fifty, and that
only because it must be finished by a certain date ;
and I have to do this, because for the moment, while
I am living abroad, I can't write anything else.   The
people at the *Sarya* office praised beyond measure a
little story that I published in that journal.   Even
the newspaper critics (on the *Golos,* the *Peter-
bourgskaya Listok,*[2] etc.) were most benevolent.   But
you will hardly believe how it revolts me to write
that kind of thing when I have so many fully formed
ideas in my mind : that is, to write something quite
different from what I want to be at.   You can surely
understand, Sonetchka, that that alone is great
torment, and added to it is the desperate state of my
affairs.   Since I have been absent from Petersburg,
all my business matters and connections there have
been frightfully neglected (although "The Idiot" did
miss fire, several publishers wanted to buy the rights
of the second edition from me ; they offered me
relatively good terms—from a thousand five hundred
to two thousand roubles).   But all these projects fell
through, for I had no one in Petersburg to look after

---

[1] "The Possessed."   [2] *Petersburg News.*

the business for me.   Well, that's how it stands with
me.   And I say nothing of how very much I grieve
for Anna Grigorovna, longing so terribly as she does
for Russia.   I can't possibly tell everything in this
letter.   But I *have* finally resolved to return to
Russia, in any event, in the autumn of this year, and
shall quite decidedly get it done somehow.   Of course,
too, I shall come to Moscow (for business reasons, if
for no others) ; that is, if the creditors do not put me
in a Petersburg prison so soon as I arrive *there*.   In
any case I hope to see you all again, my dears, at the
beginning of the winter.

In truest love :

FYODOR DOSTOEVSKY, ANYA, AND LYUBA.

LVII
To Nikolay Nikolayevitch Strachov

DRESDEN,
June 11 [23], 1870.

[In the first half of the letter Dostoevsky complains
of Kachpirev, who has not agreed to his proposal
with regard to " The Life-Story of a Great Sinner."]

By chance the *Viestnik Europi*[1] for the current
year fell into my hands, and I looked through all the
numbers that have appeared.   I was amazed.   How
can this unbelievably mediocre journal (which at its
best can only be classed with the *Northern Bee* of
Bulgaria) have such vogue with us (6,000 copies in
the second edition !).   It is because they know their
business.   How deftly they adopt the popular tone !
An insipid pattern for Liberalism !   These are the

[1] *The European Gazette :* a monthly.

things we like.   But the paper is, nevertheless, very
well managed.   It appears punctually each month,
and has a varied staff of contributors.   I read, among
other things, "The Execution of Tropmann," by
Turgenev. You may be of a different opinion, Nikolay
Nikolayevitch, but I was infuriated by that preten-
tious and paltry piece of pathos.   Why does he keep
on explaining that he was very wrong to look on at
the execution ?   Certainly he was, if the whole thing
was a mere drama for him ; but the sons of men
have *not* the right to turn away from anything that
happens on the earth and ignore it ; no, on the
highest moral grounds they have not.   *Homo sum et
nihil humani* . . . and so forth.   Peculiarly comic is
it, when at the last moment he *does* turn away, and
thus avoids seeing the actual execution.   " Look you,
gentlemen, of what delicate upbringing I am !   I
could not endure that sight !"   All through, he
betrays himself.   The most definite impression that
one gets from the whole article is that he is desperately concerned with himself and his own peace of
mind, even when it comes to the cutting off of heads.
Oh, I spit upon the whole business.   I am fairly sick
of folk.   I consider Turgenev the most played-out
of all played-out Russian writers, whatever you,
Nikolay Nikolayevitch, may write in Turgenev's
favour : please, don't take it ill of me. . . .

LVIII

To his Niece Sfioa Alexandrovna

DRESDEN,
July 2 [14], 1870.

MY DEAR SONETCHKA,

I really wished to answer your last letter instantly, but have again delayed my reply. Blame my work and various anxieties for that. And besides, you, like all my Moscow friends, have the bad habit of giving no address in your letters.

From your letter I conclude that you have moved. Where then am I to address you? You should, you know, reckon also with the possibility of my having mislaid or lost the letter in which you gave your last address. As it is, I have spent three days looking through all my correspondence for the last three years. But I happen to remember your old address, and there I send this letter. Will it reach you, I wonder? Such doubts discourage me. I beseech you not to write your letters, at any rate not those to me, in the woman's way—that is, not to omit date and address; by God, we shall manage better so!

Your letter made a very mournful impression on me, dear. Is it really a fact that if you go into the country, they won't give you any more translation to do, even in the autumn? Why do you so torment yourself? You need happiness and healthy surroundings. You work from early morning till far into the night. You must marry. My dear Sonetchka, for Christ's sake don't be angry with me for saying that. Happiness is meted out to us but once in life; all that comes afterwards is merely pain. We must prepare ourselves for this beforehand, and arrange our lives as normally as possible. Forgive me for writing to you in this tone, when I have not seen you for three years. I don't mean it for advice ; it is only my most cherished desire. For I must love you—I cannot help it !

As for my return to Russia, it is of course but a possibility of the fancy, which *may* come true, yet nevertheless is a mere dream. We shall see. And as for the rest of your counsels (with regard to the sale of the novel, the return without money, in face of the possibility of being clapped into jail by the creditors, and so forth), I must tell you that your whole letter displays your inexperience and your ignorance of the questions at issue. I have been occupied with literature for twenty-five years, but have never yet known a case of the author himself offering the booksellers his second edition (still less through the agency of strangers, to whom it matters nothing). If one offers the wares one's-self, one gets only a tenth of their value. But if the publisher, that is to say the purchaser, comes to one of his own accord, one gets ten times as much. " The Idiot " came too late ; it should have appeared in earlier years. Then, as to the creditors, they will, as sure as death, imprison me, for therein lies their sole advantage. Believe me, these gentry know very precisely how much I can get from the *Roussky Viestnik* or the *Sarya*. They will have me imprisoned in the hope that one or the other journal, or, if not, somebody else, will get me out. That is dead certain. No— if I am to come back, I must do it quite differently.

I find it very hard to have to look on and see Anna Grigorovna consumed by home-sickness and longing as she is. That troubles me more than aught else. The child is healthy, but has not yet been weaned. Return is now my one fixed idea. If I go on living here much longer, I shall lose all power to earn anything; nobody will consent to print me. In Russia, at the worst I could edit school-books or compilations. Well, anyhow, it's not worth while wasting words upon this matter. I shall most decidedly return, even if it *is* to be put in jail. I should like just to finish the work that I am doing for the *Roussky Viestnik*, so that I might be left in peace. And yet, as things are, I can't, *in any case*, get done before Christmas. The first long half of the work I shall deliver to the office in six weeks, and get a little money. The second half I shall send at the beginning of the winter, and the third—in February. Printing will have to begin in this coming January. I am afraid that they will simply send back my novel. I shall tell them from the very first that I don't intend to alter or take out anything in the book. The idea of this novel seemed to me most attractive at first, but now I am sorry that I ever began it. Not that it does not still interest me, but I should prefer to write something else.

As often as I write to you, I feel what a long space of time divides us from one another. And by-the-bye, there's another thing: I have the most fervent desire to take, before my return to Russia, a trip to the East —that is, to Constantinople, Athens, the Archipelago, Syria, Jerusalem, and Athos. This trip would cost at least 1,500 roubles. But the expenses would not signify: I could cover them all by writing a book about the visit to Jerusalem; I know by experience that such books are very popular nowadays. But for the moment I have neither the time nor the means;

and yesterday I read, in an extra-edition, that at any moment there may be war between France and Prussia. So much combustible material has accumulated everywhere, that the war, so soon as it begins, must assume formidable dimensions. God grant that Russia may not be mixed up in any of the European entanglements ; we have enough to do at home.

I love you and yours beyond all bounds, and I hope you will believe that. Love me also a little. I do not wish to die on German soil ; I want before my death to return home, and there die.

My wife and Lyuba send kisses. It is very hot here with us, and yesterday, after a long respite, I had an attack again. To-day my head is quite muddled ; I feel as if I were crazy.

Till the next time, my dears—forget me not.

I embrace and kiss you.

Your

FYODOR DOSTOEVSKY.

P.S. If I get no answer to this letter, I shall conclude that it has not reached you. My address is : Allemagne, Saxe, Dresden, à M. Théodore Dostoevsky, Poste restante.

LIX

To his Niece Sofia Alexandrovna

DRESDEN,
August 17 [29], 1870.

MY DEAR FRIEND SONETCHKA,

Forgive me for not having at once answered on receiving your letter of August 3 (I got your short letter of July 28 also). I have, often, so many anxieties and disagreeables that I have not the energy

to begin anything, least of all a letter. Only my
work has to be done in any condition of mind—and
I do it; but there are times when I am not equal
even to that, and then I abandon all. My life is not
an easy one. This time I want to write to you about
my situation : to be sure I don't like letter-writing,
for I find it hard, after so many years of separation,
to write of things that are of consequence to me, and
especially to write in such a way that you will understand me. Lively letters one can write only to those
with whom one has no relations of affection.

The most important thing is that now I must
return to Russia. That idea is simple enough; but
I couldn't possibly describe to you in full detail all
the torments and disadvantages that I have to endure
in these foreign lands ; of the moral torments (the
longing for home, the necessity of being in touch with
Russian life which as a writer is essential to me, etc.),
I won't at all speak. How unbearable are the
anxieties about my family alone ! I see clearly how
Anya longs for home, and how terribly she languishes
here. At home, too, I could earn much more money ;
here we are absolutely impoverished. We have just
enough to live on, it is true; but we cannot keep a
nursemaid. A nursemaid here requires a room to
herself, her washing, and high wages, three meals a
day, and a certain amount of beer (of course only
from foreigners). Anya is nursing the baby, and
never gets a full night's rest. She has no amusements of any kind, and usually not one moment to
herself. Also her state of health leaves something to
be desired. Why do I tell you all this, though?
There are hundreds of similar little troubles, and
together they make up a heavy burden. How gladly,

for example, would I go to Petersburg this autumn
with my wife and child (as I pictured to myself early
in the year); but to get away from here and travel to
Russia I must have not less than 2,000 roubles; nor
am I therein reckoning my debts—I need so much as
that for the journey alone. Oh yes! I can see you
shrugging your shoulders and asking: "Why so
much? What is the good of this exaggeration?"
Do, my dear, for Heaven's sake get out of your
habit of judging other people's affairs without knowing all the circumstances. Two thousand roubles *are*
absolutely necessary to do the journey, and to instal
ourselves in Petersburg. You may believe me when
I say it. Where am I to get hold of the money?
And now we must be getting the child weaned, and
vaccinated too. Only think what a fresh crop of cares
for Anya, who is already run-down and feeble. I have
to look on at it all, and am nearly driven out of my
senses. And if I do get the money for the journey
in three months, the winter will just be upon us, and
one can't drag an infant over a thousand versts in
frosty weather. Consequently we shall have to wait
till early spring. And shall we even then have
money? You must know that we can scarcely
manage on our income here, and have to go into
debt for half we need. But enough of that. I want
to talk of other things now, though they're all connected with the principal subject.

I forget whether I've written to you about my
difficulties with the *Roussky Viestnik;* the fact is
that at the end of last year I published a story in the
Sarya, while I still had to work off an advance from
the *Roussky Viestnik;* it was a year since I had
promised them the work. Did I tell you how it

came about ?   How my novel got unexpectedly long,
and how I suddenly perceived that there was no time
to get anything written by the beginning of the year
for the *Roussky Viestnik ?*   They made me no reply
about the matter, but ceased to send money.   At
the beginning of this year I wrote to Katkov that
I would deliver the novel chapter by chapter from
June, so that they could print at the end of the year.
Then I worked at the utmost limit of my energy and
my powers ; I knew that if I were to break off my
literary connection with the *Roussky Viestnik,* I
should have no means of livelihood here abroad (for
it is very difficult to enter into fresh relations with
another journal from a distance).   And besides I was
frightfully distressed by the thought that they were
calling me a rogue at the office, when they had
always treated me so extraordinarily well.   The novel
at which I was working was very big, very original,
but the idea was a little new to me.   I needed great
self-confidence to get equal with that idea—and as
a matter of fact I did not get equal with it, and the
book went wrong.   I pushed on slowly, feeling that
there was something amiss with the whole thing, but
unable to discover what it was.   In July, directly
after my last letter to you, I had a whole succession
of epileptic fits (they recurred every week).   I was so
reduced by them that for a whole month I dared not
even think of working ; work might have been actually
dangerous to me.   And when, a fortnight ago, I set to
again, I suddenly saw quite clearly why the book had
gone so ill, and where the error lay ; as if possessed by
sudden inspiration, I saw in an instant a quite new plan
for the book.   I had to alter the whole thing radically ;
without much hesitation I struck out all that I had

written up to that time (about fifteen sheets in all),
and began again at the first page. The labour of
a whole year was destroyed. If you only knew,
Sonetchka, how grievous it is to be a writer—that is,
to bear a writer's lot ! Do you know that I am absolutely *aware* that if I could have spent two or three
years at that book—as Turgenev, Gontscharov, and
Tolstoy can—I could have produced a work of which
men would still be talking in a hundred years from
now ! I am not boasting ; ask your conscience and
your memory if I have ever yet boasted. The idea
is so good and so significant that I take off my own
hat to it. But what will come to pass ? I know very
well : I shall get it done in eight or nine months, and
utterly spoil it. Such a work demands at least two
or three years. (It will, even so, be very extensive—
as much as thirty-five sheets.) Separate details and
characters will perhaps come not so badly off ; but
only sketchily. Much will be " half-baked," and much
a great deal too drawn-out. Innumerable beauties I
shall have altogether to renounce getting in, for
inspiration depends in many respects upon the time
one has at disposal. And yet I am setting to work !
It is terrible ; it is like a determined suicide ! But
it's not even the most important thing : the most
important thing is that all my calculations are upset.
At the beginning of the year, I was confidently hoping
that I should succeed in sending a considerable portion
of the novel to the *Roussky Viestnik* by the first of
August, and so bettering my situation. What am
I to do now ? At earliest I shall be able to deliver
a small portion by September 1st (I wanted to send
a lot at once, so as to have an excuse for requesting
an advance) ; now I am ashamed to ask for money ;

the first part (it is to be in five parts) will consist of
only seven sheets—how can I ask for an advance?
All my calculations having thus proved false, I don't
know at this moment what on earth I am to live
on.   And it is in such a state of mind that I must
labour !

[He writes further of his somewhat strained relations with the *Roussky Viestnik.*]

All this worries me, and deprives me of the tran-
quillity that I need for the work ; and there are
other things besides, which I do not mention at all.
With this beginning of the war, all credit has very
nearly ceased, so that living is much more difficult.
But I shall get through it somehow or other.   The
most important thing, though, is health ; and my
state has considerably worsened.

With your views on war I can't possibly agree.
Without war, people grow torpid in riches and comfort, and lose the power of thinking and feeling
nobly ; they get brutal, and fall back into barbarism.
I am not speaking of individuals, but of whole races.
Without pain, one comprehends not joy.   Ideals are
purified by suffering, as gold is by fire.   Mankind
must strive for his Heaven.   France has of late
become brutalized and degraded.   A passing trial
will do her no harm ; France will be able to endure
it, and then will awake to a new life, and new ideas.
But hitherto France has been dominated on the one
hand by old formulas, and on the other by craven-
heartedness and pleasure-seeking.

The Napoleonic dynasty will be impossible henceforth.   New life and reformation of the country are
so important that even the bitterest trials are nothing

by comparison.   Do you not recognize God's hand in it ?

Also our politics of the last seventy years—I mean Russian, European, and German politics — must inevitably alter.   The Germans will at last show us their real faces.   Everywhere in Europe great changes must inevitably come—and of their own accord.

What new life will be called forth everywhere by this mighty shock !   For want of great conceptions, even science has sunk into arid materialism ; what does a passing blow signify in face of that ?

You write " People kill and wound, and then nurse the wounded."   Do but think of the noblest words that ever yet were spoken : " I desire love, and not sacrifice."   At this moment, or at any rate in a few days, there will, I believe, be much decided.   Who betrayed whom ?   Who made a strategical error ?   The Germans or the French ?   I believe, the Germans.

Or rather, ten days ago I was of that opinion. But now it appears to me that the Germans will keep the upper hand a while longer ; the French are on the verge of an abyss, into which they are bound to plunge for a time—by that I mean the dynastic interests to which the fatherland is being sacrificed.   I could tell you much of German opinion, which I can observe here, and which is very significant in the present political crisis ; but I have no time.

I greet you all.   Remember me to everyone.   I embrace you from my heart ; do not forget that no one is so cordially inclined to you as I am.   I am glad that I have been able to write to you.   Write to me, don't forget me ; I am now setting to again at my forced labour.

With heart and soul, your FYODOR DOSTOEVSKY.

When I think of the Petersburg relatives, my heart aches. I can send them nothing before the beginning of next year, though they are in great distress. This weighs heavily on my conscience ; I had promised to aid them ; about Pasha I am particularly grieved.

P.S. You don't understand my position with the creditors ; that is why you think it would not be worth their while to put me in prison. On the contrary : they will quite certainly have me arrested, for in many respects it would be of great advantage to them. I forget whether I told you that I have hopes of procuring, immediately after my arrival in Petersburg, the use of about 5,000 roubles for about three years. That would save me from imprisonment. Nor is such a hope entirely without foundation. But I must do the business personally ; if I attempted it from here, I might spoil all. The plan has nothing to do with my literary activities. At the same time, if my present novel should make a success, my hopes for these 5,000 roubles would be sensibly improved. This is all between ourselves.

Till next time, my dears.

Your
DOSTOEVSKY.

LX

To Nikolay Nikolayevitch Strachov

DRESDEN,
October 9 [21], 1870

I have not written to you till now, because I have been uninterruptedly occupied with the novel for the *Roussky Viestnik*. The work was going so badly, and I had to re-write so much, that at last I vowed to myself that I would read nothing and write nothing, and hardly even raise my head from my desk, until I had accomplished what I had set myself to do. And I am only at the beginning now ! It is true that many scenes belonging to the middle of the novel are ready written, and separate bits of what I have rejected I shall still be able to use. Nevertheless, I am still at work on the earliest chapters. That is a bad omen, and yet I mean to make the thing as good as may be. The truth is that the tone and style of a story must make themselves. But true as that is, one occasionally loses one's note, and has to find it again. In a word : none of my works has given me so much trouble as this one. At the beginning, that is at the end of last year, I thought the novel very " made " and artificial, and rather scorned it. But later I was overtaken by real enthusiasm, I fell in love with my work of a sudden, and made a big effort to get all that I had written into good trim. Then, in the summer, came a transformation : up started a new, vital character, who insisted on being the real hero of the book ; the original hero (a most interesting figure, but not worthy to be called a hero) fell into the background. The new one so inspired me that I

once more began to go over the whole afresh. And
now, when I have already sent the beginning to
the office of the *Roussky Viestnik*, I am suddenly
possessed with terror—I fear that I am not equal to
the theme I have chosen. This dread torments me
horribly. And yet I have not arbitrarily dragged in
my hero. I arranged for his entire rôle in the
synopsis of the book (I prepared a synopsis in several
sheets, and sketched therein the entire action, though
without the dialogues and comments). Therefore I
hope that I may still bring off this hero, and even
make him a quite new and original figure; I hope
and fear simultaneously. For it is really time that I
wrote something important at last. Perhaps it will
all burst up like a soap-bubble. But come what come
will, I must write; the many re-fashionings have lost
me much time, and I have very little ready . . .

[The rest is concerned with journalism and the
Sarya.]

LXI

To Apollon Nikolayevitch Maikov

DRESDEN,
December 15 [27], 1870.

I have undertaken a task to which my powers are
not equal. I attacked a big novel (a novel " with a
purpose " — most unusual for me), and at first I
thought I should manage it quite easily. But what
has been the issue? When I had tried about ten
settings, and saw what the theme demanded, I got
very much out of heart with the thing. The first
part I finished because I simply had to (it is very
long, about ten sheets; and there are to be four parts

in all), and sent it off. I believe that that first part is
empty and quite ineffective. From it the reader
can't at all perceive what I'm aiming at, or how the
action is to develop. The *Roussky Viestnik* people
expressed themselves quite flatteringly about this
beginning. The novel is called "The Possessed"
(they are the same "possessed" about whom I wrote
to you before), and has a motto from the Gospels. I
want to speak out quite openly in this book, with no
ogling of the younger generation. I can't possibly
say all I should like in a letter.

[He then speaks of his account with the publisher
Stellovsky.]

LXII

To Apollon Nikolayevitch Maikov

DRESDEN,
December 30, 1870.

Yes, I am resolute to return, and shall certainly be
in Petersburg early in the year. Here, I am constantly in such a frightful state of mind that I can
hardly write at all. Work is dreadfully difficult to
me. I follow Russian and German happenings with
feverish interest ; I have been through much in these
four years. It has been a strenuous, if a lonely,
existence. Whatever God shall send me in the
future, I will humbly accept. My family, too,
weighs heavily on my mind. In a word, I need
human intercourse.

Strachov has written to me that everything in our
society is still fearfully puerile and crude. If you
knew how acutely one realizes that from here ! But

if you knew, besides, what a deep-drawn repulsion,
almost approaching hatred, I have conceived for the
whole of Western Europe during these four years!

My God, how terrible are our prepossessions with
regard to foreign countries! Are Russians simple-
tons, then, that they can believe it is through their
schooling that the Prussians have come off con-
querors? Such a view is positively sinful: it's a fine
schooling whereby children are harassed and tormented, as it were by Attila's horde, and even worse.

You write that the national spirit of France is in
revolt against brute force. From the beginning I
have never doubted that if only the French will not
hasten to make peace, if they will but hold out for as
much as three months, the Germans will be driven
forth with shame and ignominy. I should have to
write you a long letter if I tried to give you a
series of my personal observations—for example,
of the way in which soldiers are sent to France,
how they are recruited, equipped, housed and fed,
transported. It is extraordinarily interesting. An
unfortunate poverty-stricken woman, say, who lives
by letting two furnished rooms (rooms are all "furnished" here; she would have about twopence worth
of furniture of her own) . . . such a woman is
forced, because she "has her own furniture," to
supply quarters and food for ten soldiers. The
quartering lasts a day, or two, or three—at most a
week. But the business costs her from twenty to
thirty thalers.

I have myself read letters from German soldiers in
France to their parents (small business-folk). Good
God, the things they have to tell! O, how ill they
are, and how hungry! But it would take too long to

relate.   One more observation, though, I'll give you :
at first, one often heard the people in the streets
singing the "Wacht am Rhein": now, one *never
hears it at all*.   By far the greatest excitement and
pride exists among the professors, doctors, and
students ; the crowd are but little interested.   Indeed, they are very quiet.   But the professors are
extraordinarily arrogant.   I encounter them every
evening in the public library.   A very influential
scholar with silver-white hair loudly exclaimed, the
day before yesterday, " Paris must be bombarded !"
So that's the outcome of all their learning.   If not of
their learning, then of their stupidity.   They may be
very scholarly, but they're frightfully limited !   Yet
another observation : all the populace here can read
and write, but every one of them is terribly unintelli-
gent, obtuse, stubborn, and devoid of any high ideals.
But enough of this.   Till we meet.   I embrace you
and thank you in anticipation.   For God's sake don't
forget me, and do write to me.

Your
DOSTOEVSKY.

LXIII

To Apollon Nikolayevitch Maikov

DRESDEN,
March 2 [14], 1871.

[At first the topic is a pending transaction between
Dostoevsky and the publisher Stellovsky.]

I was delighted by your very flattering opinion of
the beginning of my novel.   My God, how I feared
for that book, and how I still fear !   By the time you
read these lines, you will have seen the second half of

the first part in the February number of the *Roussky Viestnik*. What do you say to it? I am terribly anxious. I can't at all tell if I shall get on with the sequel. I am in despair. There are to be only four parts in all—that is, forty sheets. Stepan Trofimovitch[1] is a figure of superficial importance; the novel will not in any real sense deal with him; but his story is so closely connected with the principal events of the book that I was obliged to take him as basis for the whole. This Stepan Trofimovitch will take his "benefit" in the fourth part; his destiny is to have a most original climax. I won't answer for anything else, but for *that* I answer without limitations. And yet I must once more say: I tremble like a frightened mouse. The idea tempted me, and I got tremendously carried away by it; but whether I shall bring it off, whether the whole novel isn't a [. . .[2]]—well, that's my great trouble.

Only think: I have already had letters from several quarters congratulating me on the first part. This has enormously encouraged me. I tell you quite truthfully, with no idea of flattering you, that your judgment has more weight with me than any other. In the first place, I know that you are absolutely frank; in the second, your letter contains an inspired saying: "*They are Turgenev's heroes in their old age.*" That's admirably said! As I wrote, some such idea hovered before me; but you have expressed it in a word or two, in a formula, as it were. Aye—for those words I thank you; you have illuminated the whole book thereby. The work goes very heavily forward; I feel unwell, and soon now

---

[1] Verchovensky in "The Possessed."

[2] Here is the letter D and four dots.

returns the period of my frequent attacks. I am afraid I shall not be ready in time. But I do not mean to hurry. True, I have thoroughly constructed and thoroughly studied my plan; nevertheless, if I hurry, I may spoil the whole thing. I have quite decided to return in the spring.

[Henceforth he writes of the journals *Besyeda* and *Sarya*.]

LXIV

To Nikolay Nikolayevitch Strachov

DRESDEN,
April 23 [*May* 5], 1871.

[In the first half of the letter Dostoevsky advises Strachov on no account to abandon his critical work.]

As a consequence of the colossal revolutions which are taking place in politics as well as in the narrower literary sphere, we behold general culture and capacity for critical judgment momentarily shattered and undone. People have taken it into their heads that they have no time for literature (as if literature were a pastime—fine culture, that!); in consequence of which the level of literary taste is so terribly low that no critic of to-day, however remarkable he may be, can have his proper influence on the public. Dobrolyubov's and Pissarev's successes really derive from their having totally ignored any such thing as literature, that sole domain of intellectual and spiritual vitality here below. But one must not reckon with such phenomena; one is bound to continue

one's critical work.   Forgive my offering you advice :
but that is how I should act, were I in your place.

In one of your brochures there was a wonderful
piece of observation which nobody before you has
made, namely, that every writer of any significance,
any authentic talent, has finally yielded to national
sentiment and become a Slavophil.   Thus, for
example, the facile Pushkin created, long before any
of the Slavophils, that figure of the Chronicler in
the monastery at Tchudov [1] — that is to say, he
grasped, far better than all the Kireyevskys, Chom-
yakovs, etc., the inmost essence of Slavophilism.
And then, look at Herzen : what a longing, what a
need, to strike into the true path !   Only because of
his personal weaknesses did he fail to do it.   Nor is
that all : this law of the conversion to nationality is
not only to be observed in writers and poets, but in
all other directions.   So that one can in the end set
up yet another law : if any man has genuine talent,
he will have also that impulse to return to the people
from the crumbling upper regions of society ; but if
he has no talent, he will not only remain in those
crumbling regions, but even exile himself to foreign
lands, or turn to Catholicism, or what not.

Bielinsky, whom you even to-day admire, was, as
regards talent, feeble and impotent ; therefore he condemned Russia and, in full consciousness of what he
was doing, reviled his native land (people will have
much to say of Bielinsky in the future, and then
you'll see).   But I want only to say one thing more :
that idea which you have expressed is enormously
important, and demands further and more specialized
treatment.

[1] A scene in Pushkin's drama of " Boris Godounov."

Your letters give me great delight. But about your last opinion on my novel I want to say this to you : first, you praise far too highly those excellencies which you find therein ; second, you point with admirable acumen to its principal fault. Yes, that was and ever is my greatest torment—I never can control my material. Whenever I write a novel, I crowd it up with a lot of separate stories and episodes ; therefore the whole lacks proportion and harmony. You have seen this astonishingly well ; how frightfully have I always suffered from it, for I have always been aware that it was so. And I have made another great mistake besides : without calculating my powers, I have allowed myself to be transported by poetic enthusiasm, and have undertaken an idea to which my strength was not equal. (N.B. The force of poetic enthusiasm is, to be sure, as for example with Victor Hugo, always stronger than the artistic force. Even in Pushkin one detects this disproportion.) But *I* destroy myself thereby.

I must further add that the move to Russia and the many anxieties which await me in the summer, will immensely injure the novel. Anyhow, I thank you for your sympathy. What a pity it is that we shall not see one another for so long. In the meantime

I am your most devoted

FYODOR DOSTOEVSKY.

LXV

To Nikolay Nikolayevitch Strachov

DRESDEN,
May 18 [30], 1871.

MUCH-ESTEEMED NIKOLAY NIKOLAYEVITCH,

So you really *have* begun your letter with
Bielinsky, as I foresaw.   But do reflect on Paris and
the Commune.   Will you perchance maintain, as
others do, that the whole thing failed simply because
of the lack of men, and as a result of unfavourable
circumstances ?   Through the whole of this 19th
century, that school has dreamed of the setting-up of
earthly paradises (for instance, the phalansteries), and
then, directly it came to action (as in the years 1848,
1849, and now), has shown a contemptible incapacity
for any practical expression of itself.   At bottom, the
entire movement is but a repetition of the Russian
delusion that men can reconstruct the world by reason
and experience (Positivism).   But we have seen enough
of it by now to be entitled to declare that such impotence as is displayed can be no chance phenomenon.
Why do they cut off heads ?   Simply because it's the
easiest of all things to do.   To say something sensible
is far more difficult.   Effort is, after all, a lesser
thing than attainment.   They desire the common
good, but when it comes to defining " good," can
only reiterate Rousseau's aphorism—that " good " is
a fantasy never yet ratified by experience.   The
burning of Paris is something utterly monstrous :
" Since we have failed, let the whole world perish !"
—for the Commune is more important than the world's
weal, and France's !   Yet they (and many others) see

in that madness not monstrosity, but only *beauty*.
Since that is so, the æsthetic idea must be completely
clouded over in the modern mind. A moral basis
(taken from Positivist teachings) for society is not
only incapable of producing any results whatever, but
can't possibly even define itself to itself, and so must
always lose its way amid aspirations and ideals.
Have we not sufficient evidence by this time to be
able to prove that a society is not thus to be built up,
that quite otherwhere lie the paths to the common
good, and that this common good reposes on things
different altogether from those hitherto accepted?
On what, then, *does* it repose? Men write and write,
and overlook the principal point. In Western Europe
the peoples have lost Christ (Catholicism is to blame),
and therefore Western Europe is tottering to its fall.
Ideas have changed—how evidently! And the fall
of the Papal power, together with that of the whole
Romano-German world (France, etc.)—what a co-
incidence!

All this would take long wholly to express, but
what I really want to say to you is: If Bielinsky,
Granovsky, and all the rest of the gang, had lived to
see this day, they would have said: " No, it was not
to this that we aspired! No, this is a mistake; we
must wait a while, the light will shine forth, progress
will win, humanity will build on new and healthier
foundations, and be happy at last!" They would
never admit that their way can lead at best but to the
Commune or to Felix Pyat. That crew was so obtuse
that even *now*, after the event, they would not be
able to see their error, they would persist in their
fantastic dreaming. I condemn Bielinsky less as a
personality than as a most repulsive, stupid, and

humiliating phenomenon of Russian life. The best
one can say for it is that it's inevitable.   I assure you
that Bielinsky would have been moved, to-day, to
take the following attitude : " The Commune has
accomplished nothing, because before all things it was
French—that is to say, was steeped in nationalism.
Therefore we must now seek out another people,
which will not have the tiniest spark of national
feeling, but will be ready, like me, to box its mother's
(Russia's) ears." Wrathfully he would continue to
foam forth his wretched articles ; he would go on
reviling Russia, denying Russia's greatest phenomena
(such as Pushkin), so that he might thus make Russia
seem to turn into an *empty* nation, which might take
the lead in universal human activities. The Jesuitry
and insincerity of our prominent public men, he would
regard as great good fortune. And then, for another
thing : you never knew him ; but I had personal
intercourse with him, and now can give his full
measure. The man, talking with me once, reviled
the Saviour, and yet surely he could never have
undertaken to compare himself and the rest of the
gentry who move the world, with Christ. He was
not capable of seeing how petty, angry, impatient,
base, and before all else covetous and vain, they,
every one of them, are. *He* never asked himself the
question : " But what can we put in His place ? Of
a surety not ourselves, so evil as we are ?" No ; he
never reflected in any sort of way upon the possibility
that he might be evil ; he was to the last degree
content with himself, and in that alone is expressed
his personal, petty, pitiable stupidity.

You declare that he was gifted. He was not, in
any way. My God, what nonsense Grigoryev did

write about him !   I can still remember my youthful
amazement when I read some of his purely æsthetic
efforts (as, for instance, on " Dead Souls ") ; he treated
Gogol's characters with incredible superficiality and
lack of comprehension, and merely rejoiced insanely
that Gogol had *accused* somebody.   In the four years
of my sojourn here abroad, I have re-read all his
critical writings.   He reviled Pushkin, when Pushkin
dropped his false note, and produced such works as
the " Tales of Bielkin," and " The Negro of Peter
the Great."   He pronounced the " Tales of Bielkin "
to be entirely valueless.   In Gogol's " Carriage," he
perceived not an artistic creation, but a mere comic
tale.   He wholly abjured the conclusion of " Eugène
Onegin."   He was the first to speak of Pushkin as a
courtier.   He said that Turgenev would never make
an artist ; and he said *that* after he had read Turgenev's very remarkable tale of " The Three Portraits."
I could give you, on the spur of the moment, countless proofs that he had not an atom of critical sense,
nor that " quivering sensibility " of which Grigoryev
babbled (simply because he too was a poet).

We regard Bielinsky and many another of our
contemporaries through the still enduring glamour of
fantastic judgments.

Did I really write you nothing about your article
on Turgenev ?   I read it, as I read all your writings,
with great delight, but at the same time with some
degree of vexation.   Once you had admitted that
Turgenev has lost grasp, that he has no idea what to
say about certain manifestations of Russian life (he
jeers at them, every one), you were bound to admit
as well that his artistic powers are at ebb in his recent
work—for it could not be otherwise.   But on the

contrary you hold that his recent work is on the
same level with his earlier. Can both statements be
accepted? Possibly I am myself mistaken (not in
my judgment of Turgenev, but in my interpretation
of your article). Perhaps you have merely expressed
yourself confusedly. . . . Know this: all that school
is no more than "Landed-proprietor's Literature."
And that kind of literature has said all it had to say
(particularly well in the case of Leo Tolstoy). It has
spoken its last word, and is exempt from further
duty. A new school that may take its place is still
to come ; we have not had time to produce it. The
Reschetnikovs[1] have said nothing. Nevertheless, the
works of a Reschetnikov demonstrate the necessity
for a new note in literature, which shall replace that
of the landed proprietors—however repellently such a
writer expresses himself.

[He then speaks of his return to Petersburg and of
the *Sarya*.]

N.B. Dostoevsky did return to Petersburg on
July 8, 1871.

LXVI

To Mme. Ch. D. Altschevsky.

PETERSBURG,
April 9, 1876.

You write that I am squandering and abusing my
talents on bagatelles in the *Diary*. You are not the
first from whom I have heard that. And now I want

---

[1] Reschetnikov, a novelist " with a purpose " of the 'sixties, one
of the foremost pioneers of the free-thinking " Narodniki " school,
which advocates absorption into the people.

to say this to you and others : I have been driven to
the conviction that an artist is bound to make himself
acquainted, down to the smallest detail, not only with
the technique of writing, but with everything—current no less than historical events—relating to that
reality which he designs to show forth.   We have
only one writer who is really remarkable in that
respect : it is Count Leo Tolstoy.   Victor Hugo,
whom I extraordinarily admire as a novelist (only
think : Tchutchev, who is now dead, once got
positively angry with me on account of this view of
Hugo, and said that my " Raskolnikov " was much
greater than Hugo's "Misérables")—is certainly prone
to be too long-winded in his description of details,
but he gives us most marvellous effects of observation, which would have been lost to the world but for
him.   As I am now purposing to write a very big
novel, I must devote myself most especially to the
study of actuality: I don't mean actuality in the literal
sense, for I am fairly well versed in that, but certain
peculiarities of the present moment.   And in this
present moment the younger generation particularly
interests me, and, as akin to it, the question of
Russian family-life, which, to my thinking, is to-day
quite a different thing from what it was twenty years
ago.   Also many other questions of the moment
interest me.

At fifty-three,[1] I might easily, were I to slacken at
all in this respect, fail to keep pace with the growing
generation.   Lately I had a chance encounter with
Gontscharov, and I asked him whether all the
phenomena of the present moment were comprehen-

[1] Discrepancy as to his age here, but so both in German and
French texts.

sible to him ; he answered quite frankly that there
was much he could not understand at all. (N.B. This
between ourselves.) Of course, I know that Gontscharov, with his remarkable intelligence, not only
understands it all, but is competent to instruct the
instructors of the day ; but in the peculiar sense in
which I put the question (and which he at once
understood) he does not even desire to grasp these
phenomena. "My ideals, and all that I have prized
in life, are far too dear to me," he added ; "and for
the few years that I have yet to live, I mean to abide
by them ; it would go too hard with me to study
these gentry" (he pointed to the crowd that was
flowing past us) "for I should be obliged to use up in
so doing the time which is so precious to me. . . ."
I don't know if you'll understand me, revered Chris-
tina Danilovna : I greatly desire to write something
more, and to do so with complete knowledge of my
subject ; for that reason I shall study a while longer
and put down my impressions in the *Diary of a
Writer*, so that nothing may be wasted. Of course
it's merely an ideal to which I aspire ! You won't
believe me at all, I daresay, when I declare that I
haven't yet discovered the right form for the *Diary*,
and don't know in the least if I shall ever really
succeed in discovering it ; the *Diary* might perfectly well run for two years longer, and yet be a
complete failure as a piece of work. For example,
imagine this : when I set to work, I always have
from ten to fifteen themes available ; but those
themes which strike me as particularly interesting, I
always save up for another time ; if I make use of
them at once, they take up too much of my space,
they demand my whole energy (as, for example, in

the case of Kroneberg[1]), and the number turns out a
bad one—and so forth.   Therefore I write of things
that are not at all so near to me.

On the other hand, the idea of making it a genuine
Diary was really naïve in me.   A genuine Diary is
almost impossible ; it can only be a work cut about
to suit the public taste.   Every minute I come upon
facts, receive impressions, that often carry me away
—but there are some things about which one can't
possibly write. . . .

The day before yesterday, early, there come to me
quite unexpectedly two young girls, both about
twenty years old.   They come and say: " We have
long wanted to make your acquaintance.   Everyone
laughed at us, and declared that you would not
receive us, and that even if you did, you would not
care to talk with us.   But we determined to make
the attempt, and so here we are.   Our names are so-
and-so."   They were first received by my wife, I
came out later.

They told me that they were students at the
Academy of Medicine, that there were at that
Academy as many as five hundred women-students,
and that they had entered there " to obtain higher
education, so as later to be able to do useful work."
I had never before seen girls of that sort (of the
earlier Nihilists I know a number, and have studied
them thoroughly).   Believe me, I have seldom passed
my time so agreeably as in the company of those two
girls, who remained with me a couple of hours.   Such
wonderful spontaneity, such freshness of feeling, such

---

[1] *Diary of a Writer,* February, 1876 ; a sensational lawsuit
against a certain Kroneberg, who had long inhumanly treated his
seven-year-old daughter.

purity of heart and mind, such *grave sincerity, and such sincere mirth!* Through them I came, later, to know many such girls, and must confess that the impression they made on me was powerful and pleasant. But how am I to describe all that? Despite my sincerity, and the delight with which I regard these young people, I cannot possibly do it. The impression was of almost too personal a nature. But then, what impressions *am* I to put down in my *Diary?*

Or another instance: yesterday I heard the following story. A young man, a student at an institution which I do not wish to name (I happened to make his acquaintance), is visiting friends, goes accidentally into the tutor's room, and sees a *forbidden* book lying on the table; he instantly tells the master of the house, and the tutor is instantly dismissed. When, in another household, someone told this young man that he had been guilty of a *base action*, he could not in the least see it. There you have the reverse of the medal. But how am I to write about *that?* The thing is in one way of a purely personal nature; and yet the processes of reflection, and the temper, of that young man who cannot at all perceive the baseness of his action, about which I should have much of interest to say, are typical wholly, and not personal at all.

But I have written too much about all this. The truth is, I find it terribly difficult to write letters; I have no talent for it. Forgive me, also, for the bad handwriting; I have a headache, it is *la grippe*—my eyes have been paining me all day, and I write this almost without seeing my characters.

LXVII

To Vsevolod Solovyov [1]

Ems,
July, 1876.

On my departure I left several quite personal and even pressing affairs unattended to. But here, at this tedious spa, your letter has literally refreshed me and gone straight to my heart ; I was already feeling much troubled—I don't myself know why it should be so, but every time I come to Ems, I undergo a mood of tormenting, wholly groundless, more or less hypochondriacal, depression. Whether it arises from my isolation in the crowd of 8,000 " patients," or from the climate of this place, I can't decide ; but I am always in a worse state here than almost anybody else is. You write that you must speak with me, and how dearly I should like to see you !

The June number of the *Diary* pleased you, then. I am glad of that, and for a special reason. I had never yet permitted myself to follow my profoundest convictions to their ultimate consequences in my public writing—had never said my *very last word.* A very intelligent correspondent in the provinces once, indeed, reproached me for opening up so many important questions in my *Diary*, yet never thoroughly discussing them ; he encouraged me, and urged me to be more daring. So I decided that I *would* for once say the last word on one of my convictions— that of Russia's part and destiny among the nations —and I proclaimed that my various anticipations would not only be fulfilled in the immediate future, but were already partly realized.

[1] Vsevolod Solovyov, author of some popular historical novels ; brother of Vladimir Solovyov, the philosopher.

And then there happened precisely what I had
expected : even those newspapers and magazines
which are friendly to me raised an outcry, saying that
my whole article was hopelessly paradoxical ; while
the others bestowed not the smallest attention on it—
and here am I, who believe that I have opened up
the most important of all questions ! That's what
happens when one attempts to carry an idea to its
issue ! One may set up any paradox one likes, and
so long as one doesn't carry it to its ultimate conclusion, everyone will think it most subtle, witty,
comme il faut ; but once blurt out the last word, and
quite frankly (not by implication) declare : "This is
the Messiah !" why, nobody will believe in you any
more—for it was so silly of you to push your idea to
its ultimate conclusion ! If many a famous wit, such
as Voltaire, had resolved for once to rout all hints,
allusions, and esotericisms by force of his genuine
beliefs, to show the real Himself, he would quite
certainly not have had a tithe of the success he
enjoyed. He would merely have been laughed at.
For man instinctively avoids saying his last word ; he
has a prejudice against "thoughts said."

"Once said, the thought turns lie !" [1]

Now you can judge for yourself how precious to
me are your friendly expressions about the June
number. For you have understood my words and
taken them exactly as I thought them myself. I
thank you for that ; for I was already a little dis-
illusioned, and was reproving myself for my pre-
cipitancy. If there are but a few members of the
public who understand me as you do, I have done
what I aimed at doing, and am content—my words

[1] From a poem by Tchutchev.

have not been in vain. . . . But the rest at once proclaimed with cries of joy : " He *is* so frightfully paradoxical !" And the folk who say it are precisely those who never had an idea of their own in their lives. . . .

I remain here till August 7 (Old Style). I am drinking the waters, and indeed would never be able to make up my mind to endure this place were I not convinced that the cure is really good for me. It's certainly not worth while to describe Ems ! I have promised the public to bring out a double number of the *Diary* in August ; as yet I haven't written a single line ; from sheer boredom I've got so apathetic that I regard the work before me with reluctance, as if it were an imminent misfortune. I already feel that the number will be very bad. At any rate, write to me again while I'm here, my dearest fellow. . . .

LXVIII

To Mlle. Gerassimov

PETERSBURG,
March 7, 1877.

MUCH-HONOURED MLLE. GERASSIMOV !
Your letter has tormented me terribly, because I could not answer it for so long. What can you have thought of me ? In your dejected state, you will perhaps have taken my silence as an affront.

You must know that I am almost overwhelmed with work. Besides the work for the periodically appearing *Diary*, I have to get through a quantity of letters. I receive daily several letters of the same kind as yours, which cannot possibly be disposed of in a few lines. Moreover, I have lately suffered from three attacks of epilepsy, and those of such violence and quick recurrence as I have not had for years. After each attack, I was bodily and mentally so shattered that for two and three days I could not work or write, or even read. Now you know that, you will forgive my long silence.

I did not think your letter by any means *childish* or *stupid*, as you assume. For that mood is now general, and there are many young girls suffering like you. But I don't mean to write much on that theme; I shall only lay before you my fundamental ideas upon the subject, both in general, and as it concerns you personally. If I advise you to settle down, to stay in your parents' house, and take up some intelligent occupation (corresponding to the course of your education), you won't be much inclined to listen to me. But why are you in such a hurry, why should you so dread any delay? You want to do something *useful* as soon as possible. And yet, with your ardour (I am taking it for granted that it is genuine), you could—if you don't act precipitately, but pursue your education a little longer—prepare yourself for activities which would be a *hundred times* more useful than the obscure and insignificant rôle of a sick-nurse, midwife, or woman-doctor. You urgently desire to enter the Medical High School for Women here. I should like to advise you decidedly not to do so. You will get no education there, but quite the contrary. And what do you gain, if you actually do become a mid-wife or woman-doctor? Such a calling—if you really do expect so much from it—you could quite well take up later on; but would it not be better now if you pursued other ends, and took pains with your general education? Do but look at all our specialists (even the University professors); why are they all losing ground, and whence comes the harm that they do (instead of doing good) to their own profession? It is simply because the majority of our specialists are shockingly ill-educated people.　In other lands it is quite different: there we find a Humboldt or a Claude Bernard, persons with large ideas, great culture and knowledge outside of their special job. But with us, even highly-gifted people are incredibly uneducated; for example, Syetchenov,[1] who at bottom is uneducated and knows nothing beyond his narrow special subject; of his scientific adversaries (the philosophers) he has no notion whatever; therefore his scientific efforts are more harmful than useful.　And the majority of our students—men and women—have no true education.　How then can they be useful to humanity!　They study only just enough to get paid appointments as soon as may be. . . .

LXIX
To A. P. N.

May 19, 1877.

MUCH-HONOURED ALEXANDER PAVLOVITCH,

Will you be so very good as to excuse my not having answered you for so long?　Not until to-day have I been able to leave Petersburg for a while; I have been terribly busy, and my illness added to my troubles.　But what am I to write to you now? You are intelligent enough to perceive that the questions you put to me are abstract and nebulous; besides, I have no personal knowledge whatever of you. I too strove for sixteen years with doubts similar to yours; but somehow or other I was certain that

---

[1] A renowned Russian physiologist.

sooner or later I should succeed in finding my true path, and therefore did not torment myself overmuch. It was more or less unimportant to me what position I might come to occupy in literature; in my soul was a certain flame, and in that I believed, troubling myself not at all as to what should come of it. There are my experiences, since you ask me for them.

How should I know your heart? If you will hear my counsel, I advise you to trust without hesitation to your own inward impulse; perhaps destiny may point you to a literary career. Your claims are indeed most modest, for you ask no more than to be a worker of the second rank. I should like to add this: my own youthful impulse hindered me in no wise from taking a practical grasp of life; it is true I was a writer, not an engineer; nevertheless, during my whole course at the College of Engineering, from the lowest to the highest class, I was one of the best students; later I took a post for a while, although I knew that sooner or later I should abandon that career. But I saw nothing in the career itself which could thwart that to which I aspired; I was even more convinced than before that the future belonged to me, and that I alone should control it. In the same way, if an official position does not hinder you in the pursuit of your literary vocation, why should you not temporarily undertake such an one?

Naturally I write all this at random, since I do not know you personally; but I want to be of service to you, and so answer your letter as frankly as possible. As to all the rest, it is, in great part, exaggeration.

Permit me to press your hand.

Your

FYODOR DOSTOEVSKY.

LXX
To N. L. Osmidov

PETERSBURG,
February, 1878.

MY DEAR AND KIND NIKOLAY LUKITCH,

Let me beg you, first, to forgive my having, by reason of illness and various bothers, taken so long to answer you. In the second place, what can I say in reply to your momentous question, which belongs to the eternal problem of humanity? Can one treat such matters in the narrow compass of a letter? If I could talk with you for some hours, it would be a different thing; and even then I might well fail to achieve anything. Least of all by words and argument does one convert an unbeliever. Would it not be better if you would read, with your best possible attention, all the epistles of St. Paul? Therein much is said of faith, and the question could not be better handled. I recommend you to read the whole Bible through in the Russian translation. The book makes a remarkable impression when one thus reads it. One gains, for one thing, the conviction that humanity possesses, and can possess, no other book of equal significance. Quite apart from the question of whether you believe or don't believe. I can't give you any sort of idea. But I'll say just this: Every single organism exists on earth but to live—not to annihilate itself. Science has made this clear, and has laid down very precise laws upon which to ground the axiom. Humanity as a whole is, of course, no less than an organism. And that organism has, naturally, its own conditions of existence, its own laws. Human reason comprehends those laws. Now suppose that there is no God, and no personal immortality (personal immortality and God are one and the same—an identical idea). Tell me then: Why am I to live decently and do good, if I die irrevocably here below? If there is no immortality, I need but live out my appointed day, and let the rest go hang. And if that's really so (and if I am clever enough not to let myself be caught by the standing laws), why should I not kill, rob, steal, or at any rate live at the expense of others? For I shall die, and all the rest will die and utterly vanish! By this road, one would reach the conclusion that the human organism alone is not subject to the universal law, that it lives but to destroy itself—not to keep itself alive. For what sort of society is one whose members are mutually hostile? Only utter confusion can come of such a thing as that. And then reflect on the " I " which can grasp all this. If the " I " can grasp the idea of the universe and its laws, then that " I " stands above all other things, stands aside from all other things, judges them, fathoms them. In that case, the " I " is not only liberated from the earthly axioms, the earthly laws, but has its own law, which transcends the earthly. Now, whence comes that law? Certainly not from earth, where all reaches its issue, and vanishes beyond recall. Is *that* no indication of personal immortality? If there were no personal immortality, would you, Nikolay Lukitch, be worrying yourself about it, be searching for an answer, be writing letters like this? So you can't get rid of your " I," you see ; your " I " will not subject itself to earthly conditions, but seeks for something which transcends earth, and to which it feels

DOSTOEVSKY'S STUDY IN PETERSBURG.

DOSTOEVSKY, PETERSBURG, 1879.

itself akin.   But whatever I write falls short altogether—as it must.   I cordially press your hand, and take my leave.   Remain in your unrest—seek farther—it may be that you shall find.

Your servant and true friend,

F. DOSTOEVSKY.

LXXI

To a Mother

PETERSBURG,
March 27, 1878.

MUCH-HONOURED LADY!

Your letter of February 2nd I am answering only to-day, after a month's delay.   I was ill and very much occupied, and so beg you not to take amiss this dilatoriness.

You set me problems which one could treat only in long essays, and assuredly not in a letter.   Moreover, life itself can alone give any answer to such questions.   If I were to write you ten sheets, some misunderstanding, which would easily be cleared up in a verbal interview, might cause you to take me up quite wrongly, and therefore to abjure my whole ten sheets.   Can one, in general, when wholly unacquainted, and especially in a letter, treat of such matters at all?   I consider it quite impossible, and believe that it may do more harm than good.

From your letter I gather that you are a good mother, and are very anxious about your growing child.   I cannot, though, at all imagine of what service to you would prove the solution of the questions with which you have turned to me: you set yourself too hard a task, and your perplexities are exaggerated and morbid.   You should take things much more simply. You ask me, for instance, "What is good, and what is not good?" To what do such questions lead? They concern you alone, and have nothing whatever to do with the bringing-up of your child. Every human being, who can grasp the *truth* at all, feels in his conscience what is good and what is evil. Be good, and let your child realize that you are good; in that way you will wholly fulfil your duty towards your child, for you will thus give him the immediate conviction that people ought to be good. Believe me, it is so. Your child will then cherish your memory all his life with great reverence, it may be often with deep emotion as well. And even if you do something wrong—that is, something frivolous, morbid, or even absurd—your child will sooner or later forget all about it, and remember only the good things. Mark me: in general, you can do no more than this for your child. And it is really more than enough. The memory of our parents' *good* qualities —of their love of truth, their rectitude, their goodness of heart, of their freedom from false shame and their constant reluctance to deceive—all this will sooner or later make a new creature of your child: believe me. And do not think that this is a small thing. When we graft a tiny twig on a great tree, we alter all the fruits of the tree thereby.

Your child is now eight years old; make him acquainted with the Gospel, teach him to believe in God, and that in the most orthodox fashion. This is a *sine qua non;* otherwise you can't make a fine human being out of your child, but at best a *sufferer*, and at worst—a careless lethargic "success," which is a still more deplorable fate. You will never find anything better than the Saviour anywhere, believe me.

Suppose now that your child at sixteen or seventeen (after some intercourse with corrupted school-friends) comes to you or to its father, and puts this question: " Why am I to love you, and why do you represent it as my duty ?" Believe me : no sort of " questions" or knowledge will help you then ; you won't be able to give any answer. Therefore it is that you must try to act so that it *will never once occur to your child to come to you with that question*. But that will be possible only if your child is attached to you by such love as would prevent such a question from ever coming into its head ; true, that at school such views may be for a while your child's, but you will find it easy to separate the false from the true ; and even if you *should* really have to listen to that question, you will be able to answer with just a smile, and quietly go on doing well.

If you grow superfluously and exaggeratedly anxious about your children, you may easily affect their nerves and become a nuisance to them ; and that might happen even though your mutual love were great ; therefore you must be careful and cultivate moderation in all things. It seems to me that in this respect you have no sense at all of moderation. In your letter, for example, occurs the following sentence : " If I live for them (that is, my husband and children), it is an egotistic life ; dare I live thus egotistically, when all round me are so many people who need my help?" What an idle and unprofitable thought ! What hinders you from living for others, and yet remaining a good wife and mother ? On the contrary : if you live for others also and share with them your earthly goods and the emotions of your heart, you set your children a

radiant example, and your husband will necessarily
love you still better than before.   But since such
questions come into your head at all, I must assume
that you consider it to be your duty so to cleave to
your husband and your children that thereby you
forget all the rest of the world—that is to say, without any moderation.   In that way you could but
become a burden to your child, even if it loved you.
It may easily befall that your sphere of activity will
suddenly seem to you too narrow, and that you will
aspire to a wider one, perhaps a world-wide one.
But has anyone at all any right to aspire to that ?

Believe me : it is uncommonly important and
useful to set a good example even in a narrow sphere
of activity, for in that way one influences dozens and
hundreds of people.   Your purpose, never to lie but
to live in truth, will make those who surround you
think, thus influencing them.   That in itself is a great
deed.   In such ways you can do an enormous
amount.   It were truly senseless to throw all aside,
and rush with such questions to Petersburg, meaning
thereafter to enter the Academy of Medicine or the
High School for Women.   I meet here daily such
women and girls ; what frightful narrowness I see in
them !   And all who once were good for something
are ruined here.   Seeing no serious activity in their
environment, they begin to love humanity theoretic-
ally, by the book as it were ; they love humanity, and
scorn the individual unfortunate, are bored in his
company, and therefore avoid him.

I really don't know how I am to answer your
questions, for I don't understand these matters at all.
When a child betrays an evil character, it is of course
attributable to the evil tendencies which are inborn in

him (it is beyond doubt that every human being is born with evil tendencies), as well as to those who have his bringing-up in hand, and are either incapable or lazy, so that they neither *suppress* those tendencies nor (by their own example) lead them into other directions. Of the usefulness of *that* work I really need not speak. If you inculcate good propensities in your child, the work will bring its own delight. Now enough : I have written you a lot, and have tired myself, yet have really said little ; but you will no doubt understand me.

With all respect, your most obedient servant,

FYODOR DOSTOEVSKY.

P.S. Peter the Great, with his revenue of one and a half millions, might well have led an easy lethargic existence at the Tsar's Palace in Moscow ; and yet he worked hard all his life. He always wondered at those who do not work.

LXXII

To a Group of Moscow Students[1]

PETERSBURG,
April 18, 1878.

MUCH-HONOURED GENTLEMEN,

Forgive my not having answered you for so long ; I was definitely ill, and other circumstances besides delayed my answer. I wished, originally, to reply to you through the newspapers ; but it appeared that, for reasons against which I am powerless, this

---

[1] On April 3, 1878, students demonstrating against the arrest of some colleagues at Kiev, were assaulted and beaten in the public streets by the butchers (the Moscow meat-market is near the University). A group of the students appealed to Dostoevsky in a letter of protest.

was not feasible; and, anyhow, I could not have
treated your questions with the necessary circumstan-
tiality in the press.   But indeed, what can I say to
you in any kind of a letter ?   Your questions touch
upon the *whole* interior life of Russia : do you want
me to write you a book ?   Am I to make you my
full confession of faith ?

Well, finally I have decided to write you this
short letter, wherein I risk being completely misunderstood by you—a result which would be most
painful to me.

You write : " It is of paramount importance that
we should solve the problem of how far we are to
blame in the affair, and what conclusions society, no
less than we ourselves, should draw from these incidents ?"

You go on to indicate very adroitly and precisely
the true significance of the relations between the
contemporary Russian press and the younger generation at the Universities.

In our press there prevails (with regard to you) " a
tone of condescension and indulgence."   That is very
true ; the tone is indeed condescending, and fashioned
in advance upon a certain pattern, no matter what
the case ; in short, it is to the last degree insipid and
antiquated.

You write further : " Plainly we have nothing
more to expect from these people, who for their part
expect nothing more from us, and so turn away,
having pronounced their annihilating judgment of us
as ' savages.' "

That also is true : *they do indeed turn away from
you*, and dismiss you, for the most part, from their
thoughts (at any rate, the overwhelming majority do

so). But there *are* men, and those not few in number both on the press and in society, who are horribly perturbed by the thought that the younger generation has broken with *the people* (this, first in importance) and with society. For such is actually the case. The younger generation lives in dreams, follows foreign teaching, cares to know nothing that concerns Russia, aspires, rather, to instruct the fatherland. Consequently it is to-day *beyond all doubt* that our younger generation is become the prey of one or other of those political parties which influence it wholly from outside, which care not at all for its interests, but use it simply as a contribution —as it were lambs for the slaughter—to their own particular ends. Do not contradict me, gentlemen, for it is so.

You ask me, gentlemen : " How far are we students to blame for the incidents ?" Here is my answer : I hold that you are in no wise to blame. For you are but children of the very society from which you now turn away, as from " an utter fraud." But when one of our students thus abjures society, he does not go to the people, but to a nebulous " abroad "; he flees to Europeanism, to the abstract realm of fantastic " Universal Man," thus severing all the bonds which still connect him with the people : he scorns the people and misjudges them, like a true child of that society with which he likewise has broken. And yet—with the people lies our whole salvation (but this is a big subject). . . . Nevertheless, the younger generation should not be too harshly blamed for this rupture with the people. What earthly opportunity has it had, before entering on practical life, to form any ideas whatever *about* the people ? The worst of

it is, though, that the people has already perceived
that the younger Russian intelligences have broken
with it; and still worse again is the fact that those
young men whom it has marked down, are by it
designated as "students." The people have long, so
long as from the beginning of the 'sixties, been watch-
ful of these young men; all those among them who
"went to the people" have been abhorred by the
people. The people call them "these young gentlemen." I know for certain that they are so called. As
a matter of fact, the people also are wrong, for there
has never yet been a period in our Russian life when
the young men (as if with a foreboding that Russia
has reached a certain critical point, and is on the
edge of an abyss) were, in the overwhelming majority
of cases, so honest, so avid for the truth, so joyfully
willing to devote their lives to truth, and every word
that truth can speak, as they are now. In ye is
veritably the great hope of Russia! I have long felt
it, and have already long been writing in that sense.
But what has come of it now, all at once? Youth is
seeking that truth of which it is so avid—God knows
where! At the most widely diverse sources (another
point in which it resembles the utterly decadent
Russo-European society which has produced it); but
never in the people, never in its native soil. The
consequence is that, at the given decisive moment,
neither society nor the younger generation *knows the
people*. Instead of living the life of the people, these
young men, who understand the people in no wise,
and profoundly scorn its every fundamental principle
—for example, its religion—go to the people *not* to
learn to know it, but condescendingly to instruct and
patronize it: a thoroughly aristocratic game! The

people call them " young gentlemen," and rightly.
It is really very strange ; all over the world, the
democrats have ever been on the side of the people ;
with us alone have the democratic intellectuals
leagued themselves with the aristocrats against the
people ; they go among the people " to do it good,"
while scorning all its customs and ideals. Such scorn
cannot possibly lead to love !

Last winter, at your demonstration before the
Kazan Cathedral,[1] the rank and file forced their way
into the church, smoked cigarettes, desecrated the
temple, and made a scandal. " Now listen to me,"
I should have said to those students (I *have* said it to
many of them, as a matter of fact), " you do not
believe in God, and that is your own affair ; but why
do you insult the people by desecrating its temple ?"
The people once more retorted with its " young
gentlemen," and, far worse, with " students "—though
there were numbers of obscure Jews and Armenians
among the offenders (the demonstration was, as we
now know, a political one, and organized from outside). In the same way, after the Sassulitch[2] case,
the people dubbed all the revolver-heroes " young
gentlemen." That is bad, though there actually *were*
students among them. Bad is it too that the people
should have marked down the students, and should
treat them maliciously and inimically. You yourselves, gentlemen, in accord with the intellectual
press, designate the people of Moscow as " butchers."
What may that mean ? Why are " butchers " not
members of the people ? They *are*, and of the true

[1] The Cathedral of Our Lady, at Kazan in Petersburg.
[2] Vera Sassulitch, a notorious Terrorist, was tried for a political
crime, but was acquitted by the jury.

people ; was not the great Minin[1] a butcher ? Many
are at this moment enraged by the manner in which
the people has chosen to express its feelings. But
mark this : when the people is offended, it always
manifests its emotion in that manner. The people is
rough, for it consists of peasants. The whole thing
was in reality but the breaking out of a misunderstanding which has existed, time out of mind (and
has hitherto been merely unperceived), between the
people and society, that is to say, the younger generation, which stands for fieriness and rash impulses.
The thing certainly was very ill done, and not at all
as it ought to have been, for with fists one can
demonstrate nothing. But so it has been ever and
everywhere, with every people. The English often
come to blows at their public meetings ; the French
sang and danced before the guillotine, while it did its
work. But the fact remains that the people (the
whole people, not only the " butchers " ; it is poor
consolation to call names) has revolted against the
younger generation, and has marked down the
students ; on the other hand, it is true, we must
acknowledge the no less perturbing fact (and very
significant it is) that the press, society, and the young
men have conspired to misjudge the people, and to
say : " This is no people, but a mob."

Gentlemen, if you find anything in my words which
contravenes your views, your best plan will be not to
get angry with me about it. There is trouble enough
without that. In our putrid society, nothing reigns
but sheer deception. It can no longer hold together
by its own strength. The people alone is strong and
steadfast, but between society and the people there

[1] Minin was a national hero in the interregnum of 1610-13.

have reigned for the last ten years most terrible misunderstandings.   When our sentimentalists freed the
people from serfdom, they believed, in full tide of
emotion, that the people would instantly take to its
bosom that European fraud which they call civilization.
But the people showed itself to be very independent,
and now it is beginning to realize the insincerity of
the upper stratum in our society.   The events of the
last couple of years have but strengthened it, and
made many things clear to its eyes.   Nevertheless,
the people *can* distinguish between its enemies and
its friends.   Assuredly many sad and deplorable facts
must be recognized : sincere, honest young men,
earnestly seeking the truth, went on their quest to
the people, trying to alleviate its woes.   And what
happened ?   The people drove them away, and refused
to recognize their honest efforts.   For those young
men hold the people to be otherwise than as it is ;
they hate and despise its ideals, and offer it remedies
which it cannot but regard as senseless and crazy.

With us in Petersburg the devil is indeed let
loose.   Among the young men reigns the cult of the
revolver, and the conviction that the Government is
afraid of them.   The people, now as ever, despises the
young men, and reckons not at all with them ; but
they do not perceive that the people has no fear of
them and will never lose its head.   What, when
another encounter takes place, will come of it ?
Gentlemen, we live in disquieting times !

I have written you, gentlemen, what I could.   At
any rate I have, though not sufficiently at length,
answered your question : In my view, the students
are in no wise to blame, but the contrary ; our youth
was never yet so sincere and honest as now (a fact

which has its significance, great and historical). But unhappily our youth bears about with it the whole delusion of our two centuries of history. Consequently it has not the power thoroughly to sift the facts, and is in no sense to blame, particularly as it is an interested party in the affair (and, moreover, the offended party). Blessed, none the less, be those who shall find the right path in these circumstances ! The breach with environment is bound to be much more decisive than the breach between the society of to-day and to-morrow, which the Socialists prophesy. For if one wants to go to the people and remain with the people, one must first of all learn not to scorn the people ; and this it is well-nigh impossible for our upper class to do. In the second place, one must believe in God, which is impossible for Russian Europeans (though the genuine Europeans of Europe do believe in God).

I greet you, gentlemen, and, if you will permit me, grasp your hands. If you want to do me a great pleasure, do not, for God's sake, regard me as a preacher who sets up to lecture you. You have called upon me to tell you the truth with my soul and conscience, and I have told you the truth as I see it, and as best I can. For no man can do more than his powers and capacities permit him.

Your devoted,
FYODOR DOSTOEVSKY.

LXXIII
To Mlle. N. N.

PETERSBURG,
April 11, 1880.

MUCH-HONOURED AND GRACIOUS LADY,

Forgive my having left your beautiful kind letter unanswered for so long; do not regard it as negligence on my part. I wanted to say something very direct and cordial to you, but my life goes by, I vow, in such disorder and hurry that it is only at rare moments that I belong to myself at all. Even now, when at last I have a moment in which to write to you, I shall be able to impart but a tiny fragment of all that fills my heart, and that I should like to touch upon with you. Your opinion of me is extraordinarily precious to me; your lady-mother has shown me the passage in your letter to her which relates to myself, and your words moved me profoundly, nay! even astonished me: for I know that as a writer I have many faults, and even I myself am never satisfied with myself. I must tell you that in those frequent and grievous moments wherein I seek to judge myself, I come to the painful conclusion that in my works I never have said so much as the twentieth part of what I wished to say, and perhaps *could*, actually, have said. My only refuge is the constant hope that God will some day bestow upon me such inspiration and such power as are requisite to bring to full expression all that fills my heart and imagination. Recently there took place here the public debate by the young philosopher Vladimir Solovyov (a son of the renowned historian) of his

thesis for Doctor's degree; and I heard him make
the following profound remark: "I am firmly convinced that mankind *knows much more* than it has
hitherto expressed either in science or art." Just so
it is with me: I feel that much more is contained in
me than I have as yet uttered in my writings. And
if I lay all false modesty aside, I must acknowledge
that even in what I *have* written, there is much that
came from the very depth of my heart. I swear to
you that though I have received much recognition,
possibly more than I deserve, still the critics, the
literary newspaper critics, who certainly have often
(no, rather, very seldom) praised me, nevertheless
have always spoken of me so lightly and superficially
that I am obliged to assume that all those things
which my heart brought forth with pain and tribula-
tion, and which came directly from my soul, have
simply passed unperceived. From this you can
divine what a pleasant impression must have been
made upon me by the delicate and searching comments on my work which I read in your letter to
your lady-mother.

But I am writing only of myself, which after all in
a letter to the discerning and sympathetic critic whom
I perceive in you is natural enough. You write
to me of the phase which your mind is just now
undergoing. I know that you are an artist—a painter.
Permit me to give you a piece of advice which truly
comes from my heart: stick to your art, and give
yourself up to it even more than hitherto. I know,
for I have heard (do not take this ill of me) that you
are not happy. To live alone, and continually to
reopen the wounds in your heart by dwelling upon
memories, may well make your life too drear for

endurance. There is but one cure, one refuge, for that
woe : art, creative activity. But do not put it upon
yourself to write me your confession : that would
assuredly tax you too far. Forgive me for offering
you advice ; I should very much like to see you and
say a few words face to face. After the letter that
you have written, I must necessarily regard you as
one dear to me, as a being akin to my soul, as my
heart's sister—how could I fail to feel with you ?
But now to what you *have* told me of your inward
duality. That trait is indeed common to all . . .
that is, all who are not wholly commonplace. Nay,
it is common to human nature, though it does not
evince itself so strongly in all as it does in you. It
is precisely on this ground that I cannot but regard
you as a twin soul, for your inward duality corre-
sponds most exactly to my own. It causes at once
great torment, and great delight. Such duality
simply means that you have a strong sense of yourself, much aptness for self-criticism, and an innate
feeling for your moral duty to yourself and all mankind. If your intelligence were less developed, if you
were more limited, you would be less sensitive, and
would not possess that duality. Rather the reverse :
in its stead would have appeared great arrogance.
Yet such duality is a great torment. My dear, my
revered Mlle. N. N., do you believe in Christ and in
His commandments ? If you believe in Him (or at
least have a strong desire to do so), then give yourself
wholly up to Him ; the pain of your duality will be
thereby alleviated, and you will find the true way
out—but belief is first of all in importance. Forgive
the untidiness of my letter. If you only knew how
I am losing the capacity to write letters, and what a

difficulty I find it ! But having gained such a friend as you, I don't wish to lose her in a hurry.

Farewell. Your most devoted and heartfelt friend,

F. DOSTOEVSKY.

LXXIV

To Frau E. A. Stackenschneider

STARAYA-ROUSSA,
July 17, 1880.

MUCH-ESTEEMED ELENA ANDREYEVNA,

I must call upon all your humanity and indulgence when I ask you to forgive me for having left your beautiful kind letter of June 19 so long unanswered. But I shall beg you to consider facts ; you may then perhaps find it in your power to be indulgent even to me. On June 11 I returned from Moscow to Staraya-Roussa, was frightfully tired, but sat down at once to the " Karamazovs," and wrote three whole sheets at one blow. After I had sent off the MS., I applied myself to the reading of all the newspaper articles that dealt with my speech at Moscow (I had been so busy till then that I had had no time for them), and I decided to write a rejoinder to Gradovsky ; it was to be not so much an answer to him as a manifesto of our faith for all Russia : for the significant and moving crisis in the life of our society which declared itself at Moscow, during the Pushkin celebrations, was deliberately misrepresented by the press, and thrust of set purpose into the background. Our press, particularly that of Petersburg, was alarmed by this new development, which is indeed without parallel : society has plainly shown that it has had enough of the everlasting jeering and spitting at Russia, and is consequently desirous of something different.   But that fact had of course to be distorted, hushed-up, laughed at, misrepresented: "Nothing of the sort!   It was but the general beatitude after the opulent Moscow banquets.   The gentlemen had simply over-eaten themselves."   I had already decided, at Moscow, to publish my speech in the *Moskovskoie Viedomosti*,[1] and to bring out a number of the *Diary* immediately afterwards in Petersburg; in that number, which, by-the-bye, will be the only one this year, I thought of printing my speech, with a preamble, moreover, which occurred to me the very instant I had finished speaking—on the platform itself, at the moment when, together with Aksakov and the rest, even Turgenev and Annenkov rushed up to cover me with kisses, and then shook hands with me, protesting over and over again that I had done great things.   God grant they're of the same opinion still!

I can vividly imagine how they *now* criticize my speech, having recovered from their first enthusiasm —and indeed this is precisely the theme of my preamble.   When the speech, with the preamble, had been sent to the printers in Petersburg, nay, when I actually had the proofs in my hands, I suddenly resolved to write yet another chapter for the *Diary* in the shape of my *profession de foi* for Gradovsky; it grew into two sheets, I put my whole soul into the article, and have sent it to the printers only this very day.   Yesterday was Fedya's birthday. We had visitors, but I sat apart and finished the article.   So you see that you must not take it ill that

[1] *The Moscow News.*

I am answering your letter only now. I dearly love you, as you well know! I could never give my Moscow impressions in a letter, still less my present state of mind. I am filled up with work—it is real hard labour. I want to have the fourth and last part of " The Brothers Karamazov " ready in September at all costs, and when I return to Petersburg in the autumn, I shall be comparatively free for a while ; in that clear time I want to get myself ready for the *Diary*, with which I propose to go on in the coming year 1881.

Are you on a summer holiday ? How did the Moscow news reach you ? I don't know what Gayevsky may have told you, but the affair with Katkov was not a bit like what you think. The Society of Lovers of Russian Literature, which organized the festival, seriously insulted Katkov by asking him to return the invitation-card which he had originally received ; Katkov had made his speech at the banquet held by the Town Council, and at the Town Council's request. Turgenev had no grounds whatever for anticipating any affront from Katkov ; Katkov was much more justified in dreading some sort of annoyance. For Turgenev there had been prepared so colossal a reception (by Kovalevsky and the University people) that he really had nothing to fear. Turgenev insulted Katkov first. When, after Katkov's speech, such men as Ivan Aksakov went up to clink glasses with him (even his opponents did that), Katkov stretched out his hand with the glass in it to Turgenev, that they, too, might clink ; but Turgenev drew his hand away, and would not. So Turgenev himself told me.

You ask me to send you my speech. But I have

DOSTOEVSKY, MOSCOW, 1880.

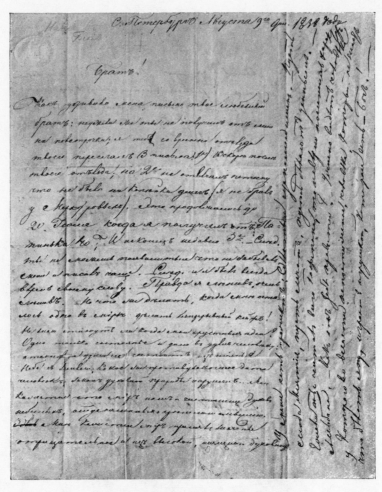

DOSTOEVSKY'S HANDWRITING IN 1838.
(LETTER TO HIS BROTHER MICHAEL, AUGUST 9.)

not a single transcript of it, and the only copy is at the printers, where the *Diary* is now being set up. The *Diary* will appear about August 5 ; bestow some attention on that number, and show it, also, to my dear collaborator, Andrey Andreyevitch. I should like to hear his opinion too.

Your devoted
DOSTOEVSKY.

LXXV
To N. L. Osmidov

STARAYA-ROUSSA,
August 18, 1880.

MUCH-ESTEEMED NIKOLAY LUKITCH !

I have read your letter very attentively ; but how am I to answer it ? You remark yourself, most justly, that one can't really say anything at all in a letter. I too am of opinion that one can deal only with quite ordinary matters in any satisfactory way. But besides that, it really would be idle for you to come even personally for advice to me, for I don't consider myself competent to resolve your questions. You write that hitherto you have given your daughter nothing that is purely literary to read, lest her fancy should become over-developed. This does not appear to me entirely a right point of view ; for fancy is an inborn capacity of human beings ; in a child, it outweighs all others, and should most undoubtedly be nourished. For if we give a child's imagination no nourishment, it may easily die out, or, on the other hand, may over-develop itself from its own sheer force, which is no less undesirable. For such an abnormal over-development prematurely exhausts the child's mental powers. And impressions of the beautiful, moreover, are precisely in childhood of the greatest importance.

When I was ten years old, I saw at Moscow a performance of " Die Räuber,"[1] with Motchalov in one of the chief parts, and I can only say that the deep impression which that performance made upon me has worked most fruitfully ever since upon my whole mental development.   At twelve, I read right through Walter Scott during the summer holidays ; certainly such reading did extraordinarily stimulate my imagination and sensibility, but it led them into good, not evil, paths ; I got from it many fine and noble impressions, which gave my soul much power of resistance against others which were seductive, violent, and corrupting.   So I advise you to give your daughter *now* the works of Walter Scott, and all the more, because he is for the moment neglected by us Russians, and your daughter, when she is older, will have neither opportunity nor desire to make acquaintance with that great writer ; therefore hasten now, while she is still in her parents' house, to introduce him to her.   Besides, Walter Scott has a high educational value.   She should also read all Dickens's works without exception.   Make her acquainted, too, with the literature of past centuries (" Don Quixote," " Gil Blas," etc).   It would be best for her to begin with poetry.   She should read all Pushkin, verse as well as prose.   Gogol likewise.   If you like, Turgenev and Gontscharov as well ; as to my own works, I don't think that all of them are suitable for your daughter. It would be well for her to read Schlosser's " Weltgeschichte," and Solovyov's Russian history ; nor should she omit Karamsin.   Don't give her Kosto-

[1] A tragedy by Schiller.

marov as yet.   The "Conquest of Peru and Mexico"
by Prescott is most necessary.   In general, historical
works have immense educational value.   She should
read Leo Tolstoy all through; also Shakespeare,
Schiller, and Goethe; these writers are to be had in
good Russian translations.   That will be enough for
the present.   With time, in a few years, you will see
yourself that there is much besides.   Journalistic
reading should, in the beginning at any rate, be kept
from her.   I don't know if my advice will commend
itself to you.   I write after much reflection, and out
of my own personal experience.   I shall be very glad
if it is really of use to you.   I think a personal visit
from you is quite superfluous at present, and the
more, because I am very much occupied.   But I
must say once again that I am not particularly competent in such matters.

The number of the *Diary* that you asked for
has been sent to you.   It comes, with postage, to
35 kopecks; so the balance of 65 kopecks stands to
your credit with me.

Yours truly and faithfully

F. DOSTOEVSKY.

LXXVI

To I. S. Aksakov

STARAYA-ROUSSA,
August 28, 1880.

MY DEAR AND HONOURED IVAN SERGEYEVITCH,

I meant to answer your first letter by return,
and now, having received your second, so *precious* to
me, I see that I have a great deal to say to you.
Never yet in my life have I found a critic who was so

sincere, and so very sympathetic for my work. I had
almost forgotten that there could be such critics, and
that they actually exist. I don't mean to say by this
that I see absolutely eye-to-eye with you in all things,
but I must, at any rate, point out the following fact :
Although I have been issuing my *Diary* for two years
now, and consequently have some experience, I am
still beset by doubts in many respects—as to what
I am to say about certain matters, what tone I am to
adopt, and on what subjects I should keep silence
altogether. Your letter came just in such a moment
of hesitation, for I have firmly resolved to continue
my *Diary* in the coming year, and so I am much
perturbed, and often put up my prayer to Him on
whom one should ever call for the needful strength,
and above all the needful ability. Thus it peculiarly
rejoices me to have *you ;* for now I see that I can
impart to you at least a portion of my questionings,
and that you can always answer me with something
most frank and far-seeing. This conviction I have
gained from your two last letters. Unfortunately
I should have to write you a lot about all this, and
just now I am very busy, and not at all inclined for
letters. You simply can't imagine how frightfully
busy I am, day and night ; it is real hard labour !
For I am now finishing the " Karamazovs," and consequently summing up the entire work, which is
personally very dear to me, for I have put a great
deal of my inmost self into it. I work, in general,
very nervously, with pain and travail of soul. Whenever I am writing, I am physically ill. And now
I have to sum up all that I have pondered, gathered,
set down, in the last three years. I must make this
work good at all costs, or at least as good as *I* can.

I simply don't know how anyone can write at great speed, and only for the money's sake. Now the time is come when I must wind up this novel, and that without delay. You will hardly believe me: many a chapter, for which I had been making notes all those three years, I was obliged, after finally setting it down, to reject, and write anew. Only separate passages, which were directly inspired by enthusiasm, came off at first writing; all the rest was hard work. For these reasons I can't possibly write to you at the moment, despite my ardent desire; I am not in the requisite state of mind, and moreover I do not wish to dissipate my energies. I shall not be able to write to you until about September 10, when I shall have the work behind me. In the meantime, I shall thoroughly ponder my letter, for the questions in hand are weighty, and I want to present them as lucidly as may be. So do not be angry with me, nor accuse me of indifference; if you only knew what an error that would be on your part!

In the meantime I embrace you, and thank you from my heart. I need you, and must therefore love you.

Your truly devoted
F. DOSTOEVSKY.

LXXVII

To Doctor A. F. Blagonravov[1]

PETERSBURG,
December 19, 1880.

HONOURED ALEXANDER FYODOROVITCH,

I thank you for your letter. You judge very rightly when you opine that I hold all evil to be

[1] Doctor Blagonravov had given Dostoevsky his opinion (from a

grounded upon disbelief, and maintain that he who
abjures nationalism, abjures faith also. That applies
especially to Russia, for with us national consciousness is based on Christianity. " A Christian peasant-
people "; "believing Russia ": these are our
fundamental conceptions. A Russian who abjures
nationalism (and there are many such) is either an
atheist or indifferent to religious questions. And the
converse : an atheist or indifferentist cannot possibly
understand the Russian people and Russian nationalism. The essential problem of our day is : How are
we to persuade our educated classes of this principle ?
If one but utters a word in such a sense, one will
either be devoured alive, or denounced as a traitor.
And whom shall one have betrayed ? Truly, naught
but a party which has lost touch with reality, and for
which not even a label can be found, for they know
not themselves what to call themselves. Or is it the
people whom one shall have betrayed ? No ; for
I desire with the people to abide, for only from the
people is anything worth while to be looked for—not
from the educated class, which abjures the people,
and is not even " educated."

But a new generation is on the way, which will
desire union with the people. The first sign of true
fellowship with the people is veneration and love for
that which the great mass of the people loves and
venerates—that is to say, for its God and its faith.

This new Russian intelligence is beginning, as it
seems to me, to lift its head, and precisely *now* is its
co-operation in the common task essential ; and this
it is coming, itself, to perceive.

physician's point of view), upon the masterly description of the
hallucination of Ivan Karamazov in the last part of the novel.

Because I preach faith in God and in the people, the gentry here would like to see me disappear from the face of the earth. Because of that chapter in the " Karamazovs " (of the hallucination) with which you, as a physician, are so pleased, it has already been sought to stamp me as a reactionary and fanatic, who has come to believe in the Devil. The gentlemen here, in their simplicity, imagine that the public will cry out with one voice : " What ? Dostoevsky has begun to write about the Devil now, has he ? How obsolete and *borné* he is !" But I believe that they will find themselves mistaken. I thank you for having, as a physician, attested for me the authenticity of my description of the psychical sickness of my hero. The opinion of one who is an expert in the matter is very valuable to me ; you will, I doubt not, allow that Ivan Karamazov, in the given circumstances, could have had no different hallucination. I mean to give, in the very next number of the *Diary*, some of the critical pronouncements on that particular chapter.

With the assurance of my sincere respect, I remain

Yours most faithfully
FYODOR DOSTOEVSKY.

Recollections of Dostoevsky
by his Friends

FROM THE REMINISCENCES OF
D. V. GRIGOROVITCH
1837—1846

It is a mystery to me to this day how I, innately the most extraordinarily nervous and timid of boys, ever got through my first year in the College of Engineering, where one's comrades were far more ruthless and cruel even than one's teachers.

Amongst the young men who were admitted to the College after I had been there about a year, was a youth of some seventeen summers, of middle height, full figure, blond hair, and sickly, pale countenance. This youth was Fyodor Michailovitch Dostoevsky. He had come from Moscow to Petersburg with his elder brother Michael. The latter did not enter the College, but joined the Corps of Sappers, and was later sent to Reval on his promotion to commissioned rank. Many years later Michael Dostoevsky took his discharge, and returned to Petersburg. There he started a cigarette manufactory, but at the same time busied himself in literature, translated Goethe, wrote a comedy, and, after Fyodor's return from banishment, became editor of the *Epoch*.

I made friends with Fyodor Dostoevsky the very first day that he entered the College. It's half-a-century ago now, but I can well remember how much

more I cared for him than for any of the other friends
of my youth.　Despite his reticent nature and general
lack of frankness and youthful expansion, he appeared
to reciprocate my affection.　Dostoevsky always held
himself aloof, even then, from others, never took part
in his comrades' amusements, and usually sat in a
remote corner with a book ; his favourite place was a
corner in Class-Room IV. by the window.　Out of
school-hours, he nearly always sat with a book by
that window.

I had, as a boy, a pliant character, and was easily
influenced ; thus my relations with Dostoevsky were
those of not merely attachment, but absolute sub-
jection.　His influence was extraordinarily beneficial
to me.　Dostoevsky was much more advanced in all
knowledge than I was, and the extent of his reading
amazed me.　The many things he told me about the
works of writers, whose very names to me were
unknown, came as a revelation.　Hitherto I had, like
the rest of my colleagues, read nothing but text-
books and abstracts of lectures ; not only because
other books were forbidden in the College, but from
lack of interest in literature.

The first Russian books with which I made
acquaintance I got from Dostoevsky ; they were a
translation of Hoffmann's " Kater Murr " and " The
Confessions of an English Opium-Eater," by Maturin
[sic] ; the latter was especially prized by Dostoevsky.
His literary influence was not confined to me alone ;
three of my colleagues came equally under his spell—
Beketov, Vitkovsky, and Berechetzky ; in this way
a little circle was formed, which gathered round
Dostoevsky in every leisure hour.

This reading, and the interchange of ideas which

it brought about, took from me all inclination for my studies.   Nor did Dostoevsky rank among the best pupils.   Before the examinations he always made the most tremendous efforts, so as to get into a higher class.   But he did not invariably succeed ; in one examination he failed entirely, and was unpromoted. This failure worried him so much that he fell ill, and had to go to hospital for a while.

In 1844 or '45 I met him quite by chance in the street ; he had then completed his studies, and had exchanged military uniform for civilian dress.   I clasped him in my arms with cries of joy.   Even Dostoevsky seemed glad, but behaved with some reticence.   He never was, indeed, given to public displays of emotion.   My delight at this unexpected meeting was so great and genuine that it never even occurred to me to feel hurt by his cool behaviour. I told him about all my acquaintances in literary circles, about my own literary attempts, and at once invited him to come to my abode and hear my latest production.   He willingly agreed.

When I had read him my story he seemed pleased with it, but gave me no very extravagant praise ; with one passage he found fault.   This was how it ran : " When the organ stopped, an official threw a copper coin out of his window, which fell at the organ-grinder's feet."   " No, that's not right," said Dostoevsky, " it is much too dull : ' The copper coin fell at the organ-grinder's feet.'   You should say, ' The copper coin fell *clinking* and *hopping* at the man's feet ' " . . .   That remark struck me as a revelation.

As time went on, I saw more and more of Dostoevsky.   At last we decided to set up house together. My mother sent me fifty roubles a month, Dostoevsky got nearly as much from his relatives in Moscow. As things were then, a hundred roubles was quite enough for two young fellows ; but we did not understand housekeeping, and the money usually lasted us only for the first fortnight ; for the rest of the month we fared on rolls and coffee. The house we lived in was at the corner of Vladimir and Grafen Streets ; it consisted of a kitchen and two rooms, whose three windows looked out on Grafen Street. We had no servants ; we made our own tea, and bought all food ourselves.

When we set up house, Dostoevsky was working at the translation of Balzac's "Eugènie Grandet." Balzac was our favourite writer ; we both considered him by far the most important of the French authors. Dostoevsky succeeded, I know not how, in publishing his translation in the *Book-Lovers' Library ;* I can still recollect how vexed Dostoevsky was when that number of the magazine reached him—the editor had shortened the novel by a third. But that was what Senkovsky, then the editor of the *Library*, always did with his collaborators' works, and the authors were so glad to see themselves in print that they never protested.

My enthusiasm for Dostoevsky was the reason why Bielinsky, to whom Nekrassov introduced me, made quite a different impression upon me from what I had expected. Properly tutored by Nekrassov, I regarded the impending visit to Bielinsky as a great joy ; long beforehand I rehearsed the words in which I should describe to him my admiration for Balzac. But scarcely had I mentioned that my housemate Dostoevsky (whose name was still unknown to Bielinsky) had translated "Eugènie Grandet" than

Bielinsky began to abuse our divinity most terribly :
he called him a writer for the bourgeois, and said that
there was not a page of " Eugènie Grandet " without
some error in taste.   I was so nonplussed that I
forgot every word of the beautifully rehearsed speech.
Probably I impressed him as a stupid boy who could
not say a word in defence of his own opinion.

At that time Dostoevsky would spend whole days,
and sometimes nights, at his desk.   He never said a
word about what he was working at ; he answered
my questions unwillingly and laconically, and I soon
ceased to interrogate him ; I merely saw countless
sheets covered with Dostoevsky's peculiar writing—
every letter as if drawn.   I have seen no writing like
it, except that of Dumas *père*.   When Dostoevsky
was not writing, he would sit crouched over a book.
For a while he raved about the novels of Soulié,
particularly the " Mémoires des Démons."   As a consequence of his hard work and the sedentary life he
led, his health was getting worse and worse ; those
troubles which had occasionally shown themselves
even in his boyhood now became increasingly frequent.   Sometimes he would even have a fit on one
of our few walks together.   Once we chanced to come
on a funeral.   Dostoevsky insisted on turning back
at once ; but he had scarcely gone a few steps when
he had such a violent fit that I was obliged to carry
him, with the help of some passers-by, into the nearest
shop ; it was with great difficulty that we restored
him to consciousness.   Such attacks were usually followed by a state of great depression, which lasted two
or three days.

One morning Dostoevsky called me into his room ;
he was sitting on the divan which served as bed also,

and before him on the little writing-table lay a thickish manuscript-book, large size, with speckled edges.

" Sit down here a while, Grigorovitch ; I only wrote it out fair yesterday and I want to read it to you ; but don't interrupt me," said he, with unusual vivacity.

The work which he then read to me at one breath, with no pauses at all, soon afterwards appeared in print under the title of " Poor Folk."

I always had a very high opinion of Dostoevsky ; his wide reading, his knowledge of literature, his opinions, and the deep seriousness of his character, all extraordinarily impressed me ; I often asked myself how it was that, while I had already written and published a good deal, and so could account myself a literary man, Dostoevsky did not yet share this distinction.   But with the first pages of " Poor Folk " it was borne in on me that this work was incomparably greater than anything that I had so far written ; that conviction increased as he read on.   I was quite enchanted, and several times longed to clutch and hug him ; only that objection of his to effusions of feeling, which I knew so well, restrained me—but I could not possibly sit there in silence, and interrupted him every moment with exclamations of delight.

The consequences of that reading are well-known. Dostoevsky has himself related in his *Diary* how I tore the manuscript from him by force, and took it to Nekrassov forthwith. He has indeed out of modesty said nothing of the reading to Nekrassov. I myself read the work aloud. At the last scene, when old Dyevuchkin takes leave of Varenyka, I could no longer control myself, and broke into sobs. I saw that Nekrassov also was weeping. I then pointed out to him that a good deed should never be put off, and that, in spite of the late hour, he should instantly betake himself to Dostoevsky, to tell him of his success and talk over the details of the novel's appearance in the magazine.

Nekrassov too was very much excited; he agreed, and we really did go straight off to Dostoevsky.

I must confess that I had acted rashly. For I knew the character of my housemate, his morbid sensibility and reserve, his shyness—and I ought to have told him all quite quietly next morning, instead of waking him in the middle of the night, and, moreover, bringing a strange man to visit him.

Dostoevsky himself opened the door to our knocking; when he saw me with a stranger, he was frightfully embarrassed, turned pale, and for a long time could make no response to Nekrassov's eulogiums. When our guest had gone, I expected that Dostoevsky would overwhelm me with reproaches. But that did not happen; he merely shut himself up in his room, and for a long time I heard him walking excitedly up and down.

After Dostoevsky had in this way come to know Nekrassov, and through him Bielinsky too (for the latter, also, soon read " Poor Folk " in manuscript), he was suddenly as if metamorphosed. During the printing of the novel he was continually in a state of the most excessive nervous excitement. His reserve went so far that he never told me a word of what further ensued between him and Nekrassov. I heard indirectly that he exacted from Nekrassov that his novel should be set up in quite peculiar type, and that every page should have a sort of framing. I was not present at the negotiations, and cannot therefore say whether these rumours were founded on truth.

One thing I can decidedly say : the success of "Poor Folk," and still more the extravagant eulogiums of Bielinsky, had a bad influence on Dostoevsky, who till then had lived wholly shut in with himself and had associated only with people who took no interest at all in literature. How could such a man as he have remained in his normal condition of mind, when at his very first entrance to the literary career, an authority like Bielinsky prostrated himself before him, and loudly proclaimed that a new star had arisen in Russian literature ? Soon after " Poor Folk," Dostoevsky wrote his novel " Mr. Prochartchin," which likewise was read aloud to Nekrassov ; I was invited to the reading. Bielinsky sat opposite the author, listened greedily to every word, and now and then expressed his delight—saying over and over again that nobody but Dostoevsky was capable of such psychological subtleties.

But perhaps Bielinsky's enthusiasm had less effect on him than the subsequent complete revulsion in Bielinsky's appreciation and that of his circle.

About that time Bielinsky said in a letter to Annenkov : " Dostoevsky's ' Mistress of the Inn ' is terrible stuff ! He has attempted a combination of Marlinsky[1] and Hoffmann, with a dash of Gogol. He has written other novels besides, but every new work of his is a new calamity. In the provinces they can't stand him at all, and in Petersburg even ' Poor Folk ' is abused ; I tremble at the thought that I

---

[1] Alexander Bestuchev (pseudonym, Marlinsky), 1795-1837, a novelist very popular at that period.

shall have to read this novel once more. We've been well taken in by our ' gifted ' Dostoevsky !"

So Bielinsky wrote, the most honest man in the world, and he meant every word of it most honestly and thoroughly. Bielinsky never flinched from declaring his opinion of Dostoevsky, and all his circle echoed him.

The unexpected transition from idolization of the author of " Poor Folk" to complete denial of his literary talent might well have crushed even a less sensitive and ambitious writer than Dostoevsky. Thenceforth he avoided all those who were connected with Bielinsky's circle, and became more reserved and irritable than ever. At a meeting with Turgenev, who likewise belonged to Bielinsky's set, Dostoevsky unhappily lost control of himself, and all the anger which had gathered in him flamed forth ; he said that he was not afraid of any one of them, and would tread them all into the mud in time. I forget what was the immediate cause of the outbreak ; I think they were speaking of Gogol, among others. But in any case I am convinced that Dostoevsky was to blame. Turgenev was never given to quarrelling ; he might rather be reproached with too great pliancy and gentleness of character.

After the scene with Turgenev it came to an open breach between Dostoevsky and the Bielinsky set. Now they overwhelmed him with derision and biting epigrams, and he was accused of monstrous conceit ; they said too that he was jealous of Gogol, whom in justice he should adore, since on every page of " Poor Folk " the influence of Gogol was unmistakable.

This last reproach, if it *is* a reproach for a novice, was not quite unjustified. Old Dyevuchkin in " Poor

Folk" does undoubtedly recall Poprischtschin the functionary, in the "Memoirs of a Madman" of Gogol; in the scene where Dyevuchkin loses a button in the presence of his superiors and, much embarrassed, tries to pick it up, one cannot but think of that scene of Gogol's where Poprischtschin tries to pick up the handkerchief which his superior's daughter has dropped, and comes to grief on the parquet floor. Not only the constant use of the same word over and over again, but the whole composition, betrays Gogol's influence.

Once, I forget why, he and I fell out. The consequence was that we decided to give up living together. But we parted on good terms. Later I often met him with acquaintances, and we treated one another as old friends.

FROM THE REMINISCENCES OF
A. P. MILYUKOV
1848—1849

I MADE Dostoevsky's acquaintance in the winter of 1848. That was a momentous period for enthusiastic and cultured youth. After the February Revolution in Paris, the reforms of Pius IX., the risings in Milan, Venice, and Naples, the victory of liberal ideas in Germany and the revolutions of Berlin and Vienna, everyone believed in the renaissance of the whole European world. The rotted pillars of reaction were crumbling one after the other, and all over Europe new life seemed to be in bud. Yet in Russia, at that time, prevailed the most crushing reaction: Science, no less than the Press, could hardly breathe beneath the heavy yoke of the administration, and every sign of mental vitality was stifled. From abroad, a quantity of liberal writings, partly scientific, partly literary, were smuggled into the country. In the French and German papers, people, despite the Censorship, were reading stirring articles; but among ourselves all scientific and literary activity was rendered well-nigh impossible, and the Censorship tore each new book to pieces. Naturally all this had a highly exciting effect upon the younger generation, who on the one hand were, through these foreign books and journals, making acquaintance not only with Liberal ideas, but with the most extreme Socialist doctrine ; and on the other, were finding that the most harmless notions of Liberalism were relentlessly persecuted in their own country—they would read the flaming speeches made in the French Chamber and at Frankfort, and at the same time see how, among ourselves, someone was punished like a criminal every day for an incautious word or a " forbidden " book. Almost every foreign post brought news of fresh rights gained for themselves by the people, while in Russian society one heard only of fresh "special decrees" and persecutions. All who remember that time will know the effect this had upon the younger generation.

There now began to form, in Petersburg, little groups of young men, who for the most part had but recently left the High Schools. These assembled solely to discuss the latest news and rumours, and to express opinions freely. In these groups, new acquaintances were made, and old ones renewed.

I happened in this way to be present at an assembly which took place at the abode of the young writer A. N. Plechtcheyev. I there entered into relations with a set of men whose memories I shall ever cherish. Among others were present : Porfiry Lamansky, Sergey Dourov, Nikolay Monbelli and Alexander Palm, both of whom were officers of the Guards— and the brothers Michael and Fyodor Dostoevsky. All these young men were extraordinarily sympathetic to me. I became particularly intimate with the two Dostoevskys and Monbelli. The latter then lived in barracks, and we used to assemble at his quarters too. I made further acquaintances among his circle, and

learnt that large assemblies took place at the abode
of one M. V. Butachevitch-Petrachevsky, whereat
speeches on political and social questions were made.
Someone offered to take me to Petrachevsky ; but
I declined, not from timidity or indifference, but
because Petrachevsky, whose acquaintance I had
recently made, had not particularly attracted me ; he
held quite too paradoxical opinions, and showed a
certain aversion for all things Russian.

On the contrary I very willingly accepted an
invitation to enter the little group which gathered
about Dourov ; he attracted many who belonged also
to Petrachevsky's set, but embraced more moderate
opinions. Dourov lived at that time with Palm in
Gorochovoya Street. At his small abode there
assembled every Friday an organized circle of young
men, among whom the military element was represented. As the host was of modest means, and the
guests always remained until three o'clock in the
morning, each had to pay a monthly contribution
towards the entertainment, and the hire of a piano.
I attended these evenings regularly, until in consequence of the arrest of Petrachevsky and the members
of his circle, they were suspended.

Dostoevsky also frequented these evenings at
Dourov's. Our circle occupied itself with no revolutionary plans of any kind, and had no written statutes
at all ; in short, it could not possibly be described as
a secret society. We assembled to exchange the then
proscribed books, and to discuss questions which were
not permitted to be openly touched on. Most of all
were we interested in the question of the emancipation of the peasants, and at our meetings we always
spoke of the ways and means to this reform. Some

thought that in view of the reaction which had been
brought about in our country by the European revolutions, the Government would never decide to carry
out the emancipation of the peasants, and that it
would come rather from below than from above ;
others, on the contrary, maintained that our people
had no desire whatever to follow in the footsteps of
the European revolutionaries, and would patiently
await the decision of their fate by the Government.
In this sense, Fyodor Dostoevsky expressed himself
with particular emphasis.   When anybody in his
vicinity declared that the emancipation of the peasants
by the lawful path was most doubtful, he would retort
that he believed in no other path.

We talked too of literature, but chiefly with
reference to remarkable newspaper articles.   Occasionally the older writers were discussed, and very
severe, one-sided, and mistaken judgments often
found expression.   Once when the subject happened
to be Dershavin, and somebody declared that he was
much more of a turgid and servile ode-maker and
courtier than the great poet for which his contemporaries and the schools had taken him, Dostoevsky
sprang up as if stung by a wasp, and cried : " What !
No poetic rapture, no true ardour, in Dershavin ?
His not the loftiest poetry ? "

And forthwith he declaimed from memory a poem
of Dershavin's with such power, with such ardour,
that the singer of Catherine the Great rose at once
in our estimation.   Another time he delivered some
poems of Pushkin and Victor Hugo, similar in subject,
and proved to us, with great success, that our poet
was a much more remarkable artist than the French-
man.

Dourov's circle included many fervent Socialists. Intoxicated by the Utopias of certain foreign theorists, they saw in this doctrine the dawn of a new religion, which one day should remodel the world on the basis of a new social order.   Everything that appeared in French on the question was discussed hotfoot by us. We were always talking about the Utopias of Robert Owen and Cabet, but still more, perhaps, of Fourier's phalanstery, and Proudhon's theory of progressive taxation.   We all took an equal interest in the Socialists, but many refused to believe in the possibility of practically realizing their teachings.   Among these latter was, again, Dostoevsky.   He read all the works on Socialism, it is true, but remained wholly sceptical.   Though he granted that all these doctrines were founded on noble ideals, he nevertheless regarded the Socialists as honest, but foolish, visionaries.   He would say again and again that none of these theories could have any real meaning for us, and that we must find our material for the development of Russian society not in the doctrines of foreign Socialists, but in the life and customs, sanctified by centuries of use, of our own people, in whom had long been apparent far more enduring and normal conceptions than were to be found in all the Utopias of Saint-Simon.   To him (he would say) life in a commune or in a phalanstery would seem much more terrible than in a Siberian prison.   I need not say that our Socialists stuck to their opinions.

All new laws and other actions of the Government were also discussed and severely criticized by us.   In view of the arbitrary rule which prevailed in our country, and the grand events which were coming off in Western Europe, and inspiring us with the hope

of a better and freer mode of existence, our discontent
is wholly comprehensible. In this respect Dostoevsky
showed the same zeal and the same rebellious spirit
as the other members of our circle. I cannot now
remember the actual content of his speeches, but I do
recollect that he ever protested against all measures
which in any way implied the oppression of the
people, and was especially infuriated by those abuses
from which the lowest ranks of society and the
students equally suffered. One could always recognize the author of " Poor Folk " in his judgments.
One of us proposed that discourses should be held in
our assemblies ; each was to write an indictment of
the Government, and read it aloud to the rest ;
Dostoevsky approved this plan, and promised to do
something of the kind. I forget whether he carried
out his promise. The first discourse, which was
given by one of the officers, dealt with an anecdote
which was at that time common talk ; Dostoevsky
found fault both with the subject and the form of
this effort. On one of the evenings, I read a passage
from Lamennais' " Paroles d'un Croyant," which I
had translated into " Church-Russian." Dostoevsky
assured me that the grave Biblical language of my
translation sounded much more impressive than that
of the original. Later on, we resolved to print
several copies of some of our members' papers, and
circulate them widely ; but this plan was never carried
out, for just then the majority of our friends, and
those in particular who had attended the Petrachevsky
evenings, were arrested.

Shortly before the break-up of the Dourov circle,
one of its members had been in Moscow, and had
brought from there a transcript of the famous letter

which Bielinsky had written to Gogol in the course of his "Correspondence with Friends." Fyodor Dostoevsky read this letter aloud both in our circle and in the houses of several of his friends, and also gave it to different people to be transcribed anew. This was subsequently the main pretext for his arrest and banishment. Bielinsky's letter, in its paradoxical one-sidedness, would scarcely impress anyone much at this time of day, but it then produced a remarkable effect upon all minds. Along with this letter, there was then circulating in our set a humorous article by Alexander Herzen (similarly brought from Moscow), in which our two capitals were contrasted no less wittily than maliciously. On the arrest of the Petrachevsky group, I know that numerous copies of these two works were seized. Besides our evenings for discussion and reading, we had musical ones. At our last assembly, a very gifted pianist played Rossini's overture to " William Tell."

On April 23, 1849, I heard, through Michael Dostoevsky, of the arrest of his brother Fyodor, as well as of Dourov, Monbelli, Filippov, and others. A fortnight later, I was told one morning that Michael Dostoevsky also had been arrested the night before. His wife and children were left wholly without means of support, for he had no regular income whatever, and lived entirely by his literary work. As I knew the tranquil and reserved character of Michael Dostoevsky, I was really but little concerned as to his fate ; it is true that he had frequented Petrachevsky, but he had been in disagreement with most members of the circle. So far as I knew, there could be little against him. Therefore I hoped that he would soon be set at liberty. As a matter of fact, he was, at the end of May ; and came to me, early in the morning, to look up his son Fedya, whom I had housed. In the evening of the same day he gave me many particulars of his arrest, of his stay in the fortress, and of the questions which had been put to him by the Committee of Investigation. From these questions we could gather what would be the indictment against Fyodor. Although he was charged only with some rash utterances against high personages and with the dissemination of proscribed writings, and the momentous Bielinsky letter, these things could, with ill-will, be given a very serious turn ; in that case, a grievous fate awaited him. True, that gradually many of those arrested were being set free ; but it was said that many were threatened with banishment.

The summer of 1849 was a sad time for all of us. I saw Michael Dostoevsky every week. The news about our incarcerated friends was very vague ; we knew only that they were all in good health. The investigating committee had now ended its labours, and we daily expected the decision. But the autumn went by, and not until shortly before Christmas was the fate of the prisoners made known. To our utter amazement and horror, they were all condemned to death. The sentence was not, however, as all the world knows, executed ; capital punishment was at the last moment altered to other penalties. Fyodor Dostoevsky got four years' hard labour in Siberia, and after completion of that sentence was to be enrolled as a private in one of the Siberian regiments of the line. All this was done so hastily and suddenly that neither I nor his brother could be present at the proclamation of the sentence on Semyonovsky Square ; we heard of the fate of our friends only when all was at an end,

and they had been taken back to the Petropaulovsky
fortress (except Petrachevsky, who was sent straight
from the tribunal to Siberia).

The prisoners were despatched in parties of two and
three from the fortress to their exile. On the third
day after the sentence, Michael Dostoevsky told me
that his brother was to depart that very evening, and
that he wanted to go and say good-bye to him at the
fortress. I too wished to say good-bye to Fyodor
Dostoevsky. We both went to the fortress, and
applied to Major M., whom we had known in past
days, and through whose mediation we hoped to
obtain permission to see the prisoners. He told us
that it was true that Dostoevsky and Dourov were
to be sent that very evening to Omsk. But permission to see our friends could be got only from the
Commandant of the fortress.

We were conducted into a large room on the
ground-floor of the Commandant's quarters. It was
already late, and a lamp was burning in the room.
We had to wait a very long time, and twice heard
the cathedral-bell of the fortress ring out the hour.
At last the door opened, and there entered, accompanied by an officer, Fyodor Dostoevsky and Dourov.
We greeted them with a mighty shaking of hands.

Despite the long, solitary confinement, neither had
changed at all appreciably ; the one seemed quite as
grave and calm, the other as cheerful and friendly,
as before the arrest. Both already wore the travelling - clothes—sheepskins and felt boots—in which
prisoners were dressed for transportation. The officer
sat unobtrusively at some distance from us on a chair,
and did not disturb our conversation. Fyodor talked
first of all of his joy that his brother had escaped a

similar fate to his ; then he asked with warm interest
for Michael's family, and about all the details of his
life.   During the meeting, he several times recurred
to that theme.   Dostoevsky and Dourov spoke with
genuine liking of the Commandant of the fortress, who
had treated them most humanely and done all that
was in his power to alleviate their lot.   Neither the
one nor the other complained of the stern tribunal, or
the harsh sentence.   The life which awaited them in
prison did not alarm them ; they could not then
foresee the effect which the punishment was to have
upon their health.

When the Dostoevsky brothers took leave of one
another, it was clear to me that not he who had to
go to Siberia, but he who remained in Petersburg,
suffered the more.   The elder brother wept, his lips
trembled, while Fyodor seemed calm and even consoled him.

" Don't do that, brother," he said ; " why, you
know me.   Come, you are not seeing me to my
grave ; even in prison there dwell not beasts but
men, and many of them are possibly better and
worthier than I am. . . .   We shall see one another
again, I am sure of it ; I confidently hope for that,
I have no doubt at all that we shall meet again. . . .
Write to me in Siberia, send me books ; I'll send
word to you from there what books I need ; I shall
surely be allowed to read there. . . .   And when
once I have the prison behind me, I'll write regularly.
During these months I have lived through much in
my soul ; and think of all I shall see and live through
in the future !   I shall truly have plenty of material
for writing. . . ."

He gave one the impression of regarding the impending punishment as a pleasure-trip abroad, in the course of which he should see beautiful scenery and artistic treasures, and make new acquaintances in perfect freedom. He never seemed to realize that he was to spend four years in the " House of the Dead," in chains, in the company of criminals ; perhaps he was full of the thought that he would find in the most fallen criminal those human traits, those sparks of divine fire that, though heaped over with ashes, still glimmer, still are unextinguished—those sparks which, according to his conviction, burn even in the most outcast of mankind, in the most hardened of criminals.

This final meeting lasted over half - an - hour ; although we spoke of many things, the time seemed short. The melancholy bell was sounding again when the Major entered, and said the interview was at an end. For the last time we embraced. I did not then imagine that I should never see Dourov again, and Fyodor Dostoevsky only after eight years

FROM THE MEMORANDA OF P. K. MARTYANOV,[1] AT THE HOUSE OF THE DEAD

1850—1854

THE hardest office which was assigned to us who had been transferred on punishment was keeping guard in the prison.   It was the same one that Dostoevsky has described in his " House of the Dead."   Of those who had been implicated in the Petrachevsky affair, there were then in the prison Fyodor Michailovitch Dostoevsky and Sergey Fyodorovitch Dourov. Whether they had formerly been much known in Petersburg, we are not aware ; but during their stay in the prison their Petersburg friends took the greatest interest in them, and did everything possible to alleviate their lot.

The two young men, once so elegant, made a sad spectacle in the prison.   They wore the usual convict-dress : in the summer, vests of striped grey and black stuff with yellow badges on the back, and white caps with no brims ; in the winter, short sheepskins, caps with ear-flaps, and mittens.   On their arms and legs were chains which clanked at every movement ; so

---

[1] Martyanov's memoranda are based on verbal information from several naval cadets who, on account of participation in the movement of 1849, were degraded, and transferred to the line regiment at Omsk as privates.

that they were in no way externally distinguished from the other prisoners. Only one thing marked them out from the mass : the ineffaceable signs of good education and training. Dostoevsky looked liked a strong, somewhat thickset, well-disciplined working-man. His hard fate had, as it were, turned him to stone. He seemed dull, awkward, and was always taciturn. On his pale, worn, ashen face, which was freckled with dark-red spots, one never saw a smile ; he opened his lips only to utter curt, disconnected remarks about his work. He always wore his cap dragged down on his forehead to his eyebrows ; his glance was sullen, unpropitiating, fierce, and mostly directed on the ground. The prisoners did not like him, though they recognized his moral force ; they looked askance at him, but with no malice, and would tacitly avoid him. He perceived this himself, and so kept aloof from all ; only on very rare occasions, when he was beyond himself with misery, would he draw any of the prisoners into conversation. Dourov, on the contrary, looked like a fine gentleman even in prison clothes. He was well grown, held his head proudly aloft, his large black eyes looked friendly despite their short-sightedness, and he smiled on all and sundry. He wore his cap pushed back on his neck, and even in the worst hours preserved an unalterably cheerful aspect. He treated each individual prisoner amiably and cordially, and all of them liked him. But he suffered much, and was frightfully run down—so much so that sometimes he could not stir a foot. And yet he remained good-tempered, and tried to forget his physical pain in laughter and joking.

From the prison-guard was then demanded much

care, energy, and vigilance.   The guard had to escort
the prisoners to the working-places, and also to super-
vise them in the prison.   The captain of the guard
had to report every morning on the condition of the
prisoners, to look after the cleanliness and discipline
in the prison and the barrack-rooms, to make surprise-
inspections, and prevent the smuggling-in of schnaps,
tobacco, playing-cards, and other forbidden articles ;
his duties, therefore, were arduous and responsible.

The naval cadets of that period were nevertheless
ready to assume these duties in place of the officers,
for in that way they obtained an opportunity of
coming continually under the notice of their superiors,
and at the same time of alleviating, so far as was
feasible, the hard lot of the prisoners.   Most of these
worked outside the prison at the building of the
fortress ; but some were daily kept in to do the
house-work.   These latter came under the immediate surveillance of the guard, and would remain,
unless they were sent to do work of some kind, either
in the orderly-room or in their cells.   In this way the
naval cadets could always keep back any particular
prisoner if they so desired.   For instance, Dostoevsky
and Dourov were often kept back for " house-work ";
the captains of the guard would then send for them
to the orderly-room, where they would tell them the
news, and give them any presents, books, or letters
that might have come for them.   We let them come
into the orderly-room only at such times as we were
sure that no superior officer was likely to appear ;
but, in case of accident, we always kept a soldier in
readiness to take them back to work.   General
Borislavsky, who superintended the labours, and the
Commandant of the fortress, General de Grave, were

made aware of this proceeding by the physician, Doctor Troizky.

According to the cadets' reports, the character of Dostoevsky was not attractive; he always looked like a wolf in a trap, and avoided all the prisoners; even the humane treatment shown by his superiors, and their efforts to be useful to him and alleviate his lot, he took as an injury. He always looked gloomy, and amid the noise and animation of the prison held himself aloof from all; only of necessity did he ever speak a word. When the cadets summoned him to the orderly-room, he would behave with much reserve; he paid no heed to their suggestion that he should sit down and rest, answered most unwillingly the questions put to him, and almost never permitted himself any frankness of speech. Every expression of sympathy he met with mistrust, as if he suspected in it some secret purpose. Even the books that were offered him he hardly ever accepted; only in two cases (they were " David Copperfield " and " the Pickwick Papers ") did he show any interest in the books, or take them to hospital with him. Doctor Troizky explained Dostoevsky's unsociability by the morbid state of his whole organism, which, as everyone knows, was shattered by his nervous troubles and epileptic fits, but outwardly he looked healthy, active, and vigorous; he shared, too, in all the labours of the other convicts. The cadet from whom I obtained this description accounted for Dostoevsky's unsociability by his fear that any relations with others, and the solicitude shown for him, might come to the knowledge of the authorities and injure him with them. Dourov, on the contrary, was universally liked. Despite his sickly, frail appearance, he took an interest in everybody, gladly entered into relationship with people outside the prison, and was cordially grateful for any alleviation or aid that was offered him. He talked, and even argued, freely upon all sorts of subjects, and often succeeded in carrying his audience with him. His open, cordial, and energetic character was apparent to us all, and so he was much better liked than Dostoevsky was.

The cadets observed with amazement that Dostoevsky and Dourov hated one another with all the force of their beings ; they were never seen together, and during their whole time in the prison at Omsk they never exchanged a word with one another. When they both happened to be in the orderly-room at the same time, they would sit in opposite corners and answer any questions they were asked with no more than a Yes or No. This was noticed, and they were thenceforth summoned separately.

When Dourov was interrogated as to this odd behaviour, he answered that neither would condescend to address the other, because prison-life had made enemies of them. And Dostoevsky, though he speaks in his " House of the Dead " of many interesting convicts who were in the prison during his time, never once mentions Dourov, either by his full name or by initials. And when he is obliged to refer to him, he does it thus : " We, that is, I and the other prisoner of noble birth who came to the prison at the same time as I did . . ." Or thus : " I observed with terror one of my prison-mates (of noble birth) who was visibly going out like a candle. When he came to the prison, he was young, handsome, and attractive ; he left it a broken, grey-haired, lame, and asthmatic creature." The head - physician, Doctor Troizky, showed great interest in the political prisoners. He often sent them word by the cadets that they might (one or the other of them) come to him in hospital for cure ; and they frequently did go to hospital for several weeks, and there got good food, tea, wine, and other such things, either from the hospital kitchen or the doctor's own. According to what Doctor Troizky told one of the cadets, Dostoevsky began his " House of the Dead " in hospital, with the doctor's sanction ; for the prisoners were not allowed writing materials without express permission ; the first chapters of that work were long in the keeping of one of the hospital orderlies. General Borislavsky also showed favour to those two, through the medium of his adjutant, Lieutenant Ivanov. By his permission they were put only to the easier labours, except when they themselves desired to share the work of the other convicts. Among these easier labours were included painting-work, the turning of wheels, the burning of alabaster, shovelling of snow, etc. Dostoevsky even got permission to do secretarial work in the office of the Engineering Department ; but when Colonel Marten, in a report to the officer commanding the corps, expressed a doubt whether political offenders condemned to hard labour should be employed in such a manner, this arrangement came to an end.

Once when Dostoevsky had remained behind in the prison for " house-work," there suddenly came into his cell Major Krivzov (whom Dostoevsky later described as a " brute in human form "), to find him lying on his plank-bed.

" What is the meaning of this ? Why is he not at his labour ?" cried the Major.

" He is ill, sir," answered a cadet, who happened to

have accompanied the Major in his capacity as officer of the guard. " He has just had an epileptic fit."

" Nonsense ! I am aware that you indulge him too much. Out to the guard-room with him this instant ; bring the rods !"

While he was being dragged from his plank and pushed along to the guard-room, the cadet despatched an exempt to the Commandant with a report of the occurrence. General de Grave came at once to the guard-room and stopped the whipping ; while to Major Krivzov he administered a public reprimand, and gave orders that in no circumstances were ailing prisoners to be subjected to corporal punishment.

FROM THE REMINISCENCES OF BARON ALEXANDER VRANGEL[1]

1854—1865

WHEN I lived in Petersburg before my transfer to Siberia, I was not acquainted with Fyodor Dostoevsky, though I knew his favourite brother, Michael. I went to see the latter before I left ; when I told him that I was going to Siberia, he begged me to take with me for his brother, a letter, some linen, some books, and fifty roubles. Apollon Maikov also gave me a letter for Fyodor Dostoevsky.

When I reached Omsk at the end of November, I found that Fyodor Dostoevsky was no longer there ; he had completed his time in prison, and had been sent as a private soldier to Semipalatinsk. Soon afterwards, I was obliged, in the course of my duty, to settle for quite a long time at Semipalatinsk.

Destiny thus brought me, exactly five years after the scene on Semyonovsky Square, at which I had happened to be present and which had been so momentous for Dostoevsky, again into contact with him, and that for some years.

On my way to Semipalatinsk I visited Omsk again. There I made the acquaintance of Mme. Ivanova,

---

[1] Baron Alexander Vrangel, as a young student, was present on December 22, 1849, at the ceremony in Semyonovsky Square. He went to Siberia in 1854 as District-Attorney.

who had been very kind to Dostoevsky during his time in prison. She was the daughter of the Decembrist Annenkov and his wife, Praskovya Ivanovna, a Frenchwoman by birth, who, like many another of the Decembrists' wives, had followed her husband into exile. Mme. Ivanova's husband was an officer of the Gendarmerie. She was a wonderfully kind and highly cultured woman, the friend of all unfortunate folk, but particularly of the political prisoners. She and her mother had made Dostoevsky's acquaintance first at Tobolsk, whither he had been brought from Petersburg in the beginning of the year 1850. Tobolsk was then the clearing-house for all offenders transported from European Russia; from Tobolsk they were sent to the other Siberian towns. Mme. Ivanova provided Dostoevsky with linen, books, and money while he was at Tobolsk; at Omsk, too, she looked after him and alleviated his durance in many ways. When, in 1856, I returned to Petersburg, Dostoevsky asked me to visit her, and convey his gratitude for all the goodness she had shown him.

I must observe that the political offenders of that time were, in most cases, much more humanely and cordially treated by their official superiors and by the gentry than in later years. In the reign of Nicholas I. the whole of Siberia was crammed with political offenders, Russians as well as Poles; these were all cultured, liberal persons, absolutely sincere and convinced. But Fyodor Dostoevsky awakened quite peculiar sympathy. He told me himself that neither in the prison nor later during his military service was ever a hair of his head hurt by his superiors or by the other prisoners or soldiers; all the newspaper reports that declare otherwise are pure invention. For it has frequently been maintained that Dostoevsky's fits were brought on by the corporal chastisement he received ; and many appear to believe this legend.

In November, 1854, then, I came to Semipalatinsk. On the morning after my arrival, I betook myself to the Military Governor, Spiridonov. He at once sent his adjutant to look out for rooms for me; and within a few hours I had settled down in my new home. I inquired of the Governor how and where I could find Dostoevsky, and ask him to come to tea with me that evening. Dostoevsky was then living in an abode of his own (and no longer in barracks).

At first he did not know who I was and why I had asked him to come ; so he was in the beginning very reticent. He wore a grey military cloak with a high red collar and red epaulettes ; his pale, freckled face had a morose expression. His fair hair was closely shorn. He scrutinized me keenly with his intelligent blue-grey eyes, as if seeking to divine what sort of person I was. As he confessed to me later on, he had been almost frightened when my messenger told him that the District-Attorney wished to see him. But when I apologized for not having first visited him personally, gave him the letters, parcels, and messages from Petersburg, and showed my friendly feeling, he quickly grew cheerful and confidential. Afterwards he told me that on that first evening he had instinctively divined in me an intimate friend-to-be.

While he read the letters I had brought, tears came into his eyes; I too was overcome by that mysterious sense of despair and desolation which I had so often felt during my long journey. As I was talking with Dostoevsky, a whole pile of letters from my relatives and friends in Petersburg was brought to me. I ran through the letters and suddenly began to sob ; I was at that time unusually emotional and greatly attached to my family. My separation from all who were dear to me seemed insupportable, and I was quite terrified of my future life. So there we were together, both in a desolate and lonely condition. . . . I felt so heavy-hearted that I forgot my exalted position as District-Attorney, and fell on the neck of Fyodor Michailovitch, who stood looking at me with mournful eyes. He comforted me, pressed my hand like an old friend, and we promised one another to meet as often as possible. Dostoevsky was, as is known, discharged from prison early in the year 1854, and sent to Semipalatinsk as a private. At first he lived with the other soldiers in barracks ; but soon, through the influence of General Ivanov, he got permission to live in a private house near the barracks, under the supervision of his Captain, Stepanov. He was under surveillance by his sergeant as well, but the latter left him alone, on receipt of a trifling " recognition."

The early days were the worst for him; the absolute isolation seemed unbearable. But gradually he came to know some of the officers and officials, though there was no close intercourse. Naturally, after the prison, this new condition of things seemed a paradise. Some cultured ladies in Semipalatinsk showed him warm sympathy, most particularly Mme. Maria Dmitryevna Issayev, and the wife of his Captain, Stepanov. The Captain, a frightful drunkard, had been transferred from Petersburg to Siberia for this offence. His wife wrote verses, which Dostoevsky was called upon to read and correct. Mme. Issayev, after her husband's death, became, as everyone knows, Dostoevsky's wife.

In my time, Semipalatinsk was something between a town and a village. All the houses were built of wood. The population was between five and six thousand, including the garrison and the Asiatic merchants. On the left bank of the river there lived about three thousand Circassians. There was an Orthodox church, seven mosques, a large caravanserai, a barracks, a hospital, and the Government offices. Of schools there was only a district one. In some of the shops one could buy anything, from tin-tacks to Parisian perfumes; but there was no book-shop, for there was nobody to buy books. At the most, from ten to fifteen of the inhabitants subscribed to a newspaper; nor was that any wonder, for at the time people in Siberia were interested only in cards, gossip, drinking-bouts, and business. Even in the Crimean War they took no interest, regarding it as an alien, non-Siberian affair.

I subscribed to three papers: a Petersburg one, a German one, and the *Indépendance Belge*. Dostoevsky delighted in reading the Russian and the French ones; he took no particular interest in the German paper, for at that time he did not understand much German, and he always disliked the language.

Between the Tartar and the Cossack suburbs lay the actual Russian town; this region was called the " Fortress," although the fortress had long been razed; only one great stone gate remained. In this region all the military lived; here lay the battalion of the Line, the Horse-Artillery, here were all the authorities, the main guard, and the prison, which was under my control. Not a tree nor a shrub was to be seen; nothing but sand and thorny bush. Dostoevsky lived in a wretched hovel in this part of the town.

Living was then very cheap; a pound of meat cost half a kopeck, forty pounds of buckwheat groats, thirty kopecks. Dostoevsky used to take home from barracks his daily ration of cabbage-soup, groats, and black bread; anything left over, he would give to his poor landlady. He often lunched with me and other acquaintances. His hovel was in the dreariest part of the town. It was of rough timber, crazy, warped, without any foundations, and with not one window looking on the street.

Dostoevsky had a quite large, but very low and badly-lit room. The mud-walls had once been white; on both sides stood broad benches. On the walls hung fly-spotted picture-sheets. To the left of the doorway was a large stove. Behind the stove stood a bed, a little table, and a chest of drawers, which served as a dressing-table. All this corner was divided from the rest of the room by a calico curtain. In the windows were geraniums, and curtains hung there which had once been red. Walls and ceiling were blackened by smoke, and it was so dark in the room that in the evenings one could scarcely read by the tallow candle (wax candles were then a great luxury, and petroleum lamps not known at all). I can't even imagine how Dostoevsky contrived to write for whole nights by such illumination. The lodgings had yet another great attraction: on the tables, walls, and bed there were always perfect flocks of beetles, and in summer the place swarmed with fleas.

Every day made us greater friends. Dostoevsky visited me several times a day, as often as his military and my official duties permitted; he often lunched with me, and particularly enjoyed an evening at my house, when he would drink a vast quantity of tea, and smoke endless cigarettes.

My intercourse with Dostoevsky soon attracted attention in the circle most concerned. I noticed that my letters were delayed for some days in transmission to me. My enemies, and I had not a few among the venal officials, often asked me ironical questions about Dostoevsky, and expressed their surprise at my consorting with a private. Even the Governor warned me, and said that he was afraid of the evil influence which the revolutionary Dostoevsky might have on one of my youth and inexperience.

The Military Governor, Spiridonov, was an uncommonly pleasant, humane, and unaffected man, and noted for his unusual hospitality. Being of such high rank, he was naturally the most important person in the town. I lunched with him every other day, and enjoyed his fullest confidence. I wanted him to have the opportunity of knowing Dostoevsky better, and begged for permission to bring the exile to his house. He pondered this a while, and said: " Well, bring him some time, but tell him that he is to come quite without ceremony in his uniform."

Spiridonov very soon grew to like Dostoevsky; he helped him in every way he could. After the Military Governor had set the example, the better families of Semipalatinsk opened their doors to Dostoevsky.

There were no amusements of any sort in the town. During the two years of my stay, not a single musician came to the place; the one piano

was regarded more as a rarity than anything else.
Once the regimental clerks got up amateur theatricals
in the riding-school. Dostoevsky was very useful in
giving them advice, and persuaded me to be present
on the night. The whole town assembled in the
riding-school.   The fair sex was particularly well
represented.   This performance ended in a great
scandal.   In the pause between two acts, some regimental clerks appeared as soloists, and offered such
indecent ditties for the company's amusement that
the ladies took flight, though the officers, led by the
commander of the battalion, one Byelikov, roared
with laughter.

I can't remember a single dance, picnic, or organized
excursion. Every one lived for himself. The men
drank, ate, played cards, made scandals, and visited
the rich Tartars of the neighbourhood ; the women
busied themselves chiefly with gossip.

In Semipalatinsk there were other political offenders
—Poles and whilom Hungarian officers of Russian-
Polish origin. When Gorgey in 1848 surrendered
with his army to Russia, Tsar Nicholas I. treated the
officers who had been taken prisoners in the war as
though they had been formerly his subjects, and sent
them to Siberia. The Poles kept to themselves, and
held no intercourse with others. The rich ones looked
after the poor, and there prevailed in general great
solidarity among them. Fyodor Dostoevsky did not
like these Poles, and usually avoided them ; we
became acquainted with only one, the engineer
Hirschfeld, who often visited us, and brought a
certain variety into our monotonous life.

I grew fonder and fonder of Dostoevsky ; my
house was open to him day and night.   When I

returned from duty, I often found him there already, having come to me from the drill-ground or the regimental office. He would be walking up and down the room with his cloak unfastened, smoking a pipe, and talking to himself; his head was always full of new ideas. I can still remember distinctly one such evening; he was then occupied with "Uncle's Dream" and "Stepanchikovo Village."

He was in an infectiously cheerful mood, laughing, telling me of his "Uncle's" adventures, singing operatic airs; when my servant Adam brought in some amber-coloured sturgeon soup, he declared that he was hungry, and urged Adam to hurry up with the rest of the meal. He greatly liked this Adam— always stood up for him, and would give him money, which afforded my Leporello, a terrible drunkard, quite superfluous opportunities for "one more."

Fyodor Dostoevsky's favourite authors were Gogol and Victor Hugo. When he was in a good temper he liked to declaim poetry, and especially Pushkin's; his favourite piece was "The Banquet of Cleopatra," from the "Egyptian Nights." He would recite it with glowing eyes and ardent voice.

I must observe that at that time I was little interested in literature; I had devoted myself wholly to dry erudition, and this often made Dostoevsky angry. More than once he said to me: "Do throw away your professorial text-books!" He often sought to convince me that Siberia could have no future, because all the Siberian rivers run into the Arctic Sea.

At that time Muravyov's achievements on the Pacific Coast were unknown to the world, and of the great Siberian Railway no one had so much as dared to dream ; such a plan would have been taken for the delirium of a madman. I myself could not help laughing when Bakunin, whose acquaintance I made in 1858, unfolded the idea to me.

More and more I grew to care for Dostoevsky. How highly I esteemed him is evident from my letters to my relatives ; these I have at hand to-day. On April 2, 1856, I wrote from Semipalatinsk : " Destiny has brought me into contact with a man of rare intellect and disposition—the gifted young author Dostoevsky. I owe him much ; his words, counsels, and ideas will be a source of strength to me throughout all my life. I work daily with him ; at the moment we think of translating Hegel's 'Philosophy' and the ' Psyche ' of Carus. He is deeply religious ; frail of body, but endowed with iron will. Do try, my dear papa, to find out if there is any idea of an amnesty."

In a letter to one of my sisters I read : " I beg of you to persuade papa to find out, through Alexander Veimarn, whether any prisoners are to be pardoned on the occasion of the Coronation festivities, and whether one could do anything for Dostoevsky with Dubelt, or Prince Orlov.[1] Is this remarkable man to languish here for ever as a private ? It would be too terrible. I am sorely distressed about him ; I love him like a brother, and honour him like a father."

Dostoevsky's indulgence for everyone was quite extraordinary. He found excuses for even the worst of human traits, and explained them all by defective education, the influence of environment, and inherited temperament.

[1] Dubelt was Chief of the Police ; Orlov of the Gendarmerie.

"Ah, my dear Alexander Yegorovitch, God has made men so, once for all!" he used to say. He sympathized with all who were abandoned by destiny, with all the unhappy, ill, and poor. Everyone who knew him well knows of his extraordinary goodness of heart. How pathetic is his solicitude, for instance, about his brother Michael's family, about little Pasha Issayev, and many others besides !

We often spoke of politics too. Of his trial he did not care to talk, and I never alluded to it of my own accord. All I heard from him was that he had never liked Petrachevsky or approved his plans; he had always been of opinion that there should be no thought of a political upheaval in Russia at that period, and that the idea of a Russian Constitution on the model of those of West-European States was, considering the ignorance of the great mass of the people, nothing less than ridiculous.

He often thought of his comrades, Dourov, Plechtcheyev, and Grigoryev. He corresponded with none of them, though ; through my hands went only his letters to his brother Michael, once in a way to Apollon Maikov, to his Aunt Kamanina, and to young Yakuchkin.

And now I must relate what I know of his epileptic fits. I never, thank God, saw one of them. But I know that they frequently recurred ; his landlady usually sent for me at once. After the fits he always felt shattered for two or three days, and his brain would not work. The first fits, as he declared, had overtaken him in Petersburg ; but the malady had developed in prison. At Semipalatinsk he would have one every three months. He told me that he could always feel the fit coming on, and always experienced beforehand an indescribable sense of well-being. After each attack he presented a woefully dejected aspect.

Fyodor Dostoevsky led a more sociable life than I did ; he went particularly often to the Issayevs'. He would spend whole evenings at that house, and among other things gave lessons to the only son, Pasha, an intelligent boy of eight or nine. Maria Dmitryevna Issayev was, if I am not mistaken, the daughter of a schoolmaster, and had married a junior master. How *he* had come to be in Siberia I cannot say. Issayev suffered from pulmonary consumption, and was, moreover, a great drunkard. Otherwise he was a quiet, unpretentious person. Maria Dmitryevna was about thirty, an extremely pretty blonde of middle height, very thin, passionate, and *exaltée*. Even then one often saw a hectic flush on her cheek ; some years later she died of consumption. She was well read, not unaccomplished, witty and appreciative of wit, very good-hearted, and uncommonly vivacious and romantic. She took a warm interest in Fyodor Michailovitch. I do not think that she highly esteemed him ; it was more that she pitied him. Possibly she was attached to him also ; but in love with him she most decidedly never was. She knew that he had epileptic attacks, and that he suffered dire poverty ; she often said he was " a man without a future." But Fyodor Michailovitch took her compassion and sympathy for love, and adored her with all the ardour of his youth. He would spend whole days at the Issayevs', and tried to induce me to go there too, but the family did not attract me.

In the beginning of March, Squadron-Adjutant Achmatov came to Omsk (he had done the journey from Petersburg in ten days) with news of the decease of Tsar Nicholas I. The news reached us in Semipalatinsk on March 12.

Rumours of the clemency and mildness of the new Tsar had already penetrated to Semipalatinsk. I went with Dostoevsky to the Requiem Mass. The general demeanour was grave enough, but one saw not a single tear; only some old officers and soldiers so much as sighed. Dostoevsky now began to hope for a change in his fate, for an amnesty. Most of all we discussed the question of whether the Crimean War would go on.

In the summer I went into the country with Dostoevsky to the so-called "Kasakov Gardens." The place lay on the high bank of the Irtich. We built a bathing-box close to the bank among bush, underwood, and sedge, and began bathing as early as May. We also worked hard in the flower-garden. I can see Dostoevsky now, watering the young plants; he would take off his regimental cloak, and stand among the flower-beds in a pink cotton shirt. Round his neck hung a long chain of little blue glass beads— probably a keepsake from some fair hand. On this chain he carried a large bulbous silver watch. He was quite fascinated with gardening, and took great delight in it.

The summer was extraordinarily hot. The two daughters of Dostoevsky's landlady in the town often helped us with our gardening. After some hours of work we would go to bathe, and then drink tea up above. We read newspapers, smoked, talked about our Petersburg friends, and abused Western Europe.

The Crimean War still lasted, and we were both in a gloomy frame of mind.

I passionately loved riding; one day I succeeded in persuading Dostoevsky to try a mount, and placed one of the gentlest of my horses at his disposal; for this was the first time in his life that he had ever been on horseback. Comical and awkward as he looked in the saddle, he soon grew to like riding, and thenceforth we began to take long canters over the steppes.

Dostoevsky's love for Mme. Issayev was by no means cooling all this time. He went to her house as often as he could, and would come back in a perfect ecstasy. He could not understand why I failed to share his enchantment.

Once he returned in utter despair and told me that Issayev was to be transferred to Kusnezk, a town five hundred versts distant from Semipalatinsk. "And she is quite calm, appears to see nothing amiss with it. . . . Isn't that maddening?" he said bitterly.

Issayev was really transferred soon after that to Kusnezk. Dostoevsky's despair was immeasurable; he nearly went out of his mind; he regarded the impending good-bye to Maria Dmitryevna as a good-bye to life. It turned out that the Issayevs were heavily in debt; when they had sold all they had in payment of these obligations, they had nothing left over for the journey. I helped them out, and at last they started.

I shall never forget the leave-taking. Dostoevsky wept aloud like a little child. Many years afterwards, in a letter to me of March 31, 1865, he alluded to that scene.

Dostoevsky and I decided to go part of the way with the Issayevs. I took him in my carriage, the

Issayevs sat in an open diligence. Before the departure, they all turned in to drink a glass of wine at my
house. So as to enable Dostoevsky to have one last
talk undisturbed with Maria Dmitryevna before she
went, I made her husband properly drunk. On the
way I gave him some more champagne, thus getting
him wholly into my power—then took him into my
carriage, where he forthwith fell asleep. Fyodor
Michailovitch went into Maria Dmitryevna's. It was
a wonderful clear moonlight night in May; the air
was filled with soft perfume. Thus we drove a long
way. At last we were obliged to part. Those two
embraced for the last time, and wiped the tears from
their eyes, while I dragged the drunken and drowsy
Issayev over to the carriage; he at once went off
again, and never knew in the least what had been
done with him. Little Pasha was fast asleep too.
The diligence set off, a cloud of dust arose, already
we could see it no more and the sound of the little
bells was dying away in the distance; but Dostoevsky
stood stark and dumb, and the tears were streaming
down his cheeks. I went up to him, took his hand—
he awoke from his trance and, without saying a word,
got into the carriage. We did not get back till dawn.
Dostoevsky did not lie down and try to sleep, but
kept walking to and fro in his room, talking to himself. After that sleepless night, he went to camp for
drill. Home again, he lay there the whole day,
neither eating nor drinking, and smoking pipe after
pipe.

Time did its work, and Dostoevsky's morbid despair
came to an end. He was in constant communication
with Kusnezk, but that did not always bring him
happiness. Fyodor Michailovitch had gloomy fore-

bodings. Mme. Issayev, in her letters, complained of bitter poverty, of her own ill-health and the incurable sufferings of her husband, of the joyless future which awaited her; and all this sorely depressed Dostoevsky. He failed more and more in health, became morose, irritable, and looked like the shadow of a man. He even gave up working at " The House of the Dead," which he had begun with such ardour. Only when, on warm evenings, we lay in the grass and looked up to the star-sown sky, did he know relative well-being. Such moments had a tranquillizing effect on him. We seldom spoke of religion. He was at heart religious, though he rarely entered a church; the popes, and especially the Siberian ones, he could not stand at all. Of Christ he would speak with moving rapture. His manner in speech was most peculiar. In general he did not speak loudly, often indeed in a whisper; but when he grew enthusiastic, his voice would become louder and more sonorous; and when he was greatly excited, he would pour forth words, and enchain his hearers by the passion of his utterance. What wonderful hours I have passed with him! How much I owe to my intercourse with that greatly gifted man! In the whole of our life together there never was a single misunderstanding between us; our friendship was untroubled by one cloud. He was ten years older, and much more experienced, than I. Whenever, in my youthful crudity, I began, terrified by the repellent environment, to lose heart, Dostoevsky would always tell me to take courage, would renew my energies by his counsel and his warm sympathy. I cherish his memory especially on account of the human feeling with which he inspired me. After all this, the reader will understand that I could not be an indifferent witness of the unhappy frame of mind into which his unfortunate relation with Mme. Issayev had brought him.

I made up my mind to distract him from it in every way I could. On every opportunity, I brought him about with me, and made him known to the engineers of the lead and silver mines that lie near by. But I found it very hard to woo him from his mournful brooding. He had got superstitious all of a sudden, and would often tell me tales of somnambulists, or visit fortune-tellers; and as I, at twenty, had my own romance, he took me to an old man, who told fortunes by beans.

About this time I heard from Petersburg that the new Tsar was gracious and unusually clement, that people were feeling a new spirit in things, and expecting great reforms. This news had a most encouraging effect on Dostoevsky; he grew more cheerful, and much more rarely refused the distractions that I offered him.

One day there came tidings from Omsk that in consequence of the political tension on the southern border and the unrest among the Circassians, the Governor of Omsk was coming to Semipalatinsk, to review the troops; it was said that on this occasion he would also review the rest of the Siberian garrisons.

So Dostoevsky, like the rest, had to prepare for the possible campaign in every way; he had to get boots, a waterproof coat, linen, and other indispensable clothing—in a word, to equip himself afresh from head to foot; for he possessed no clothes but those he had on. Again he needed money, again he racked his brains to think where to get it. These cursed money-worries never left him. From his brother Michael and his aunt he had just then had a small sum ; so he could not possibly ask *them* again. Such anxieties tormented him terribly ; and from Kusnezk the news grew more troubling every day. Mme. Issayev was dying of loneliness beside her sick and ever-drunken husband, and complained in all her letters of isolation and want of someone to talk to. In her more recent letters there often occurred the name of a new acquaintance, an interesting young teacher, and colleague of her husband. In each suc-ceeding letter she spoke of him with more enthusiasm and pleasure ; she praised his kindness, his fidelity, and his remarkable powers of affection. Dostoevsky was tortured by jealousy ; and his dark mood had, moreover, a harmful influence on his state of health.

I was sorely distressed about him, and resolved to arrange a meeting with Maria Dmitryevna at Smiyev, half-way between Kusnezk and Semipalatinsk. I hoped that an interview might put an end to the unhappy state of affairs. But I had set myself a difficult task ; how was I to take Dostoevsky from Semipalatinsk to Smiyev, without anybody's know-ledge ? The authorities would never permit him so long a journey. The Governor and the Colonel had already twice refused his applications for leave. It reduced itself simply to taking our chance. I wrote at once to Kusnezk and asked Maria Dmitryevna to come to Smiyev on a certain day. At the same time I spread a rumour in the town that Dostoevsky had been so run down by several violent epileptic attacks that he was obliged to keep his bed. I also informed his Colonel that he was ill, and under treatment by

the military doctor, Lamotte. This Lamotte, however, was our good friend, and in our confidence. He
was a Pole, formerly a student at the University of
Vilna, and had been sent to Siberia for some political
misdemeanour. My servants were instructed to say
to everyone that Dostoevsky was lying ill in my
house. The shutters were shut, " to keep the light
from disturbing the invalid." Nobody was allowed
to enter. Luckily for us, all the commanding
officers were away, from the Military Governor
downwards.

Everything was in our favour. We started about
ten o'clock at night. We drove like the wind ; but
poor Dostoevsky thought we were going at a snail's
pace, and conjured the coachman to drive still faster.
We travelled all night, and reached Smiyev by morning. How terrible was Dostoevsky's disappointment
when we were told that Maria Dmitryevna was not
coming ! A letter from her had arrived, in which she
told us that her husband was worse, and moreover
that she had no money for the journey. I can't
attempt to convey the despair of Dostoevsky ; I had
to rack my brains to tranquillize him in any sort of
way.

That same day we returned, having done the
300 versts in twenty-eight hours. Once at home, we
changed our clothes and instantly went to see some
acquaintances. So nobody ever knew anything about
our prank.

Our life went monotonously on ; Dostoevsky was
mostly in dejected mood, and at times worked very
hard ; I tried to divert him as well as I could. There
was no variety at all in our way of life ; we walked
daily to the bank of the Irtich, worked in the garden,

bathed, drank tea, and smoked on the balcony.
Sometimes I would sit with a rod by the water,
while Dostoevsky lay near me on the grass and read
aloud; all the books I had were gone through countless times in this way. Among others he read to
me, " for my instruction," Aksakov's " Angling," and
" A Sportsman's Sketches." There was no library
in the town. The numerous books on zoology and
natural science that I had brought from Petersburg,
I knew almost by heart. Dostoevsky preferred fine
literature, and we eagerly devoured any new book.
The monotony of our lives was redeemed, however,
by the hours in which Dostoevsky's creative inspiration came over him. In such hours, he was in so
uplifted a state that I too was infected by it. Even
life in Semipalatinsk seemed not so bad in those
moments; but alas! the mood always went as suddenly as it had come. Every unfavourable report
from Kusnezk brought it to an end at one blow;
Dostoevsky instantly collapsed, and was seedy and
wretched again.

As I have already mentioned, he was then working
at " The House of the Dead." I had the great good
luck to see Dostoevsky in his inspired state, and to
hear the first drafts of that incomparable work from
his own lips; even now, after all these years, I recall
those moments with a sense of exaltation. I was
always amazed by the superb humanity that glowed
in Dostoevsky's soul, despite his grievous destiny,
despite the prison, the exile, the terrible malady, and
the eternal want of money. Not less was I astonished
by his rare guilelessness and gentleness, which never
left him even in his worst hours.

[Baron Vrangel goes on to tell of the arrival of the

Governor-General, Hasford, at Semipalatinsk, and of his arrogant and domineering manner.]

I was invited to lunch with the other officials at the Governor's. I had known his wife in Petersburg. She received me very cordially, and offered me a place by her side.

At table the Governor assumed quite a different tone, and behaved like an ordinary mortal. He seemed in good spirits, asked me about my acquaintances, and let fall the remark that he was well aware of my relations with Dostoevsky. I made up my mind to play upon his better temper, and win him to Dostoevsky's cause. Dostoevsky had shortly before written a poem on the death of Tsar Nicholas I.; we wanted to send it through General Hasford to the widowed Tsarina. The poem began, if I remember rightly, in this way:

> " As evening-red dies in the heavens,
> So sank thy glorious spouse to rest. . ."

To my most respectfully proffered request, Hasford replied with an energetic " No," and added: " I'll do nothing for a whilom enemy of the Government. But if they take him up in Petersburg of their own accord, I shall put no obstacle in the way."

The poem reached the Tsarina, nevertheless, and that in the following way. I wrote two or three times to my father and my influential relations, and begged them to discover some means of bringing it to the Tsarina's notice. My endeavours were finally crowned with success: Prince Peter Georgyevitch von Oldenburg undertook to deliver the poem. The Prince was an impassioned musician and a bad composer; at that time he consorted much with the

well-known pianist, Adolf Henselt, who had to correct his compositions. This Henselt had been for
many years teaching music in our family. My relatives applied to him, and he willingly acceded to our
request. The poem really did reach the Tsarina ;
this was told me later by a high official. Dostoevsky
wrote yet another poem : " On the Accession of
Alexander II." This I later gave personally to
General Eduard Ivanovitch Totleben.

Dostoevsky was now terribly affected by his
malady ; often he feared for his reason. He clearly
perceived the aim of his life to be literary work. But
so long as he was in exile, he would not be allowed
to publish his works ; in his despair he even begged
me to let them appear under my name. That I did
not agree to this proposal, flattering as it was for me,
I need not say. Literature, moreover, was his only
means of earning money. He was longing at this
time for a personal life ; he wanted to marry, and
hoped thereby to find "boundless happiness." For
many years he had suffered the direst need ; who
knows—if Dostoevsky had not taken that step for
which his stern critics so severely blame him, one of
the greatest Russian writers, the pride of Russia,
might have languished to death in the deserts of
Siberia.

The projected campaign never came off. The
Governor-General departed, and our Semipalatinsk
society sank back into its lethargy. After their
urgent activities before the Governor-General, the
soldiers needed some rest, and so Fyodor Michailovitch had a little spare time. We settled down again
in our " Kasakov Garden," and once more the days
were all alike. From Kusnezk came the gloomiest

tidings; Dostoevsky went no more to the sooth-
sayers, bored himself to death, was always in bad
spirits, and took no pleasure in work. He simply did
not know how to kill the time. Then there occurred
to his mind a certain Marina O., the daughter of an
exiled Pole. When he used to go to the Issayevs',
he had interested himself in this girl at Maria
Dmitryevna's request, and given her some lessons.
Now he went to her father, who after some time
declared himself willing to send her daily to Kasakov
Gardens for instruction. Marina was then seventeen,
and had grown into a blooming, pretty creature.
She brought life into our house, was quite at her
ease, laughing and romping, and coquetting with her
teacher.

I was at that time absorbed in a love-affair, and
sought diversion from it in long journeys. I was for
two months absent from Semipalatinsk, and in that
time covered more than 2,000 versts.

Dostoevsky stayed behind alone in the summer
weather, changeable of mood, teaching Marina, working, but not over-diligently, and keeping up a lively
correspondence with Maria Dmitryevna; his letters
to her were as thick as exercise-books.

When, before my departure, I saw how eagerly
Dostoevsky was interesting himself in the girl, who
was evidently in love with her teacher, I began to
hope that intercourse with Marina would woo him
from his fatal passion for Maria Dmitryevna. But
when I came back from my trip, I heard of a real
tragedy.

On my first view of Marina after my return, I was
shocked by her aspect; she was hollow-eyed, emaciated, and shrunken. And Dostoevsky told me that

he had observed this alteration, but that no efforts had enabled him to learn from her the cause of such a metamorphosis. Now, however, we both set ourselves to question the girl, and at last she poured out the following story :

The son of the Mayor of Semipalatinsk, a youth of eighteen, had long had an eye for the pretty maiden ; by the intervention of my housekeeper, he succeeded in making her his own ; the scoundrel stuck to her for a while, and then deserted her. But that was not the worst. The boy's coachman, a rascally old Circassian, knew of these relations ; he had often gone for the girl by his master's orders, to drive her to the rendezvous. On one such transit, he threatened that he would tell of the matter to her father and stepmother if she did not yield herself to him. The terrified Marina, who had very little force of character, consented. The coachman was now blackmailing her, and plundering her as he alone could ; she hated and feared him, and implored us to save her from the clutches of this scoundrel.

The case cried to Heaven. I made use of my official powers, and expelled the Circassian from Semipalatinsk.

A year later, Marina was forced to marry, against her will, a boorish old Cossack officer, selected for her by her father. She hated him, and flirted as before with anyone she came across. The old man pestered her with his jealousy. Later on, when Dostoevsky was married, this Marina was the cause of quarrels and scenes of jealousy between him and Maria Dmitryevna ; for Marina still would flirt with him, and this terribly enraged Maria Dmitryevna, who was even then marked for death.

When I returned from a trip to Barnaul, I found
Dostoevsky still more broken-down, emaciated, and
desperately depressed. He always got a little more
cheerful in my company, but soon he was to lose
heart altogether, for I had to tell him that I should
be compelled to leave Semipalatinsk for ever.

[Vrangel left Semipalatinsk "for ever" in the
New Year of 1855.]

The last days before my departure went by very
quickly. By the end of December I was ready for
the road. Dostoevsky was with me the whole day,
and helped me to pack; we were both very sad.
Involuntarily I asked myself if I should ever see him
again.

After my departure he wrote me a succession of
moving, affectionate letters, and said that he suffered
frightfully from loneliness. In a letter of December 21 he writes : " I want to talk with you as we
used to talk when you were everything to me—friend
and brother ; when we shared every thought of each
other's heart. . . ." Our parting grieved me bitterly.
I was young, strong, and full of roseate hopes ; while
he—great, God-given writer—was losing his only
friend, and had to stay behind as a common soldier,
sick, forsaken, desolate—in Siberia !

The day of my departure arrived. So soon as
evening fell, Adam carried out my baggage ; Dostoevsky and I embraced and kissed, and promised
never to forget one another. As at our first meeting,
both our eyes were wet. I took my seat in the
carriage, embraced my poor friend for the last time,
the horses started, the troika glided away. I took a
last look back ; Dostoevsky's tragic figure was scarcely
to be discerned in the failing light.

In February I came to Petersburg. And now began an unbroken correspondence between us. His fate was not even yet quite decided. I knew that there would be a general amnesty at the Coronation, but how far this would affect those concerned in the Petrachevsky affair was as yet uncertain. Even the highest officials of the police could give me no information. This uncertainty agitated Dostoevsky terribly. His impatience increased from hour to hour. He *would* not see that I, an insignificant little Siberian lawyer, could not possibly have any influence on the course of events, and that even my powerful relatives could do nothing to expedite his case. I did not want to pester them too incessantly, lest I should spoil all. But in his nervous excitement Dostoevsky could not understand that. I did everything that I at all could ; but Count Totleben was the most urgent of any in his cause.

I had known Count Eduard Ivanovitch Totleben from my school-days ; and had often met him at the house of my great-uncle Manderstyerna, then Commandant of the Petropaulovsky Fortress. He had attended the College of Engineering at the same time as Dostoevsky, and his brother Adolf had even been intimate with the latter. Directly I arrived in Petersburg I looked up Totleben, told him of Dostoevsky's insupportable lot, and begged for his support. I visited his brother Adolf also. Both showed warm sympathy for Dostoevsky, and promised me to do all they could. The name of Totleben was then in everyone's mouth, not only in Russia, but over all Europe. As a private individual, he was unusually attractive. The high honours with which he had been overwhelmed, had altered his character in no wise.

He was still the same friendly, good-humoured, and humane person as when I had known him before the war.   He did much for Dostoevsky by his intercession with Prince Orlov and other powerful men in Petersburg.

Dostoevsky esteemed Totleben very highly, and was much moved by his sympathy.   In his letter to me of March 23, 1856, he writes : " He is through and through of knightly, noble, and generous nature. You can't at all imagine with what joy I am following all that such splendid fellows as you and the Totleben brothers are doing for me."

But the greatest influence on Dostoevsky's fate was that of Prince Peter von Oldenburg.   He had known me since my school-days.   He was Proctor of the school, and came there nearly every day.   And now, therefore, I was called upon again to turn to Adolf Henselt.   I delivered to the Prince, through Henselt, the new poem that Dostoevsky had written on the Coronation.   He mentions this poem in his letter to me of May 23, 1856 :

" It would be, I think, clumsy to try unofficially for permission to publish my works, unless I offer a poem at the same time.   Read the enclosed, then ; paraphrase it, and try to bring it under the monarch's notice in some way or other."

I did all I could.   The Prince gave the poem to the Tsarina Maria Alexandrovna ; whether it ever reached the Tsar's hands, I know not.

At the same time Dostoevsky informed me that he was going to send me an article, " Letters upon Art," that I might deliver it to the President of the Academy, the Grand-Duchess Maria Nikolayevna.[1]

[1] See p. 98.

I never received that article.

In the same letter he writes of another article, which he had begun while we were still together—one " On Russia."[1] I never received that one, either.

All Dostoevsky's thoughts were now set on one thing—whether, in case of his pardon, he would be permitted to publish his works. Not only his passion for literary activity, but also his great need, obliged him to strive for recognition in the highest quarters. He then required much money, and had none at all. He had numerous debts, and only that one hope—of earning something by means of the many stories and novels with which his brain was always filled.

In January 1860 Dostoevsky at last got permission to settle in Petersburg. As the climate there was harmful to his wife's health, he left her behind in Moscow, and came alone to Petersburg. He took rooms in Gorochovaya Street. We saw one another very often, but only in flying visits, for we were both carried away by the whirl of Petersburg life. Moreover I was then engaged to be married, and spent all my free time with my betrothed, while Dostoevsky was working day and night. So our short interviews were chiefly taken up with loving memories of the past.

On one of our meetings we spoke of a forthcoming public event in Petersburg. I intended to make a speech "upon the liberties and rights accorded by the Tsarina Catherine II. to the Russian nobility." Dostoevsky instantly sketched a brilliant discourse for me ; but at the meeting I controlled myself, and did not deliver it.[2]

[1] See p. 97.
[2] Some " emancipated " speeches were made on this occasion, for which the orators were afterwards punished.

DOSTOEVSKY, MOSCOW, 1863.

DOSTOEVSKY ON HIS DEATH-BED, JANUARY 29, 1881.

I was once present at a public reading by Dostoevsky. He read Gogol's "Revisor." I already knew his masterly art in delivery. The room was packed. Dostoevsky's appearance and his reading were greeted with thunders of applause. But I was not satisfied with his performance that evening; I saw that he was not in the right mood; his voice sounded dead, and was sometimes barely audible. After the reading, he sought me out among the audience, and told me that he had *not* been in the mood; but that the organizer of the evening had urged him not to abandon the reading, and he never could say "No" to anyone. If I am not mistaken, that was his first reading after his return from banishment.

When in 1865 I returned to Copenhagen from my summer leave, I found a despairing letter of Dostoevsky's from Wiesbaden. He wrote that he had gambled away all his money, and was in a desperate situation—he had not a penny left, and creditors were pressing him on every side. This craze of Dostoevsky's for play was somewhat surprising to me. In Siberia, where card-playing is so universal, he had never touched a card. Probably his passionate nature and shattered nerves needed the violent emotions which gambling afforded him. At all events, now I had to help my old friend out of his fix; I sent him some money, though I had not a great deal myself. With it I wrote, and said that he must positively come to me at Copenhagen.

He did actually come to Copenhagen on October 1, and stayed a week with me. He extraordinarily pleased my wife, and was much devoted to the two children. I thought him thin and altered. Our meeting gave us both great joy; we refreshed old

memories, of course, recalled the " Kasakov Gardens,"
our love affairs, etc.   We spoke much of his first
wife, Maria Dmityrevna, and of the fair Marina, of
whom she had been so terribly jealous.

In this intimate talk we touched almost inevitably
on his family-life, and the strange relation (to this
day a mystery for me) between him and his first wife.
In one of his earlier letters, he wrote to me : " We
were both thoroughly unhappy, but could not cease
from loving one another ; the more wretched we
were, the more we clung together."   At the meeting
in Copenhagen he confirmed that saying.   I had
never believed that Dostoevsky would find happiness
in that marriage.   Every kind of torment—the whole
grievous burden that he fastened on himself by that
connection—robbed him of all peace of mind for long
and long. . . .   At Semipalatinsk I had often tried to
reason him out of his morbid passion for Maria
Dmitryevna, but he would listen to nothing.   Maria
Dmitryevna was invested with a radiant halo in his
eyes.

Among other things, he expounded his views on
women in general, and gave me corresponding advice.
Once, in talking of our Siberian acquaintances, I
mentioned a frivolous and insidious lady of Semipalatinsk ; Dostoevsky thereupon remarked : " We
should be eternally grateful to a woman whom we
have loved, for every day and hour of joy which she
has given us.   We may not demand from her that
she think of us only all her life long ; that is ugly
egoism, which we should subdue in ourselves."

As I have said, Dostoevsky looked very ill during
his stay at Copenhagen ; before that, he had complained in his letters of his state of health : " Besides

the epilepsy, I am a martyr to violent fever ; every
night I have shivering fits and fever, and lose ground
day by day."

Even a perfectly sound man could not have borne
the harassed life that Dostoevsky was then leading !
Eternally in want of money, anxious not only for his
own family, but also for that of his brother Michael,
pursued by creditors, in constant fear of being clapped
in prison, he knew no rest day nor night ; by day he
was running from one newspaper-office to the other,
and by night he was writing, as he said himself, " to
order, under the lash." Naturally all that was bound
to have a hurtful effect on his health as well as his
character.

He told me of one incident, among others, which
will show how nervous and irritable he sometimes
was. When in Paris, it had occurred to him to pay
a visit to Rome. To do this, he had to have his passport signed by the Papal Nuncio in Paris. Dostoevsky went twice to the Nuncio's, but on neither
occasion found him. When he went for the third
time, he was received by a young abbé, who asked
him to wait a while, as Monsignor was just breakfast-
ing, and would take his coffee first. Dostoevsky
leaped up as though gone suddenly crazy, and cried :
" *Dites à votre Monseigneur, que je crache dans son
café—qu'il me signe mon passeport, ou je me précipiterai
chez lui avec scandale !*" The young abbé stared at
him in consternation ; he rushed into his chief's apart-
ment, came back with another abbé, and requested
our Fyodor Michailovitch to clear out at once, and
let the porter of his hotel come and see about the
passport.

" Yes—I was too hot-tempered that time !" concluded Dostoevsky, with a shy smile. But evidently this irritability long endured ; for in one of his later letters he writes : " I have become frightfully nervous and irritable ; my character gets worse every day, and I can't imagine what it will end in." [1]

[1] He used the incident at the Nuncio's in his book, " The Gambler."

FROM THE REMINISCENCES OF SOPHIE KOVALEVSKY[1]

1866

ANYUTA was so delighted by her first literary success that she at once began another story.   The hero of this tale was a young man who had been brought up far away from home in a monastery by his uncle, a monk. The hero, whose name was Michael, had some resemblance to Alyosha in the " Brothers Karamazov." When I read that novel, some years afterwards, I was instantly struck by the resemblance ; I spoke of it to Dostoevsky, whom I very often met at that time.

"I believe you are right !" said he, striking his forehead.   " But I give you my word of honour that I never once thought of this Michael, when I created my Alyosha. . . . Perhaps he was unconsciously in my memory," he added, after a pause.

When this second story of Anyuta's appeared in print, the catastrophe arrived ; a letter of Dostoevsky's fell into my father's hands, and there was a great fuss.

[1] Sophie Kovalevsky, the renowned mathematician, tells of the intercourse of Dostoevsky with her elder sister, Anna Korvin-Kovalevsky, who had sent him her earliest literary effort without her parents' knowledge.   Later, not without opposition from her parents, she made his acquaintance.   Sophie, who at that time was little more than a child, fell in love with Dostoevsky.   This episode belongs to the year 1866.

We had hardly returned to Petersburg from the country before Anyuta wrote to Dostoevsky asking him to call. And he came—on the very day she fixed. I can still remember with what feverish impatience we awaited his arrival, and how, for a whole hour before he could be expected, we jumped at every tingle of the bell. But this first visit of Dostoevsky's was a complete failure.

Our father had a great prejudice against all literary men. It is true that he allowed my sister to make acquaintance with Dostoevsky, but it was not without secret anxiety. When we were going back to town (he stayed in the country), he said, on parting, to my mother:

" Do reflect, Lisa, on the great responsibility you are undertaking. Dostoevsky does not belong to our circles. What do we know of him, after all? Only that he is a journalist, and has been in prison. A nice recommendation! We shall have to be very cautious about him."

Father especially enjoined on mother that she should never leave Anyuta a moment alone with Dostoevsky. I begged for permission to be present at this first meeting. Our two old German aunts came into the room every minute on one pretext or another, and stared at our guest as if he were some strange animal; finally they both sat down on the sofa and stayed there till he went.

Anyuta was furious that her first meeting with Dostoevsky, on which she had set such high hopes, should be taking place in such circumstances; she looked cross, and would not speak. Dostoevsky too was very uncomfortable in the presence of the two old ladies. It was clear that he was sharply annoyed.

He looked ill and old that day, as he always did when he was in a bad temper. He pulled nervously at his short blond beard, bit his moustache, and made dreadful faces.

Mama did her very best to get up an interesting conversation. With the friendliest conventional smile on her lips, but evidently in the greatest perplexity, she tried to say all sorts of pleasant and flattering things to him, and to ask him intelligent questions.

Dostoevsky answered monosyllabically and discourteously. At last Mama was *au bout de ses ressources*, and said no more. Dostoevsky sat with us half-an-hour; then he took his hat, bowed hastily and awkwardly to us all, but shook hands with none of us —and went.

As soon as he was gone, Anyuta ran to her room, threw herself on the bed, and began to cry. " You always spoil everything !" she said, over and over again.

Yet, some days later, Dostoevsky reappeared, and his visit this time was very opportune, for Mama and the aunts were out, and only my sister and I at home. He thawed at once. He took Anyuta by the hand, sat down beside her on the divan, and instantly they began to talk as if they were two old friends. The conversation did not, as on his first visit, drag itself with difficulty from one uninteresting theme to another. Anyuta and he had to make the best use of their time, and say as much as they possibly could to one another, so on they gabbled, joked, and laughed.

I was sitting in the same room, but taking no part in their conversation ; I stared unwinkingly at Dostoevsky, and devoured every single word he said.

This time he looked different from what he had at his first visit—young, frank, clever, and attractive. " Can he really be forty-three years old ?" thought I. " Can he really be three-and-a-half times as old as I am, and twice as old as Anyuta ? They say he's a great writer, and yet one can talk to him like a chum !" And all at once he seemed to me such a dear. Three hours went by in no time. Suddenly there was a noise in the ante-room : Mama had come back from town. She did not know that Dostoevsky was there, and came in with her hat on, laden with parcels.

When she saw Dostoevsky with us, she was surprised and a little alarmed. " What would my husband say ?" was probably her first thought. We rushed to meet her, and when she saw we were in such high spirits, *she* thawed in her turn, and asked Dostoevsky to stay for lunch.

From that day forward he came to our house as a friend. As our stay in Petersburg was not to be very long, he came frequently, say three or four times in the week.

It was particularly agreeable when he came on evenings when we had no other visitors. On such occasions he was remarkably vivacious and interesting. Fyodor Michailovitch did not like general conversation ; he could only talk as a monologuist, and even then only when all those present were sympathetic to him, and prepared to listen with eager attention. When this condition was fulfilled, he talked most beautifully—eloquent and convincing as no one else could be.

Often he told us the story of the novels he was planning, often episodes and scenes of his own life.

I can still remember clearly how, for example, he described the moment when he, condemned to death, stood with eyes blindfolded before the company of soldiers, and waited for the word " Fire !" and how instead there came the beating of drums, and they heard that they were pardoned.

Dostoevsky was often very realistic in his conversation, and quite forgot that young girls were listening, I suppose. Our mother used sometimes to be terrified. In this way he once told us a scene out of a novel he had planned in his youth. The hero was a landed proprietor of middle age, highly educated and refined ; he often went abroad, read deep books, and bought pictures and engravings. In his youth he had been very wild indeed, but had grown more staid with years ; by this time he had a wife and children, and was universally respected. Well, one morning he wakes very early ; the sun is shining into his bedroom ; everything about him is very dainty, pretty, and comfortable. He is penetrated with a sense of well-being. Thorough sybarite that he is, he takes care not to awake completely, so as not to destroy this delightful state of almost vegetable felicity. On the boundary between sleep and waking, he enjoys in spirit a series of agreeable impressions from his latest trip abroad. He thinks of the wonderful light on the naked shoulders of a St. Cecilia in one of the galleries. Then some fine passages from a book called " Of the Beauty and Harmony of the Universe " come into his mind. But in the midst of these pleasant dreams and sensations he suddenly becomes aware of a peculiar feeling of discomfort, such as that from an internal ache or a mysterious disturbance. Very much like what a man experiences who has an old wound, from which the bullet has not been extracted; in the same way, *he* has been feeling perfectly at ease when suddenly the old wound begins to smart. And now our landed proprietor speculates on what this may portend. He has no ailment, he knows of no trouble, yet here he is, utterly wretched. But there must be something to account for it, and he urges his consciousness to the utmost. . . . And suddenly it *does* come to him, and he experiences it all as vividly, as tangibly—and with what horror in every atom of his being!—as if it had happened yesterday instead of twenty years ago. Yet for all that twenty years it has not once troubled him.

What he remembers is how once, after a night of debauchery, egged on by drunken companions, he had forced a little girl of ten years old.

When Dostoevsky uttered those words, my mother flung her hands above her head, and cried out in terror: "Fyodor Michailovitch! For pity's sake! The children are listening!"

At that time I had no idea what Dostoevsky was talking about, but from my mother's horror I concluded that it must be something frightful.

Mama and Dostoevsky became good friends, all the same. She was very fond of him, though he gave her much to bear.

Before we left Petersburg Mama decided to have a farewell evening-party, and invite all our acquaintances. Of course, Dostoevsky was asked. At first he refused, but unluckily Mama succeeded in persuading him to come.

The evening was unusually dull. The guests took not the slightest interest in one another; but as well-bred people, for whom such dull evenings form an essential part of existence, they bore their tedium stoically.

One can easily divine how poor Dostoevsky felt in such company! In his personality and appearance he was frightfully alien to everybody else. He had gone so far in self-immolation as to put on a dress-coat; and this dress-coat, which fitted very badly and made him uncomfortable, ruined his temper for the whole evening. Like all neurotic people, he was very shy in the company of strangers, and it was clear that his ill-temper was to be displayed on the earliest possible opportunity.

My mother hastened to present him to the other guests; instead of a courteous acknowledgment, he muttered something inarticulate, and turned his back at once. But the worst was that he monopolized Anyuta from the very beginning. He withdrew with her into a corner of the room, plainly intending to keep her there all the time. That was, of course, contrary to all etiquette; and he behaved to her, moreover, with anything but drawing-room manners— holding her hand and whispering in her ear. Anyuta was much embarrassed, and Mama was vexed to death. At first she tried to convey to him delicately how unsuitable his conduct was. She passed the couple as if by chance, and called my sister, as if to send her into the other room on some message. Anyuta tried to get up and go, but Dostoevsky coolly held her back, and said: "No, wait—I haven't finished yet." But with that my mother's patience came to an end.

"Excuse me, Fyodor Michailovitch; she must, as daughter of the house, attend to the other guests," said she indignantly, leading my sister away with her.

Dostoevsky was furious; he stayed silently sitting in his corner, and casting malignant looks on every side.

Among the guests was one who displeased him extraordinarily from the first moment. This was a distant relative of ours, a young German, an officer in one of the Guards' regiments.

Handsome, tall, and self-satisfied, this personage excited his hostility. The young man was sitting, effectively posed, in a comfortable chair, and displaying his slender ankles, clad in close-fitting silk socks. He bent gaily towards my sister, and evidently said something very funny to her. Anyuta, who had not yet recovered from the scene between Dostoevsky and my mother, heard him with a somewhat stereotyped smile—" the smile of a gentle angel," as our English governess laughingly described it.

As Dostoevsky watched the pair, a veritable romance formed itself in his brain : Anyuta hates and scorns the German, self-satisfied fop that he is, but her parents mean to marry her to him. The whole party has of course been got up to this end alone !

He believed at once in this hypothesis, and got into a fury. That winter, people were talking much of a book by an English clergyman : " Parallels between Protestantism and [Greek] Orthodoxy." In our Russo-German circle it was exciting great interest, and the conversation grew more animated as soon as this book was mentioned. Mama, who was herself a Protestant, remarked that Protestantism had one advantage over Orthodoxy, and that was that Protestants were more conversant with the Bible.

" And was the Bible written for fashionable ladies ? "

Dostoevsky suddenly broke out, having sat stubbornly silent till now. "For in the Bible it is written, among other things : 'And God made them male and female.' And again : 'Therefore shall a woman forsake her father and mother, and shall cleave unto her husband.' That was Christ's conception of marriage ! What have *our* mothers to say to it, they who think only of how they may get rid of their daughters to the best advantage ?"

Dostoevsky said these words with uncommon pathos. The effect was stupendous. All our well-bred Germans were confounded, and stared with all their eyes. Not for some moments did they realize how unsuitable Dostoevsky's speech had been, and then they all began to talk at once, so as to obliterate the unfortunate impression.

Dostoevsky cast another malignant look on all, retired to his corner, and spoke not a word for the rest of the evening.

When he came next day, Mama tried by a cool reception to give him to understand that she felt herself to be offended. But in her great good-nature she never could long be angry with anyone, and so they soon became friends again.

But, on the other hand, the relations between Dostoevsky and Anyuta were completely altered from that evening. He lost all influence over her, at that one blow ; she now continually took it into her head to contradict and tease him. He showed, on his side, great irritation and intolerance ; he would demand an account from her of every day on which he had not been with us, and displayed much hostility to everybody whom she at all liked. He did not visit us less frequently, indeed he came oftener even than before, and stayed longer every time, though he never ceased quarrelling with my sister during his whole visit.

In the beginning of their intimacy, Anyuta used to refuse many invitations and gaieties if she knew Dostoevsky was coming on those days. Now that, too, was quite changed. When he came to us on an evening when we had other visitors, Anyuta calmly devoted herself to the other guests. And if she were invited anywhere on one of " his " evenings, she would write and put him off.

The next day, Dostoevsky was always in a bad temper. Anyuta would pretend not to notice, and take a piece of sewing. This would make him worse; he would go into a corner and sit silent. My sister would say nothing either.

" Do stop sewing !" says Dostoevsky at last, and takes her work away from her.

My sister crosses her arms on her breast, and says not a word.

" Where were you last night ?" asks Dostoevsky crossly.

" At a ball," says my sister carelessly.

" And did you dance ?"

" Naturally."

" With your cousin ?"

" With him and others."

" And that amuses you ?" Dostoevsky further inquires.

Anyuta shrugs.

" For want of anything better, it does," she answers, and begins to sew again.

Dostoevsky regards her in silence for some moments.

" You are a shallow, silly creature," he suddenly declares.

That was the tone of most of their conversations. They had their bitterest quarrels when the subject of Nihilism came up. The debates on this theme would often last till late into the night; and each would express far extremer views than either held.

" The whole younger generation is stupid and un-cultured !" Dostoevsky was wont to say. " A pair of country boots is more precious to them than the whole of Pushkin."

" Pushkin *is* out-of-date," my sister would calmly maintain. She knew that nothing put him out so thoroughly as a disrespectful remark about Pushkin.

Dostoevsky would often spring up in a rage, seize his hat, and depart with a solemn asseveration that he did not want to have anything more to do with a Nihilist, and would never again cross our threshold. But next evening he would come again, as if nothing had happened.

The more strained became the relations between Dostoevsky and my sister, the more friendly did I grow with him. I was more fascinated by him every day, and more subject to his influence. Of course he could see how I adored him, and he evidently liked it. He often told my sister that she should take example by me.

When Dostoevsky uttered some profound idea or some clever paradox, my sister frequently chose to pretend that she did not understand him ; I would be quite carried away, while she, to torment him, would make some insipid rejoinder.

" You are a poor, insignificant thing !" Dostoevsky

would then exclaim. " How different your sister is !
She is still a child, but how wonderfully she understands me !   *Hers* is a delicate, sensitive soul !"

I would get crimson all over with delight ; I would
gladly have let myself be cut in pieces to show how
well I understood him.   In the depths of my soul
I was well pleased with this change in the relation of
Dostoevsky to my sister ; but I was ashamed of the
feeling.   I accused myself of treachery to my sister,
and took great pains to make up for my secret sin by
being very nice to her.   But despite all pangs of conscience, I was always glad of every fresh quarrel
between Dostoevsky and Anyuta.   He called me
his friend, and I, in my simplicity, believed that
I was really dearer to him than my sister, and understood him better.   Even my looks he praised to the
detriment of hers.

[Finally Dostoevsky made a proposal of marriage
to the elder sister, but it was not accepted.]

Dostoevsky came once more, to take leave.   He
stayed only a short time, but was simple and friendly
in his manner to Anyuta ; they promised to write to
one another.   He said good-bye to me very tenderly.
He even kissed me, but had no idea, I am sure, of the
feelings that he had awakened in me.

After about six months, Dostoevsky wrote to my
sister to say that he had learned to know and love
a wonderful girl, who had consented to marry him.
This girl, Anna Grigorevna Snitkin, became later his
second wife.   " My word of honour : if anyone had
prophesied this to me half a year ago, I should not
have believed it !" remarks Dostoevsky naïvely at the
end of this letter.

Dostoevsky in the Judgment of his Contemporaries

I

R. P. Pobyedonoszev[1] *to I. S. Aksakov*

" January 30, 1881.

" MY DEAR FRIEND IVAN SERGEYEVITCH !

" When you wrote to me that you felt so sick at heart, you as yet knew nothing of Dostoevsky's death. But I stand by his bier, and my heart is doubly sick. I knew this man well. I had reserved for him my Saturday evenings, and he often came to talk alone with me. I even furnished him with many hints for his ' Zosima ';[2] we talked of that often and intimately. The time when he was editing *Grajdanin* was that of our intimacy. I pitied him in his desperate state, and worked together with him through a whole summer; in such a way we quickly made friends. In these times, he was the very man for our cause. He cannot be replaced, for he stood entirely alone. . . ."

[1] Pobyedonoszev, the famous Head Procurator of the Holy Synod, had a great influence on the conservative side in Russian politics of the years from 1881 to 1904. His correspondence with the Slavophil, Ivan Aksakov, is from the point of view of both very remarkable ; they saw in Dostoevsky their companion in battle against the reforms and revolutionary tendencies of the 'eighties.

[2] In " The Brothers Karamazov."

II

I. S. Aksakov to R. P. Pobyedonoszev

" Moscow,
" *February*, 1881.

"The death of Dostoevsky is a real chastisement from God. Now for the first time it is fully felt what value he had as a teacher of the younger generation. Even those who did not know him personally must perceive it. Those noble ideals which many a youth cherishes unconsciously in his soul, found in him an upholder. For 'injured and insulted' is, in very truth, only the religious and moral sense of the Russian intelligence. . . ."

III

TURGENEV ON DOSTOEVSKY

Letter to Slutchevsky of December 26, 1861

" My Bazarov, or to speak more precisely, my intentions, only two men have comprehended: Dostoevsky and Botkin."

Letter to Dostoevsky of December 26, 1861

" I am reading with great enjoyment your ' House of the Dead.' The description of the *bath* is worthy of a Dante ; in several figures (for example, in Petrov) there are many most authentic psychological subtleties. I am truly rejoiced at the success of your journal, and repeat that I shall always be glad to give it a helping hand."

Letter to Polonsky of April 24, 1871

" I am told that Dostoevsky has immortalized me in his novel;[1] I don't mind, if he likes to do that sort of thing. . . ."

[Turgenev goes on to tell of his meeting with Dostoevsky at Baden-Baden,[2] and says more than once that he considers Dostoevsky to be mad.]

Letter to Mme. Milyutin of December 3, 1872

" MY DEAR MARIA AGGEYEVNA,

" I thank you from my heart for the friendly feelings which dictated your last letter. I was not in the least surprised by Dostoevsky's proceeding : he began to hate me when we were both young and at the commencement of our literary activities, although I did nothing to call forth that hatred. But unreasoned passions are, it is said, the strongest and most persistent of all. Dostoevsky has permitted himself something worse than a parody : he has shown me, under the mask of Karmasinov, as a secret partisan of Netchayev. It is worthy of remark that he selected for this parody the only story which I published in the journal at one time conducted by him—a story for which he overwhelmed me in his letters with thanks and praise. I still have his letters. It would certainly be rather amusing to make them public now. But he knows that I shall never do so. I am sorry that he should use his undoubtedly great talent for the satisfaction of such unlovely feelings ; evidently he does not himself prize his gifts very highly, since he degrades them to a pamphlet."

[1] As Karmasinov in "The Possessed."
[2] See Dostoevsky's letter to Maikov of August 16, 1867.

Letter to Saltykov of November 25, 1875

"The theme of Goncourt's novel is very daring. As he says himself, the book is the fruit of a close scientific study of the life of prostitutes. But at all events, it's something very different from Dostoevsky's 'Hobbledehoy.' I glanced at that chaos in the last number of the *Otetschestvennia Zapiski*; my God, what a welter of hospital stinks! What a vain and incomprehensible stuttering; what a psychological rubbish-heap! . . ."

Letter to Saltykov of September 24, 1882

" I also read Michailovsky's article on Dostoevsky. He has rightly divined the characteristic mark of Dostoevsky's creative work. In French literature, too, there was a like case — namely, the famous Marquis de Sade. This latter depicts in his 'Tourments et Supplices' the sensual pleasure afforded by the infliction of refined tortures. And Dostoevsky, in one of his books, enlarges on the same sort of delights. . . . And when one thinks that all the Russian Bishops said masses for the soul of *this* Marquis de Sade, and even preached sermons about his great love for all mankind! Truly, we live in a remarkable age."

IV

Leo Tolstoy on Dostoevsky

From Tolstoy's Letters to A. N. Strachov

"*September* 26, 1880.

" Lately I was ill, and read Dostoevsky's 'House of the Dead.' I have read much, and forgotten much; but I do not know in all modern literature,

Pushkin included, any better book. Not the manner, but the point of view, is what is so remarkable; it is so frank, natural, and Christ-like. A fine, edifying book. Yesterday, when I read it, I knew such pleasure as I have not had for a long time. If you see Dostoevsky, tell him that I love him."

At the beginning of 1881 :

" I wish I had the power to say all that I think of Dostoevsky! When you inscribed your thoughts, you partly expressed mine. I never saw the man, had no sort of direct relations with him ; but when he died, I suddenly realized that he had been to me the most precious, the dearest, and the most necessary of beings. It never even entered my head to compare myself with him. Everything that he wrote (I mean only the good, the true things) was such that the more he did like that, the more I rejoiced. Artistic accomplishment and intellect can arouse my envy ; but a work from the heart—only joy. I always regarded him as my friend, and reckoned most confidently on seeing him at some time. And suddenly I read that he is dead. At first I was utterly confounded, and when later I realized how I had valued him, I began to weep—I am weeping even now. Only a few days before his death, I had read with emotion and delight his ' Injury and Insult.' "

THE WIDOW AND CHILDREN OF DOSTOEVSKY AT HIS GRAVE IN PETERSBURG.

INDEX